William Carlos Williams

THE POET AND HIS CRITICS

William Carlos Williams

THE POET AND HIS CRITICS

PAUL L. MARIANI

AMERICAN
LIBRARY
ASSOCIATION
CHICAGO

THE POET AND HIS CRITICS

A series of volumes on the meaning of the
critical writings on selected modern British
and American poets.

Edited by CHARLES SANDERS, University of Illinois, Urbana

Robert Frost by Donald J. Greiner

LIBRARY OF CONGRESS CATALOGING IN PUBLICATION DATA
Mariani, Paul L
  William Carlos Williams: the poet and his critics.

  (The Poet and his critics)
  Bibliography: p.
  1. Williams, William Carlos, 1883-1963—Criticism and
interpretation—History.
PS3545.I544Z627   818'.5'209   75-8645
ISBN 0-8389-0199-9

William Carlos Williams

COLLECTED EARLIER POEMS. Copyright 1938 by
New Directions Publishing Corporation.

PATERSON. Copyright 1946, 1948, 1949, 1951,
© 1958 by William Carlos Williams.

SELECTED LETTERS. Copyright © 1957 by William
Carlos Williams.

OTHERS, v. 6 (July 1919), 25–32.

(All) Reprinted by permission of New Directions
Publishing Corporation, publishers and agents
for Mrs. W. C. Williams.

Parts of chapter 5, "The Critical Current," appeared in an
earlier form in *Massachusetts Review* 14, no. 1 (Autumn, 1972).

Printed in the United States of America

Second printing, July 1978

To Our Sons
Paul, Mark, John

Contents

Acknowledgments

In a study of this kind, it is all but impossible to enumerate, to name, everyone who helped to "realize" the finished product. The most obvious aid, of course, came from a grant from the National Endowment for the Humanities in 1973, a grant that allowed me the time to actually write and rewrite the book itself. The seed money came from a grant given me by the Graduate Faculty Research Committee of the University of Massachusetts, which enabled me to gather the hundreds of reviews and articles written on Williams over the past sixty-odd years. The library staff at the University of Massachusetts was helpful almost beyond belief, especially in procuring copies of articles and reviews in those ephemeral but important little magazines to which Williams contributed right up to the end. I also owe a special note of thanks to the Collection of American Literature of the Beinecke Library at Yale and to the Poetry Collection of the Lockwood Library of the State University of New York at Buffalo. In particular, I would like to thank Donald Gallup, curator of the American Collection, who has been of immense help to me in working with the Williams papers over the past several years, and also Karl Gay, curator of the Lockwood Collection, and his assistants, especially Beverly Ruth Vander Kooy. I also owe a debt of gratitude to James Laughlin, of New Directions, and to Mrs. William Carlos Williams for allowing me to consult the large numbers of unpublished materials, manuscripts and typescripts, in these two major collections.

I want to thank, too, the members of the English Department's Long-Range Planning Committee, who twice lightened my teaching load so that I might write this book, and to thank in a special way Joseph Frank, head of the English Department, and Ernest Hofer, associate head, for their generous support of my various projects over the past half-dozen years. Special thanks, too, to Diane McGann for patiently typing and retyping my manuscript.

Of course, there are the commentators on Williams himself, but the text will in part attend to acknowledging the debt I owe them. My enthusiasms should be evident from the kinds of attention I have given them.

In a special way I would also like to thank several people who have helped me with their encouragement at various stages in the writing of this book. First, Allen Mandelbaum of the Graduate Center of the City University of New York, a cherished friend and continual teacher, a touchstone of critical integrity, a rare presence; Marjorie Perloff, for her critical sanity and humaneness; my colleague, David Porter, for his openness to new ideas and for his ability to listen; Emily Wallace, for her dedication to making Williams more available, more known; Richard Noland and Vincent DiMarco, colleagues, friends, who listened to me go on about Williams even beyond the limits of friendship, and whose critical skepticisms more than once made me return to the texts; Margaret and Jim Freeman, for their abiding encouragement in me, in all my projects. And, finally, my wife, Eileen, companion, muse, always my hardest and fairest critic, for keeping the thing honest, for her hand in the typing, for calling the shots as she saw them, and, always, for her presence. Where I have fallen short, I have only myself to call to task; I single out those above only for praise.

Introduction

This study will serve as an overview of the critical reception of William Carlos Williams over the last sixty years. Williams holds—to date—the unenviable distinction of being the last of the major poets of his moment to be "discovered." That moment includes Eliot, Pound, Stevens, and Crane: Eliot and Pound were recognized modern voices by the mid-twenties; Crane, leaping from the S.S. *Orizaba*, simultaneously leapt into the foreground of the critics' consciousness in the thirties; and Stevens began receiving serious academic consideration by the late forties. But Williams had to wait until the early fifties before he began to be taken at all seriously by more than an intellectual coterie. Indeed, it was not until the mid-sixties that anything like a respectable critical analysis of his real achievement became recognizable.

William Carlos Williams: The Poet and His Critics covers the critical response to Williams from its beginnings until the early seventies. It would be an intolerable disservice to the reader to insist too firmly on a separation of Williams's reception into hard topical divisions, at least not until chapter 5, which examines the decade of criticism since Williams's death. It is only here that one can define anything like a body of writing sufficiently sustained to identify separate and specific areas of critical interest. Williams was a prolific writer who tried many forms, amassing boxloads of manuscripts as though he were possessed by a demon (as indeed, in one sense, he was). He wrote short stories, novels, plays, improvisations, prose poems, reviews, criticism, essays on education, thousands of letters, and poems of every description. But the truth is that much of Williams's output was, and continues to be, largely ignored. Modern critics have been notoriously reluctant to allow serious discussion of a writer in more than one area: if the writer is a poet, then his novels and plays are treated as the works of a poet trying his hand in other modes, the dabblings of the well-intentioned amateur; or those other genres gain their significance solely or largely from an understanding of what light they shed on the development of the poet. This may not be a "bad" thing in itself, if in fact these other modes are, as is often the case, ancillary to the poetic achievement of the writer. But in Williams's case especially, critics, with few exceptions, have been unwilling to consider the man seriously as anything but a poet of significance, and even that partial victory took forty years to achieve.

When I began work on this book in 1971, there was no critical overview of Williams available. The time was ripe, in fact, over-due for such a study and, indeed, two bibliographical-critical essays on Williams appeared after my own comprehensive critical overview of Williams was all but finished. Linda Wagner's review of Williams studies, which appeared in the first issue of *Resources for American Literary Study*, was subsequently included in Jackson R. Bryer's *Sixteen Modern American Authors* and published in early 1974. The twelve-page Wagner essay follows the general format established by Bryer, discussing first the bibliographical sources and primary materials available, and then very briefly sketching in Williams's critical reception from the beginnings through early 1971. Of greater value is Charles Tomlinson's *Penguin Critical Anthology* of Williams, published in late 1972. Tom-linson—who has lived now with Williams's poetry for many years—has done an exemplary job of describing the critical re-sponse to Williams in three compact and extremely perceptive essays, followed by selections from and by Williams which chart the sharp, central arc of his achievement and reception, both here and in England.

Except for Williams's critical French reception in the twenties and his British reception, the present study does not examine European reaction to Williams. Hans Galinsky has two long, pioneering, and necessarily incomplete essays on Williams's critical reception in Germany, England, and Italy from 1912 through the mid-sixties. These were published in the *Jahrbuch für Amerika-studien* in 1966 (vol. 11, pp. 99–175) and 1967 (vol. 12, pp. 167–205) as "William Carlos Williams: Eine vergleichende Studie zur Augnahme seines Werkes in Deutschland, England und Italien (1912–65)," and appeared in revised form in 1968 in his *Weg-bereiter moderner amerikanishcher Lyrik, Interpretations und Rezeptionsstudien zu Emily Dickinson und William Carlos Wil-liams*. Williams's work has been translated into a great many languages and he exists as an important American influence in such countries as Italy, Germany, and Czechoslovakia; but the parame-ters of that influence have yet, to my knowledge, to be charted.

My study focuses primarily on Williams's reception in America. However, since Williams was fiercely aware of the need for American poetry to break from the English mold if it was ever to come into its own, this study looks also at Williams's reception (if that is the correct word) in England. Jack Hardie's fifty-page annotated "Selected Checklist" in the May, 1971, *Journal of Modern Literature* was of considerable help in ascertaining what was available on Williams in England and America, but it does not deal with foreign essays. And while there are gaps in Hardie's bibliographical coverage, his checklist supersedes the earlier, shorter checklists available on the subject, except for Galinsky's aforementioned commentary on Williams's foreign reception. While an occasional commentary may have been overlooked, some have been excluded simply because they were not responsible enough. Nevertheless, I have been sparing in such eschewals, choosing to present as complete a picture of the American (and British) critical landscape around the figure of Williams as seemed possible.

At the same time, an attempt has been made to provide a narrative on how Williams "made it" as a poet in America. And while such was not my intention, this commentary must also serve as a partial indictment of the state of literary criticism in America for taking more than a half-century to adequately recognize one of its own sons. Perhaps, given the economy and the morphology of revolutions—and Williams certainly effected no less than a revolution—fifty years is not an inordinate length of time. Certainly Williams's reputation is stronger than ever and, if the kinds of attention he is receiving now are any indication, he seems assured of maintaining his new centrality in modern American poetry as a presence comparable to Whitman. It is no exaggeration to say that Williams is, in our country, probably our most important modern poet in terms of influence and radical achievement.

The necessarily comprehensive nature of a critical study of this size will mean that at points the reader may feel as though the trees have obscured the topographical patterning we call the forest. That is one effect of the kind of artificial foregrounding possible with a modern, computerized library system, so that one could almost wish for that fire in the library which Williams dreams of in *Paterson*, a fire consigning to oblivion what belongs to oblivion. There is, philosophically, something to be said even for the anti-social activities of the Ostrogoths. On the other hand, a study like the present one has some very special virtues, and one of them is that it can present a demographic charting of one chapter of modern American intellectual history. For the artist finds himself inhabiting a very special locus, a very real space with a specific audience out there listening or not as the case may be. Looking over the six decades of criticism registered in these pages, I am aware now that this book is as much about the nature and quality of American criticism in the act of listening to its artists as it is about the unfolding of the artist's achievement itself.

It is a fact, and one that I had not foreseen, that almost none of the published criticism directed towards an understanding of Williams comes anywhere near being as perceptive or as useful, finally, as the kind of critical attention Williams himself paid to other artists. If, for example, you listen carefully to what Williams is saying about Marianne Moore in the pages of the *Dial* in 1925, you will find a critical intelligence capable of going directly to the core of that artist's poetics. No one, not even Pound or Marianne Moore herself, Williams's two best early critics, was able to articulate the precise configuration of what, exactly, a modernist poetics was after with the same kind of brilliant clarity and distinctiveness —hesitations and all—that Williams achieved. "The best work," Williams says in that essay, "is always neglected and there is no critic among the older men who has cared to champion the newer names from outside the battle. The established critic will not read. So it is that the present writers must turn interpreters of their own work." And Williams means himself as much as Marianne Moore. This may sound cranky, like, in Williams's own words, "sour grapes," but it is as true today of the way books are received here and in England as it was a half century ago. Deep down, writers know the comparative worth of the reviews in *The New York Times* Sunday literary supplement, and yet those who "know" will tell you that, "politically," a review in its pages means "more" than all the other reviews combined: X's book reaches a wider audience through this one organ than through all the other reviews, with their circulations of a few hundred or a few thousand, all put together.

Somehow, as Williams himself said, good work survives, is circulated, becomes known. But it is at a cost. For most of his life, Williams resigned himself to the idea that his work would rise through the mass of literature only after he was gone. And yet, that knowledge had a bitter taste; it made him cranky, distrustful of the "academy," of academics; it made him, on the other hand, naïvely effusive, genuinely surprised when someone did respond to him as an artist. It made him overreact to T. S. Eliot and caused him to lash out at Philip Horton, really, for the unforgivable sin of having written a good biography of Hart Crane only five years after Crane's death, at a time when critics were still calling Williams—then in his mid-fifties—a promising poet. Yet Williams also disliked bohemian preciosity and literary inbreeding as much as he distrusted the level of critical reviewing in the well-organized, efficient newspapers and nationally distributed trade magazines.

There were other battles. He had to learn how to skirt the socialist orthodoxies of the thirties, the neoformalist rigidities of the forties, and, finally, the excesses of the younger poets of the fifties, poets like the Beats, who were in the process of canonizing him according to articles of faith to which he could not subscribe. (It was also the younger generation of American poets—poets like Olson and Creeley and Levertov, but also other poets as diverse as Roethke and Lowell—who, in borrowing and learning from Williams, also account for the most important critical response to Williams. But that chapter must wait to be written.) Finally, and perhaps most damaging, in the absence of a really strong advocate-critic, Williams was studied in the sixties according to methodologies which, it is becoming increasingly clear, though well meaning, are inadequate. That situation is changing, but it will take at least another decade before Williams's total achievement even begins to be realized in any sense worthy of the man. The present study is meant as an aid towards understanding where we as readers have come from, where we are, so that we can begin the serious business of realizing the tremendous legacy Williams bequeathed us.

A word on the bibliographical methodology of this study. References cited or alluded to in a chapter will be found listed at the end of that chapter. For example, chapter 1 includes the critical bibliography on Williams for the years 1910–30: all entries are listed by author; where there are multiple listings for a single author, these are then listed chronologically. Since the bibliographical material cross-serves the function of footnoting, the author's name is set off for easier identification. Below this the following information is given: the title of the book, essay, or review; the name of the journal or paper; the date of publication; pagination; or, for a book, place of publication. The reader should be able, therefore, to see at a glance what commentaries are available on Williams for any given moment over the past sixty years. Abbreviations used in text for all journals and newspaper reviews may be found in the List of Abbreviations preceding the Index.

CHAPTER I

Williams's Initial "Impact": 1910-1930

With few exceptions, almost no one writing on William Carlos Williams between 1910 and 1945, the period covered in the first two chapters of this study, seemed willing to *listen* to him on his own terms. This is especially lamentable because Williams looked hard for intelligent criticism and, contrary to an assumption still held by many, welcomed thoughtful commentary, whether positive or negative, when he could find it. Good criticism helped not only others, it helped Williams himself to see his own aims more clearly and to proceed accordingly. Unfortunately, except for a handful of essays by avant-garde writers like Ezra Pound and Marianne Moore and, later, by a few critics writing for the national reviews, it was not until the poet was already in his mid-sixties that anything like a sufficient critical mass attached itself to Williams's work. And by that time Williams had long since been numbed by repeated dismissals into distrusting the critics, especially the academic establishment.

In the early years, between 1910 and 1915, Pound offered the most influential commentary on Williams, such as it was; and his comments, which have the sharpness of scholastic categories beneath their hurried wiseacreish delivery, at once shaped Williams's own poetics and provided initial footholds for grasping his particular distinctiveness. The New York avant-garde, including figures like Marianne Moore, Kenneth Burke, Gorham Munson, Alfred Kreymborg, and Paul Rosenfeld, tried more or less to steer Williams into courses of their own plotting: Burke, Kreymborg, and Munson, for example, all preferred Williams's classical imagism, and Rosenfeld and his group praised Williams (when they did) as an "American" bard. By the mid-twenties a small coterie of French intellectuals and poets, who had been searching for a radically new language for French poetry, were praising Williams for similar qualities, especially for his attempts to rinse the language of its dull linguistic overlay and recover his own language, a process he described metaphorically as a contact with one's own ground in *In the American Grain* (1925). In England, the truth was that, despite Pound's early championing of Williams while Pound was in London, Williams had been summarily snubbed. Even T. S. Eliot chose to ignore his American cousin, dismissing him as being merely of "some local interest perhaps."

Pound's Early Influence

Ezra Pound seems to have seen the worth of his friend William Carlos Williams more clearly than anyone else—with the possible exception of Marianne Moore—in the crucial twenty-year period from 1910 to 1930 when Williams's literary reputation was shaping. That Williams, of course, knew Pound during the same period and understood his worth is of far less importance, because Pound was early and rightly acknowledged as a force in the literary ambience of Georgian London—a force in part created by Pound himself, largely through his own assiduous campaigning for modern letters. In the story of Pound's early critical reception, Williams represents just another voice, and "only" an American one at that. But it was Pound who initially launched Williams— indeed the former is synonymous with the initial critical response to Williams, for nobody else seems to have been listening. It was Pound who criticized by letter Williams's first, thin volume of Keatsian poesies, *Poems* (1909). It was Pound who presented a selection from Williams's second volume, *The Tempers,* in the *Poetry Review* (1912); and Pound who got Elkin Mathews, his own publisher, to publish the book in England (1913). Pound then undertook to review *The Tempers* in the *New Freewoman* (1913). Pound gave Williams a further boost by dedicating his own *Ripostes* to him (1912); by publishing Williams as an "imagiste" in the first volume of *Des Imagistes* in March, 1914; and later by publishing two of Williams's poems—"In Harbour" and "The Wanderer"—in his *Catholic Anthology* late in 1915. In his "Pavannes and Divisions" essay of 1918, Pound praised Williams's "Postlude" for its imagistic purity. And, ten years later, by way of reviewing Williams's *Voyage to Pagany,* it was Pound who summed up Williams's "position" in a brilliant critical overview for the influential *Dial.*

Williams needed Pound's criticism in those crucial early years. One example of American reviewing in the provinces measured against Pound's sharp dismissal: "Verses by Dr. W. C. Williams: Poems Composed in Odd Moments by One of Rutherford's Bright Young Men" appeared in the local *Rutherford American* for Thursday, May 6, 1909. The anonymous reviewer praised with Georgian exuberance the twenty-five-year-old doctor-poet's *Poems,* that slender first volume published by a local printer at Williams's own expense in an edition mercifully limited to one hundred copies. "At odd moments Dr. Williams, one of the bright young men of whom Rutherford is justly proud, has wooed the muse to good effect, and the result is highly creditable." The reviewer hoped that the busy doctor might "find more odd moments in which to record his open-eyed interest in the things of beauty, the mind and the spirit."

"I hope to God you have no feelings," Pound shot back to Williams in a letter sent two weeks later from London. "If you have, burn this before reading. . . . Individual, original it is not. Poetic it is, but there are unnumerable poetic volumes poured out here in Gomorrah [London]. . . . Your book would not attract even passing attention here. There are fine lines in it, but nowhere I think do you add anything to the poets you have used as models."

Pound's letter seems to have had the same bracing shock value on Williams that Ford Madox Ford's rolling on the floor in helpless laughter had had on Pound after he had shown Ford some of his own work. It is the kind of acerbic criticism that can save years. With one exception, Williams never allowed any of these stillborn pieces to be reprinted; and that exception came only forty years later, when John Thirlwall collected "The Lost Poems of William Carlos Williams" (*ND* 16). In fact, so touchy and secretive was Williams about this first volume for years to come that so close a friend as Kenneth Burke thought, at least publicly, that Williams's first volume of poems had been *The Tempers.*

Nearly a year before Mathews published *The Tempers,* Pound, as mentioned earlier, prepared the way by printing a selection in the pages of the London *Poetry Review.* "God forbid that I should introduce Mr. Williams as a cosmic force," he began, adding that at least Williams was "not overcrowded with false ornament." Williams, he noted, apologetically, had "found his art very difficult," but he was determined to win through. One could only "hope that his grit is not yet exhausted." When he reviewed *The Tempers* for the London crowd in the *New Free-woman* late in 1913, Pound could praise the poems for the "vigour of their emotional colouring," as well as for their "directness of expression and honesty of emotion." But he was also troubled by Williams's not having read enough. When he did show traces in his poetry of having read something, Pound noted, it acted more as "a snare against which he struggles, rather than a support to lean upon." In spite of this, the man had a music of his own: "his metres are bold, heavily accented, and built up as part of himself."

In March, 1913, Pound had congratulated Harriet Monroe on her decision to print Williams in the pages of *Poetry*. Williams in his turn had sent her a bruising reply for meddling with his "absolute egoism" in having edited the poems he had sent her. "I'm a great poet," he told her on March 5, "and you don't think so, and there we are." But for all their mutual criticism, Williams was in no position really to insist on anything and had to listen to her advice, even to sending his poems to Pound for his "divine" editing before she would take them. But at least Williams had found an American forum, and a good one. He also continued to publish in the *Egoist* (the former *New Freewoman*) in London, again through Pound. The *Egoist* published, in several issues throughout 1914, ten of his poems, including the lengthy "The Wanderer."

In his review of current books for the London-based the *Future* (June 1918), Pound focused on four young American writers who had all been influenced by modern French literature: T. S. Eliot, Marianne Moore, Mina Loy, and Williams, giving more space to Williams than to the others. Because all of them were unknown in England, Pound quoted in full Eliot's "The Hippo-potamus" and "Conversation Galante," Moore's "Pedantic Literal-ist," Loy's "Ineffectual Marriage," and Williams's "The Old Men" and "Portrait of a Woman in Bed." He ended his review by fo-cusing on Williams, whose voice, he said, was as "distinct and as different as possible from the orderly statements of Eliot." If Moore and Loy were "difficult to follow," he had to confess that Williams's "abruptness" left him fumbling. "I do not pretend," Pound wrote, "to follow all of his volts, jerks, sulks, balks, out-blurts and jump-overs; but for all his roughness there remains with me the conviction that there is nothing meaningless in his book, not a line."

There was in Williams, he felt, "the absolute conviction of a man with his feet on the soil, on a soil personally and peculiarly

his own. He is rooted." If Williams was sometimes almost inarticulate, he was "never dry, never without sap in abundance." In six
years, Williams had managed to transform his poetry from the
opacity and "subjective reality" of "The Postlude" to a poetry of
"maximum objective reality." Focusing on Williams's "Portrait of
a Woman in Bed," Pound noted its resemblance to Rimbaud, its
superiority to Vildrac's "Auberge." Williams had condensed
"two hundred magazine stories about the comedy of slum-work"
into a single lyric. Here was work "that could be translated into
French or any other modern language and hold its own with the
contemporary product of whatever country one chose."

Early Work, 1917-1918

Part of the reason for Williams's transformation was that he
had plugged into the new literary currents alive in New York
following the 1913 Armory Show. By 1915 he had become an
intimate of the New York *Others* group which clustered around
the summer colony at Grantwood, New Jersey, under the aegis
of Alfred Kreymborg. In late 1917, when Williams's third volume
of poetry, *Al Que Quiere!*, appeared, he was a regular contributor
to four very good little magazines: *Poetry*, the *Egoist*, the *Little
Review*, and *Others*, for which he also served a stint as editor. (*Al
Que Quiere!* means, loosely, "To him who wants it" and is a play
on Alfred Kreymborg's name—Al. K—to whom Williams dedicated the book.) Williams was also contributing to such other little
magazines as *Rogue*, the *Masses*, and the *Poetry Journal*. But it was
clearly *Others* which launched Williams as one of the younger
voices of the new, brash experimental poetry beginning to be
recognized in the urban American centers by the end of World
War I.

When the Four Seas Company (Boston) published Williams's
eighty-seven-page *Al Que Quiere!*, it printed a blurb on the dust
jacket characteristic of Williams's rebellious iconoclastic stance,
largely a product of public indifference and the artist's subsequent
mask of indifference towards the bourgeoisie. And, too, Williams
felt humiliated that at thirty-four he still had to pay to have his
own poems published: "To Whom it May Concern! . . . You,
gentle reader, will probably not like it, because it is brutally powerful and scornfully crude. Fortunately, neither the author nor the
publisher care much whether you like it or not . . . But we have

the profound satisfaction of offering that which will outweigh . . .
a dozen volumes of pretty lyrics. We have the powerful satisfaction of publishing a book in which, we venture to predict, the
poets of the future will dig for material as the poets of today dig
in Whitman's *Leaves of Grass*."

From our fifty-year vantage point, the words, though strong,
are true enough. But in its own time *Al Que Quiere!* received
only a scattering of reviews, predictably in the little magazines
to which Williams contributed. Dorothy Dudley, herself a poet,
wrote a six-page favorable review for the April, 1918, issue of
Poetry. She began by blasting the publisher's preface for intimi-
dating and misleading the "gentle reader" with magnificent but
misplaced immensities. What she found in the book instead was
a poetry "at its best fibrous, marvelously observant, delicate,
haunting," and at its worst "stilted, confused, obtuse." Williams
had the ability to capture "those more intricate sensations that
nearly baffle expression." He had the "conscience of the great
artist" without his "supreme ease." As others would after her,
Dudley tended to praise the "arty" lyrical Williams of "fluid
beauty" and to reject his "obscure" and "cryptic" side, in fact his
distinctively modernist side, with its conscious undercutting of an
elevated lyrical mood. But Williams, scanning the magazines for
reviews of his book, wrote to Harriet Monroe praising Dudley's
review: "I care for no reader who does not go direct to the matter of the poem; for that reason I feel a mistaken joy, we'll say,
in driving off just the plain gentle souls. I deserve very few
readers. Dorothy Dudley seems to be one; she really seems to
have read the book and to have given it some thought. It's a rare
trait in a reviewer these days" (in Monroe's *A Poet's Life*, 1938).

John Rodker, a friend of Williams's, gave a short but intelligent
notice to *Al Que Quiere!* in the November issue of the *Little
Review* among his "List of Books." He noted that it was "the
most important book" to come out of the Imagists, and commented on the difference between the linguistic clarity of these
poems and the opaque density of Williams's "Improvisations"
which were then appearing in the pages of the *Little Review*.
However, the expatriate John Gould Fletcher had treated *Al Que
Quiere!* more harshly in the April, 1918, issue of the *Egoist*. Reviewing Williams along with Conrad "Aitken," he commented
that, "One writes about most American poets obviously more from
a sense of duty than from a feeling of abiding pleasure in their
productions." If the English were hamstrung by the weight of

tradition, Americans tended to stammer into the void, achieving "beauty by accident." A poem by Williams, he wrote, was "packed, concentrated observation," its tone tense and unhesitating. But, he added, Williams was too much the self-conscious experimenter—in short, the modernist.

Conrad Aiken's own *Scepticisms: Notes on Contemporary Poetry* (1919) contained a few pages of mild, neo-Arnoldian criticism of Williams. In chapter 18, "Confectionery and Caviar," Williams's excessive individuality—a stylistic caviar—was placed against the uninspired, the "pretty-pretty, the pious, the sacred virtues" of such figures as Edward Bliss Reed, John Cowper Powys, Theodosia Garrison, and Joyce Kilmer. And if Williams was worth more than these other minor versifiers, still, he manifested an excessive egoism and lack of depth: "What do they [the caviar poets] care how peculiar or esoteric their idiom is? Self-expression is the thing. If the crowd cannot understand, or ignores them, so much the worse for the crowd . . . Williams too seldom goes below the surface. He restricts his observations almost entirely to the sensory plane. . . . [His] world is a world of plane surfaces, bizarrely coloured, and cunningly arranged so as to give an effect of depth and solidarity; but we do not get depth itself."

Was Williams a puritan, Aiken wondered, who could not "let go" to express his emotions? Was it this fear of emotion that forced upon him a technique which tended to suppress beauty and opt for a mere prose cadence? Aiken makes a good prognosis, but Williams was looking for a good diagnostician. "What the hell do I care if a man or woman is or is not passionate or tender?," he wrote in his essay, "Belly Music," in the July, 1919, issue of *Others* with one eye on Aiken. What Williams was looking for was not grand feelings or variations on the old rhetorics, but a distinctively modern voice that could capture "a vision into the desolate PRESENT."

In September, 1918, the *Little Review* published an essay by a second-rate English critic, Edgar Jepson, called "The Western School." This was a shortened version of an essay earlier published in the *English Review* and written primarily for a British reading public. Jepson had sent the essay to Pound who was then in London. Pound, seeing some merit in Jepson's attack on the former's more fiercely chauvinistic American contemporaries in their choices for bestowing American poetry prizes on themselves, condensed the piece and sent it to Margaret Anderson at the *Little Review*. Jepson singled out for attack in particular Lindsay, Masters, and Frost as typical of the native school of poetry, even though Pound told Jepson that this triumvirate had already passed the crest by 1918 and that he might better have attended to "Williams, [Mina] Loy, [Marianne] Moore, and the worser phenomena." When Williams, that "hot-blooded Mercutio of the tribe of Others," as Harriet Monroe called him in 1920, read Jepson's piece, it summed up for him the kind of reactionary tactics by an outsider—a foreigner and an Englishman to boot—which always made Williams see red. Jepson's words might just as well have been aimed directly at Williams, particularly as Jepson had singled out T. S. Eliot's poetry for special praise. Eliot's poetry, Jepson contended, was "securely rooted in its native soil. . . . Could anything be more United States, more of the soul of that modern land than 'The Love Song of J. Alfred Pruffock [sic]'?" "La Figlia Che Piange" was certainly "the very fine flower of the finest spirit of the United States."

For these and other remarks, Williams tore into Jepson and, more or less directly, into Pound—"the best enemy" American poetry ever had—in his "Prologue" to his *Improvisations*, the prose poems he was then revising. "It is silly," he said, "to go into a puckersnatch because some brass-button-minded nincompoop in Kensington [Williams's epithet for the British critic as watchdog of poetic standards] flies off the handle and speaks openly about our United States prize poems." Jepson's attack and phraseology was, on the whole, well-merited, and nothing was good "save the new." Williams too could afford to dismiss Masters, Lindsay, and Frost. But Eliot's work, like America's prize poems, he insisted, was also rehash—a "repetition in another way of Verlaine, Baudelaire, Maeterlinck." And Pound himself was a paraphrase of Yeats, the Renaissance, Provence, and the modern French: "Men content with the connotations of their masters." (For this blast Pound retorted in his letter to Williams of September 12, 1920, that "what the French real reader would say to your 'Improvisations' is 'Voui, ç(h)a j(h)ai déjà (f)vu ç(h)a ç(h)a c'est de R(h)imb(h)aud!!' ") The New World was not, Williams insisted, the subtle clubhouse conformation to the Old World of "La Figlia Che Piange"; it was, rather, the stuff of the adobe Indian hag's lullaby and of Kandinsky's *Ueber das Geistige in der Kunst*. The artist had to express himself and his place, and in so doing express the universal. "I praise those who have the wit and courage, and the conventionality, to go direct toward their vision of perfection [London]," Williams conceded. But he would also "confine them in hell for their paretic assumption that there is no alternative but their own groove."

In the final issue of *Others* in the following July (1919), Williams turned home and took "the field against the stupidity of the critics writing in this country about poetry today." As a warm-up, he took a poke at John Gould Fletcher's "flamflam" for trying to purvey "Oxford Poetry 1918" ("oatmeal mush") on the Americans. Then he followed through with shots at such local figures as Untermeyer, Frank V. Anderson, Sandburg, Braithwait, Amy Lowell, and H. L. Mencken, and at such forums as the *Midland*, the *Lyric*, the *Liberator*, the *Pagan*, and the *Modern School*, all mushrooming amidst a paucity of good talent. He ripped out once more against "loveliness" in poetry, against Aldington's "preference" for Villon over contemporary poetry. The *Little Review* was one of the few good magazines which was "not a ragbag." He insisted, too, in the face of his nameless critics, that he was not to be tied to his early romantic effusions, his "Byronic adolescence of body and mind . . . : I began when I was twenty. I *BEGAN* then. *OTHERS* saw its inception when I was thirty (1914), when I had already proved a failure time after time. And yet I sing. And if my voice is cracked at least no one can *HEAR* singing as I can nor put it into the throat so perfectly."

He lumped American critics together in order to dismiss them as "sophomoric, puling, non-sensical," their criticism amounting to no more "than an isolated perception of certain values." Indeed, their criticism was reactionary, its tone "puling testiness in most cases or a benign ignorance in others of the purpose of the work with which they are dealing." "Where is a man who has a head for smashing through underbrush," he complained. "We are gifted among the critics of this country with men and women of neatly tailored servility." What Williams wanted was an intelligent critic, a "more able scholar, a cooler brain with a wider fund of information more acutely focused," one who could see, for example, *why* free verse was "the ONLY form that CAN CARRY THE NEW MEANING that is imperatively required today." Since such a critic did not seem forthcoming, Williams had written his belly music "to fill the gap." But the kind of criticism Williams demanded would be long in coming to American poetry—and longer to him.

When Harriet Monroe reviewed the *Others* anthology for 1919, she chose to end with Williams, placing him over against Wallace Stevens. Stevens's poems, she wrote, manifested a "com-

beauty." ("Dear fat Stevens, thawing out so beautifully at forty," had been Williams's own counterbalancing estimate in his 1918 "Prologue" to *Kora in Hell*.) Monroe felt at home with Stevens's classic lines, but Williams was "like no one else." In denying his strong Puritan strain, she asserted (as a number of other writers who knew Williams would also), that Williams had had to "play the devil, show himself rioting in purple and turquoise pools of excess." "But he doesn't need to assert his rights," she concluded, "we are all quite ready to admit them. He is a poet, indisputably."

"Though Pound soon gathered [Williams] into the 'imagist' fold, . . . no group could hold him," she was to write in *A Poet's Life* nearly twenty years later (1938). She would also recall that when *Poetry* took a cut at an *Others* anthology and Alfred Kreymborg had retorted by demanding that his poems which were to appear in *Poetry* be returned, Williams had asked her to "laugh it off." Williams's real saving grace, and he needed it for his survival as a poet, was that he "never took himself or anyone else too seriously."

Alfred Kreymborg, the man to whom Williams had dedicated *Al Que Quiere!* and the co-founder of *Others*, also recalled Williams and the *Others* days in his *Troubadour: An American Autobiography* (1925). He remembered Williams back in 1915 riding up to the artists' colony at Grantwood on Sunday afternoons in his Ford flivver, looking like some mad Don Quixote. "Shy though Bill was in person, blank paper let loose anything he felt about everything, and he frankly and fearlessly undressed himself down to the ground. Not since the days of old Walt [Whitman] had an American gone quite so far, and readers were shocked all over again." No one had given as much of himself to the *Others* endeavor as Williams had, but Kreymborg had disliked Williams's "Belly Music" essay in the last number of *Others*, which Williams had edited. "Belly Music" was a "grieving, ranting, coroner's inquest" and Williams had buried *Others* with that essay.

"I know Kreymborg, who retired from the editorship of *Others* after the first ten or twelve issues or so, thought I had sabotaged it at the end," Williams recalled hazily in his *Autobiography* (1951). "But it was finished. It had published enough to put a few young men and women on their feet . . . but had really no critical standards and offered only the scantiest rallying point for a new movement. It helped break the ice for further experimentation with the line, but that was all." The truth seems to be that long before

Others had ended, Kreymborg and Williams had drifted apart. Williams had come to regard Kreymborg as unreliable, especially after he warned Williams that a man had to look out for himself. As co-editor of the *American Caravan*, Kreymborg continued to help keep Williams visible by printing him in the pages of that annual anthology of the best American writing in the later twenties. But the distance between the two men is apparent in Kreymborg's view of Williams in his 1929 *Our Singing Strength: An Outline of American Poetry (1620–1930)*. Williams, Kreymborg said, was "the most indigenous of modern American poets." He had "achieved, in mad flights and slow steps, a poetic style peculiarly his own." But, he added, Williams's prose poems like *Kora in Hell, Spring and All,* and *The Descent of Winter* included a "set of theories fascinating in themselves, but completely out of place in a work of art. I know of nothing more annoying than these persistent interruptions to the powerful pulse of Williams' fictions, since the theories are a defense mechanism whereby the poet, scorning an audience as numskulls [sic], vilifies that audience for refusing to doff a larger hat to him. . . . Behind his bragging and public swearing, wretched uncertainty has him in thrall and knifes the poet mid-air in a glorious flight. . . . His great frankness has been the inspiration of the younger poets of the left wing; he has become their leader in the face of his steady unpopularity with critics and the public."

Williams had unfortunately followed Pound in jumping on the soap box to harangue friends and imaginary enemies, Kreymborg lamented. It would have been better for Williams if he had continued to write classical, imagistic poems. A volume like *Al Que Quiere!* had "won the affection of poets by virtue of its absolute freshness and American artistry." But since *Sour Grapes* had marked the beginning of their falling out, *Al Que Quiere!* remained for Kreymborg "one of the most distinguished contributions to an era in which distinction of one sort or another had almost become the rule." Indeed, it was more intellectually rigorous than a work of fiction like Sinclair Lewis's *Main Street*. Moreover, Williams was essentially a poet of the erotic. "But his adolescent persistence in courting fame, of explaining himself in the midst of his writing, of quoting what Ezra [Pound] says about him," Kreymborg closed by saying, was "stupidly redundant." If Williams was to keep from slipping into the second rank of poets, then, he would have to "shed Pound, his friends and disciples, along with his imaginary enemies," such as, presumably, Eliot.

One of the top contenders for the most idiosyncratic review ever published (even in an age gone Dada) must be the Baroness Elsa von Freytag-Loringhoven's two-part "Thee I call 'Hamlet of Wedding-Ring': Criticism of William Carlos Williams' 'Kora in Hell' and why . . ." which appeared in 1921 in the January-March and Autumn issues of the *Little Review*. Even Margaret Anderson and Jane Heap hesitated before deciding to print it. The story of the baroness and Williams makes fascinating reading in itself and Williams was to devote a chapter of his *Autobiography* to this woman twenty-five years after her death. Williams published a prose sketch about her in the Summer 1921 issue of *Contact*, probably in retaliation for the first barrel of her own blast, the baroness's review and Williams's sketch forming a kind of dadaist duet. It is difficult to follow the baroness' fragmentary pastiche, but it is clear that it is at least in part the love-bellows of a rejected lover. As much as he liked the baroness, Williams refused to be forced, as he phrased it, into a syphilitic bed with her. She in turn accused him of bourgeois paranoia over being labeled sentimental, inexperience, timidity, malebluster, brutality, uxoriousness, flippancy, paranoia about swinging on the trapeze, a lack of skill with juggler's balls, dancing with corpses, bourgeois abstemiousness, immaturity, and stagnation.

When the dust and garbage had settled, the baroness had charged Williams, one gathers, with being emotionally and imaginatively suppressed by his American puritanism and monogamy. She had read *Kora in Hell* as Williams's pathological scream for release from middle-class restraints. But, she warned, he was a fake performer. "From nudeness to title to crude triteness of content 'Kora in Hell' does make me scream. . . . Thee I call 'Hamlet of wedding-ring'—chasing ghost of honeymoon bliss—to detect who poisoned—killed—once live body." And in the second part, succinctly: "Husband *or* artist—W. C." There is also a marginal attack on Williams's Jewish heritage for "trying to save own tradition within family." Williams had portrayed himself in *Kora in Hell* as a child of the Rimbaudian tradition, imaginatively liberated. But for the baroness the *Improvisations* were all one big farce. She painted Williams with daredevil helmet cocked, ready for the "land of adventure after business-hours," driving down to Greenwich Village after hanging up his doctor's cloak in Rutherford. At the close of Part II, two "poems" by Abel Sanders were printed. Sanders was Pound's pseudonym, and the poems were addressed to Williams and "Else von Johann Wolfgang Loringhoren

y Fulano." Williams, Pound quipped, was really a comic interna-
tionalist: "Billy Sunday one harf Kaiser Bill one Harf" with "a
little boiled Neitzch on the sabath." Pound also saw Williams's
shrill insistence on being called a liberated artist as at least redundant: "Bad case, bad as fake southern gentlemen tells you every-
morn that he is gentleman, and that he is not black. Chineseman-
darinorlaundryman takes for granted youwillsee he is *not* Booker
T. Washington."

In the March, 1921, issue of *Poetry* Helen Birch-Bartlett's review, "Koral Grisaille," commented with pastel intensity on the
grisaille texture of *Kora in Hell:* "the image of Mr. Williams in
his sadness creating his word-impressions becomes curiously that
of a dancer waving a spotted scarf" (Williams was viewed here as
a surrogate Isadora Duncan). There was an "eastern character"
about *Kora in Hell*, Bartlett noted. But she can hardly be said to
have done justice to the book's density. Angered by Birch-Bartlett's flippant reception, Robert McAlmon, then co-editor with
Williams of *Contact*, shot off a long letter about the book to
Poetry which was published in the following issue. "Unless from
an impulse to say something keenly felt," he insisted, "writing is
without justification." In Europe Joyce was creating new forms
for a modern age. And "in America William Carlos Williams, and
he beginning only with his improvisations entitled *Kora in Hell*,
is conscious of the new form in relation to the dubiety of the day.
. . . There is in this book the spasmodic quality of the active,
imaginative, alternately frightened and reckless, consciousness." If
Kora in Hell was "unintelligible" to most people, still, it was by
far "the most important book of poetry that America has produced." The book did not "pander" to sublime beauty. It was,
rather, a "record of somebody else's conscious states by which to
check their own." It answered McAlmon's own moment and his
own place—New York, 1920—in a truer way than *Leaves of
Grass* could for those who found themselves living "in the cities
of smoke, subways, tired faces, industrialism; here with the movies
and their over-gorgeousness, and the revues and follies which grad-
ually inject their ultra coloration into vaudeville."

When John Gould Fletcher again attacked Williams, this time
in the *Freeman* for May, 1921, in his review of *Kora in Hell*,
Williams merely printed part of the review in the summer issue
of his own *Contact*, under the title, "The Italics are God's.":
"What does Dr. Williams say in effect? That literature is a bad
job and humanity in a bad way. This has been said before, ever

since Solomon. Any novel way of putting it is merely a dodge for
wrapping up platitudes in a different kind of statement. *Literature,
however, depends not on the kind but on the degree of statement. . . .*"

For Williams, of course, as McAlmon had noted, just the opposite was true. It was the *way* of saying that made one reperceive
the thing. In the same issue of *Contact*, and preceding Fletcher's
pronouncement, Williams printed Marianne Moore's perceptive
review of *Kora in Hell*. Williams's writing, she said, was characterized by "a concise, energetic disgust, a kind of intellectual
hauteur which one usually associates with the French." It had
"compression, colour, speed, accuracy." Its chief value had been
in its "acknowledgement of our debt to the imagination." Without
naming it as such, Marianne Moore saw in Williams a sophisticated
metaphysical imagination which could "see resemblances in things
which are dissimilar." If his brash "audacity" was somewhat alien
to her own sensibility, she nevertheless understood Williams's need
to take such a stance; it was, in fact, part of his realistic esthetic
of the local condition. The "abrupt" transitions between the parts
of the improvisations were part of his esthetic which demanded
"exactness" and "instant satisfaction." For all Williams's insistence
on "no school but experience," she saw that the work itself showed
an "authoritativeness, the wise silence which knows schools and
fashions well enough to know that completeness is further down
than professional intellectuality and modishness can go."

But she took issue with Williams's poetics. To his "petulant"
comment that, "Nowadays poets spit upon rhyme and rhetoric,"
she answered incisively that his own poetry provided "examples
of every rhetorical principle insisted on by rhetoricians." Nevertheless, there was in the poetry "an appetite for the essential," a
complexity, and with it a disdain for the fashionable and the "average" so great that the ordinary critic simply could not deal with
him, and the more "ambitious" critics underestimated him. She
knew that Williams disliked criticism, even from his best friends.
So, rather than argue with him, she preferred simply to remind
him that "the conflict between the tendency to aesthetic anarchy
and the necessity for self-imposed discipline must take care of
itself."

In his "American Letter," which appeared in the *Dial* in April,
1921, W. C. Blum, a pseudonym for J. S. Watson, praised Williams's poetry for its unrelenting contact, its "Chekhovian" quality
of realness. But Williams's espousal of a metaphysics of the local

"as a test for art" was "stupid," since no one, Blum maintained, could tell whether "a given piece of writing shows contact with the writer's environment." At the same time, however, he slammed into the opposing Americanist faction, the Seven Arts Group—Van Wyck Brooks, Waldo Frank, Randolph Bourne, Paul Rosenfeld—for excluding the work of such "very admirable and very American poets like Ezra Pound, Marianne Moore, and William Carlos Williams" simply because their esthetic strategies were different from the Group's.

Between Art and Pre-Art: The Early Twenties

Williams's slim volume, *Sour Grapes*, appeared at Christmas, 1921. Among those who reviewed it were Kenneth Burke, in the February, 1922, issue of the *Dial*, and Yvor Winters, in the July issue of *Poetry*. Burke's essay stressed Williams's apparent formlessness and his refusal to compromise with the intensity and randomness of the perceived moment. Williams's poetics could be reduced, in Burke's view, to an almost physical intimacy with whatever thing he chose as subject: "There is the eye, and there is the thing upon which that eye alights; while the relationship existing between the two is a poem." What Burke was describing sounds very much like an impressionist esthetics, but he was in fact slamming that "miserable crew," the Imagists. Fortunately, however, Williams had made Imagism *work* for him. The more classical *Sour Grapes* had come as a relief for Burke after the formlessness of *Kora in Hell*, for "having twenty sentences of chaos to heighten one sentence of cosmos is too much like thanking God for headaches since they enable us to be happy without them." *Sour Grapes* was the real successor to *Al Que Quiere!* because Williams's real gift was for definition, lucidity. Williams was, essentially, a poet of surface, of minute fixations, with the emotions implied. Even *Contact*, which Williams was editing, implied "man without the syllogism, . . . man with nothing but the thing and the feeling of that thing." And if *Contact* was the counterpart of culture (à la Eliot and Pound implied), "Williams becomes thereby one of our most distinguished Neanderthal men." For philosophical Burke saw his friend as a true primitive, a hater of the idea, with "a complete disinterest in form." Williams dealt characteristically with the Ur-phenomenon, with his own desires. rather than with principles with which to handle those desires. Yet, Burke was willing to admit, this relentless process of contact with the bare thing "undeniably had its beauties" too.

As Marianne Moore had done a year earlier, Yvor Winters also noted Williams's "Metaphysical" conceits: "an intellectual relationship between two objects physically unrelated, one of which fuses with the sound and takes on an image existence." At times, Winters noted, Williams's conceits could be as "perfect and as final as Herrick," as in "To Waken an Old Lady" and "The Nightingales," but they could also be redundant or overworked. Williams also knew how to use images for their own sake, without an ulterior or symbolic "meaning." Winters insisted that Williams was caught just as much as T. S. Eliot in the "tradition." Was not his very prose in the line of Flaubert? He saw too—interestingly—that Williams's greater serenity in the *Sour Grapes* volume owed something to Pound's Chinese translations. Pound's influence had worked here, but he warned Williams that that influence also had its pitfalls.

This was Winters's first published response to Williams. But with time he began to see Williams as part of the larger romantic dragon and himself as an increasingly lone St. George. Only two years later, in the July, 1924, issue of the *Modern Review*, Winters came down hard on Williams's fallacy of form, the belief that, "since America is a larger, loose, uncorrelated country, our verse must be large and loose and uncorrelated in order to express that land." A loose poem for Winters was a weak one, "inaccurate and lacking in cumulative power." It was the fallacy of "Whitman and his decadent followers, Sandburg and Anderson," and Williams had succumbed to it in his "Improvisations." Most of the early critics, then, were put off by Williams's experimental work. They preferred instead his clear, sharp imagist poems. Few of them as yet seemed to understand that the raw improvisations were necessary to Williams's more "finished" work.

In 1923 Williams published two books—*The Great American Novel* and *Spring and All*. Both were brought out by Robert McAlmon's Paris-based *Contact Editions* in expensive, limited editions of 300 copies. Neither volume had any circulation. "Paris bookshops did not show much interest in limited editions," Robert McAlmon recalled in his *Being Geniuses Together* (1938), "and such books as we published and tried to send to England or America were held up at the docks and in most cases we were not notified. In America the books were seldom commented on and if mentioned, they were mentioned as Paris and expatriate productions, even if their authors were living and had been living steadily in America." It is not surprising, therefore, that neither book had any noticeable effect on Williams's reputation, which had stalled on the *Al Que Quiere!* volume of seven years before. Since both *The Great American Novel* and *Spring and All* were almost impossible to come by in the states, there were virtually no reviews of either book. Matthew Josephson, who had met Williams and McAlmon in 1920, however, reviewed *The Great American Novel* together with Jean Toomer's *Cane* in the October, 1923, issue of *Broom*, thanks to its editor, Alfred Kreymborg. "In pyramids [of words] Williams heaps up his America," Josephson wrote. "He knows her national accent; her speech, her credulities, her prejudices burn in his ears. He is terribly *sincere* . . . and . . . his honesty drives him to the ground, where one begins with words." Where other moderns wrote as artists, Williams wrote instead for that relentless contact with things themselves.

In late 1923 Williams published an eleven-page pamphlet called *Go-Go*. Composed almost entirely of poems which had earlier that year appeared in the unobtainable *Spring and All*, a New York printer published 150 copies of the tiny pamphlet in his *Manikin* series. Normally, the little avant-garde venture would have escaped a reviewer's notice. But Marion Strobel, a young poet whom Williams had met at a poetry reading in Chicago in the spring of 1918, and for whom he wrote his "A Good Night," hit Williams hard in the November, 1923, *Poetry* in a review called "Middle-aged Adolescence." Her tone was extremely harsh, directed against such a slim volume. It was a tone, in fact, recalling the baroness' very personal attack of two years before. Williams hadn't "the guts" to be simple, and so had made "a muddle of his last poems." He was really "a person with delicate sensibilities and genuine emotion" who insisted on hiding behind words. He was a "bully-boy" whose "swaggering phrases" merely hid a "frightened spirit."

To counter this sharp blast, Marjorie Allen Seiffert, another young poet-friend of Williams's from the *Others* days and a member of the short-lived Spectric School, replied to Strobel in the April, 1924, issue of *Poetry* in her review of *Spring and All*. She called her review, pointedly, "Against the Middle-Aged Mind." Williams, she said, was one of the few poets "articulate enough to tell us what he means, what he is attempting to do." He was a modern, one of those who had already "attained an established position with the apostles of the newer forms of poetry." *Spring and All* was marked by clarity and speed, a sign that it had escaped the sclerosis of "middle age." She pointed to Williams's own definition of art as nonrepresentative, as object enjoying its own "separate existence," written out of a "condition of imaginative suspense." But, she added, besides simply writing down what occurred at such moments, the intelligence had to *shape* the material, or else one was left not with the poem but with a dream-like pre-art. Williams's method somehow worked for his poems about objects, but failed where he dealt with subjective states of mind. In spite of this, she still preferred Williams's "copies" from nature to most artists' "imitations."

Paul Rosenfeld's *Port of New York* (1924) devoted a generous chapter to Williams. Rosenfeld was music critic for the *Dial*, intimate of Stieglitz's Seven Arts Group, and an influential literary critic in New York circles in the twenties. He was considered a liberal, the forward-looker as Van Wyck Brooks was the conservative, the traditionalist. *Port of New York* presented fourteen portraits of men and women, many of them, interestingly, painters and photographers. What Rosenfeld saw in them all, however, was a new spirit, a new wealth in American life. Williams shared space with figures like Sandburg, Stieglitz, Bourne, Marsden Hartley, Georgia O'Keeffe, Van Wyck Brooks, and John Marin, all of whom were treated with Rosenfeld's ersatz impressionistic effusiveness, a style which seems to have been caught in the undertow as the twenties went out, pulling Rosenfeld under with it. "The poems of William Carlos Williams are good biting stuff," he noted. "Lyric substance has gotten a novel acidulousness of him. Scent bitter like the nasturtium's, and like the nasturtium's fresheningly pungent, mounts off his small spiky forms."

Here was Pater's style mixed, as in epilepsy, with brilliant flashes, as when Rosenfeld called Williams's stark, crisp world "some Greenland on the verge of the Arctic circle," "a world of lowish climaxes and thin releases." Williams's palate was a monotone grey, and his world too "scraggly and bare," filled with clearly defined but isolated objects . . . a solitary track of footprints in the snow, a fire in an ash-can, pools left by the tide." And yet he had risen above the poverty of these surroundings through his imagination and "selfless sympathy" to see "children, women in labor, the sick." Rosenfeld admired the man for blaming only himself for this leanness and not his place or his time, as T. S. Eliot, that "emigre" who lacked Williams's passion for truth, had done in *The Waste Land*. Williams could "give himself" without "pride, . . . give himself in his crassness, in his dissonant mixed blood, in absurb melancholy, wild swiftness of temper, man-shyness; Americano, Jerseyite, Rutherfordian; give himself with a frankness, a fearlessness, a scientific impersonality, that is bracing as a shock of needle-spray."

The Great American Novel, he said, was like *Ulysses*. It too saw its place—the American suburbs—"not as in the bestsellers, superficially," but from within: "the Sunday-afternoon family motor drive, . . . the Pullman plate-glass window in the parlor wall." Williams was the one American who had come to the New World, and not to an achieved American civilization, had come to the smoky Bayonne littoral with its "slatey weed-garden of wharves, gas-tuns, church-spires," and sent "up some wild signal rockets through the gloom" to show other American intellectuals that they could make it here.

In the American Grain

In the American Grain, published by Albert Boni in November, 1925, was Williams's "first book by a commercial publisher," as he tells us in his *Autobiography*, "and I was dancing on air—because to that point nothing I was writing had any market: I had either paid for it myself or had it accepted, for the most part, without pay. The Bonis made a beautiful book of it, for which I shall be forever grateful, but, as far as marketing it, they did next to nothing. . . . In no time at all the thing was remaindered." In spite of this, the book still managed to attract a good deal of attention.

The *Saturday Review of Literature* for December 19, 1925, for example, carried a front-page, although anonymous, review of the book. The reviewer, out to counter Williams's Rousseauvian attack on the accepted staple of American household penates, insisted (as many critics were to do) that Williams was a poet and not a historian. Unfortunately, there was just too much debunking of America in the air, in such books as *Civilization in the United States* (1921), with its chorus of thirty American malcontents who had denied the "traditional" American values. That horde loosed by Lytton Strachey had set out to attack "the moral im-

pulse as the curse of America" and to make the uncontrolled frontiersman "our only hero." Such books, the reviewer said, were not
only not history; they weren't even good sense. He was puzzled
that Williams could regard "the sober march of civilization across
the continent as an unfortunate curtailment of savage liberty," replacing it with the alternative vision of Williams dancing "naked
in the moonlight around a broached rum cask in Gramercy Park."
While much could be said against the fatted-calf image of America, "to choose rampageous Indians" like the Abenakis or Jaca-
tacqua, and "political reprobates" like Aaron Burr as "ancestral
models by way of a change from Puritans, Quakers, and Virginia
gentlemen" was "to strike a Parisian attitude which seems a little
absurd in New York." A whole world of settled attitudes lies in
that last comment, a fear endemic to the more established quar-
terlies which fifty years has not quieted.

The anonymous reviewer for the *Times* (Feb. 7, 1926) was
more ambivalent. *In the American Grain* was at once "remarkably
lucid," yet "turbid and inconsequential." Williams had taken a
number of figures from American history—mostly famous—and
judged them by their relation to America. Williams's admiration
had gone out mostly to those men who were failures in history's
eyes but whose lives were made richer for that failure: the defeated Indians, Boone, Poe, and Aaron Burr, "a fighter against the
narrow Federalism of the times." And his dislike had been aimed
against those, like the Puritans and Franklin, who had shaped the
America of his own moment. Williams was a master of a rich,
impressionistic prose, but he could also collapse into a "gracelessly
cryptic style;" in fact, for all its brilliance, the whole book spun
off, finally, into a near absurdity.

Kenneth Burke (*Books*, Mar. 14, 1926) attempted to see the
book in terms of its underlying strategy. "It is Williams' business,"
he wrote, "to see beyond the label." Williams's strategy had been
"to replace 'Columbus discovered America in 1492' with excepts
[sic] from Columbus' diary which show what it was to be ap-
proaching America at the turn of that century and to see a continent not as land, but in terms of seaweed, of river birds heard
passing in the night." (Burke may have been recalling Pound's
insistence that we see place not by map but by seaboard.) Still,
Williams's method had its shortcomings: there was too much interpretation and too little research. Ideology as an organizing principle—form again—had been insufficiently attended to. Williams saw
his country's past not defined in terms of historical pressure or

movements, but in terms of representative figures. But in place of Pound's company of geniuses, Williams sought a company of heroes. Both were driven by what seemed to be a Nietszchean will, which, beginning as a lure, finally became a goad—riding Williams's heroes until it was impossible to distinguish in them "that which is done in aggression and that which is done in defense, between power and starvation, play and malice." Unfortunately, Williams's treatment of women, while vigorous and picturesque, was often puerile. Even his masculine heroes tended to degenerate to the level of "a nun's ponderings."

In fact, Lola Ridge (*NR*, Mar. 24, 1926) found "in Williams signs of sex-antagonism." He had a "hunger" to make contact with women, not "the plush sofa variety, . . . but those of the gutters." Like most outsiders who had not come in direct contact with them, Williams had made the error of regarding New England woman as "sexless." "But," Ridge insisted, "they are no more sexless than any other women, merely encased in congealed opinion that resists thaw like the long snows that persist upon their hills." Significantly, Williams treated blacks in his writing in the same way that he treated women: inadequately. It was not that he was unsympathetic; he was simply too narrow. He tended to see them in terms of a "single gesture:" as people whose joy and beauty could not be beaten out of them. It was, really, the Indian who dominated the book, a giant figure, "a red power passing silent, subtle, into the white bodies, in and under the white skin." If the book was unequal, it was also "a great adventure, . . . a fresh and beautiful interpretation of American history, . . . an interrupted song." The Lincoln closing was a "sensitive minor note, . . . the first to touch the brooding mother in that lonely man." Raleigh, "that shadow-man," was "a song in the air . . . not again to be forgotten." Montezuma had been drawn to the very life, but Daniel Boone and De Soto remained the figures of a "boy's passion." Of Williams's Puritans, Ridge offered this two-edged comment: "He has achieved here as searching an analysis of Puritanism as was possible to one not yet quite convalescent from its effects." The book worked, finally, because it had gone beyond "mere factual truth" to "the truth that can only be proven by emotional recognition."

The anonymous reviewer in the *Saturday Review* had been the first to comment on the book's similarities to D. H. Lawrence's 1923 *Studies in Classic American Literature*. The latter had also attacked the "puritan" suppression of instinct in America and the

thwarted flowering of "a kind of old Indian devil" in the pioneer
American. In April, 1926, Lawrence himself reviewed *In the
American Grain* and underlined Williams's emphasis that good
"creative art must rise out of a specific soil and flicker with a
spirit of place." The book stressed "the Americanization of the
white men in America" rather than the "Europizing" of America.
This was important, Lawrence noted, because most of the "new
one hundred per cent" American writing, while it may have been
about Americans, was still European in its conception. For the
white American was basically European; what was different about
him was that he had gone after the spirit of the new continent,
"a woman with exquisite, super-subtle tenderness and recoiling
cruelty," a "myth-woman." There was as yet no American race,
Lawrence felt, only a "bastardized" European "consciousness with
only a flicker of a really *new* consciousness in the germ of a new
aristocracy." Difficult as it was, Williams had managed to catch
some of that life: "the strength of insulated smallness in the New
Englanders, the fascination of 'being nothing' in Negroes, the
spell-bound quality of men like Columbus, De Soto, Boone,"
glimpses of "what the vast America *wants men to be*." If Williams's view differed in some respects from his own, Lawrence was
"thankful" that the book had been written. Williams himself was
extremely pleased by Lawrence's attention and wrote telling him
so, but Lawrence never answered. Still, Lawrence had touched
Williams deeply, as his beautiful elegy to Lawrence bears witness.
That two poets so close in spirit did not pursue this opportunity to
exchange their ideas with one another is but one more of a thousand literary regrets.

   In the American Grain was particularly well received by the
French avant-garde. Eugene Jolas, the editor of *transition*, admired Williams, and so, for the first issue of his Paris-based journal,
published in April, 1927, Kay Boyle was invited to review the
book. Williams's approach to his subject was unusually "single and
detached." He had not written about "the 'wilderness' with affection, and few writers have avoided that." Boyle saw in Williams
what he himself had seen in Poe: "the strong sense of a beginning," the intensity of immediate contact with the environment
which had produced a rich and violent prose. There was an "authenticity" in the writing.

   But if Kay Boyle praised Williams's achievement, Laura Riding,
also focusing on Williams's treatment of Poe, attacked him in the
October number of *transition*. In a piece called "Jamais Plus"

(Nevermore), a chapter of a book she was writing on Poe, she regretted that Americans like Eliot and Williams had tried to salvage such "second-rate" American artists as Poe. "An inhibition composed of uneven parts of snobbism and loyalty," she wrote, "generally inspires modern Poe enthusiasts to quote Poe in his less famous achievements. In Dr. Williams it is three parts loyalty to prefer *To One in Paradise*, one of the worst of Poe's poems, to the *Raven*, the best of the worst (and all were worst); and the lesser tales to the 'popular, perfect'—*Gold-Bug* and the *Murders in the Rue Morgue*, which are undoubtedly the best." Williams had been right not to stress the sense of supernatural mystery in Poe because, finally, Poe was "plainly insignificant." Riding, together with Robert Graves, had earlier in the same year dismissed Williams's "spurious individuality" in their *A Survey of Modernist Poetry*. Scrutinizing Williams's "Struggle of Wings," which had appeared in the *Dial* in 1926, they condemned it as "obvious charlatanry." Williams's was a synthetic modernist poetry composed of ingredients plainly imitative of those "that made up the poems of more genuine writers" such as Cummings, Edith Sitwell, and Eliot. Williams himself was simply one of those "parasitical imitators," a group which included Stevens and Pound.

Williams was no doubt angry at such a libelous dismissal, but it was Riding's essay on Poe which brought his angry response in the January, 1928, *transition:* "My own essay on Poe in my book *In the American Grain*," he replied, "is full of hasty statements which Miss Riding is quite correct in checking." But she had missed the force of his argument. Writers were a community, he reminded her, and when they went after each other as she had gone after him, with a kind of hauteur and general ill will, then the cause of writing itself suffered. (Williams's larger response to Laura Riding's attack on modernist poetry, "Philosophy as Literature," written in September, 1927, while he was on board ship heading home to America, was never published but exists in typescript.)

Between Riding's attack and Williams's reply, Eugene Jolas issued a statement of purpose (Dec. 1927) which was clearly Marxist in orientation. He praised Williams as an example of the poet who had returned "to the origins of the American mythology." Williams was an American romantic, an example for others of the artist who had gone "back to his earth, that rich, fruitful loam which is now being violated by the sadistic hand of industry." What was more, he had shown the way in *In the American*

Grain to "a new faith which may help us create the myths for
which every true artist is waiting today." By returning to the
primitive ground of the New World, Williams had hoped "to
find again that impetus to the imaginative life now being choked
in sentimentality and ignorance. The Mound Builders, the Indians,
the Incas, the Azteks, the Mayas, Negro art offer a liberation of
the spirit that may help the new artistic forces of our generation."
Williams's heroes were the "great pioneers" with their "roots in
the soil." In thus emphasizing their own place, they had become
models for the "great internationalists."

Early Overviews, 1926-1928

In late 1925 Marianne Moore had asked Wallace Stevens to review *In the American Grain* for the *Dial*, but Stevens replied that
there was no time because of his new role as *pater familias*. "What
Columbus discovered is nothing to what Williams is looking for,"
he told her. "However much I might like to try to make that
out—evolve a mainland from his leaves, scents and floating bottles
and boxes—there is a baby at home." When, a year later she asked
him to write the *Dial* Award announcement for 1926 honoring
Williams, he had to turn down her offer "to act as midwife for
Williams's spirit." So Marianne Moore wrote the announcement
herself in January, 1927, quoting from Stevens's 1925 letter, from
Blum's 1921 comments, and from an old note of William Marion
Reedy's. Williams, she said, wrote of "fences and outhouses built
of barrel-staves and parts of boxes, of the 'sparkling lady' who
'passes quickly to the seclusion of her carriage,' of Weehawken, of
'The Passaic, that filthy river.' His "venomous accuracy" of
language was firmly against " 'makeshifts, self-deceptions and grotesque excuses.' "

The February number of the *Dial* carried Kenneth Burke's
"William Carlos Williams, the Methods of." "Williams has consistently manifested an almost hysterical demand for newness,"
Burke maintained, "and we may pardon his attempt to make this
a categorical imperative for all writers when we see how salubrious
it has proved to be in the case of himself." But, he warned (as
Stevens had warned ten years before) "an equipment of habitual
gestures is as necessary to verse as it is to tennis." Because he had
taken his own lonely tack, Williams had turned after *Al Que
Quiere!* to write "not lyrics but diaries" with their eschewal of

both "ceremony" and the "sustained emotional curve" of oratory—
another of Burke's jabs at the *Improvisations*. Instead, Williams's
lyrics had assumed "the qualities of conversation and the friendly
letter: moodiness, vagary, simple declarations, ellipses, and fresh
starts, an art which as Gide says of life occurs without erasure."
The strategy of the *Improvisations*, Burke noted, was "a simple
dualism," where the metaphor and its object of reference were by
turns equally prominent: variation followed by theme rather than
the reverse, with the theme itself pulling away from the overall
schema to follow instead the curve of the improvisation itself.
They were, he felt, a kind of "biological necessity," a kind of
clearing house for Williams, after which *Sour Grapes* had come
as a "recovery," where "keenness of perception" did not have to
"dislocate consistency of movement." *The Great American Novel*
he dismissed as "an entire book written incidentally while the
author searches for an opening sentence." Williams's best volume
was still his early *Sour Grapes*, all the work after it serving as
"some new and hypothetical equilibrium of the future." But how
long was this review sitting around one wonders, since there is
no mention of *In the American Grain* and, in fact, of nothing
done after 1923?

Marianne Moore's steel-web logical structures served as anti-
phon to Burke in the March number of the *Dial*. "It was Ezra
Pound's conviction some years ago," she noted in her essay, "A
Poet of the Quattrocento," "that there could be 'an age of awak-
ening in America' which could 'overshadow the quattrocento.'"
And, in fact, Pound had already praised such un-"murkn" qualities
in Williams as his "opacity," his "distinctness and color." Beyond
this, however, Williams was "a man with his feet on the soil . . .
personally and peculiarly his own." He was "rooted." And if at
times he was "almost inarticulate," still, he was "never dry, never
without sap in abundance." Moore found Pound's tree metaphor
to describe Williams fitting. For here was indeed a poet of *place*,
one who believed he could flower in his own locale.

In the fall of 1922 Gorham Munson had written in S_4N "that
the permanent expatriate type" was already "extinct." Pound's
symbolic gesture of leaving the United States (as Henry James
had done before him) was no longer necessary, for it was now
possible for the young American artist to simply secede from all
"irrelevant drains upon our energies" and to move "into purely
aesthetic concerns." During the 1910s, a new literary milieu had
been created in America with a new reading public (numbering

perhaps 20,000) which had rejected the old parasitic genteelness that had fed off English Victorianism. By 1920 naturalism and realism were exhausted forms, as were the literary canons of Sinclair Lewis and Robert Frost. American criticism was simply reactionary and "enervatingly harmonious," its leading spokesmen either mud beds of undisciplined emotionalism like Paul Rosenfeld or smartish gossips posing as "advanced" critics like Burton Rascoe. But there was a group of young writers, then in their early twenties, who were "ripe for a secession," writers who were after, in Malcolm Cowley's words, "form, simplification, strangeness, respect for literature as an art with traditions, abstractness." Munson had in mind writers like Hart Crane, Cummings, Waldo Frank, Kenneth Burke. And while Williams was then almost forty, he had found a strong following among the younger writers. He best exemplified in his own work the quality of simplification, the antithesis of the Symboliste–Mallarmean mode. Williams was, instead, the poet of the "stark hard definition," accurately rendering the immediate sensation; he was a neo-primitive, a "precultural" writer.

In his *Destinations: A Canvass of American Literature since 1900*, published six years later, Munson presented a generous overview of Williams's development in the dozen years between *The Tempers* (1913) and *In the American Grain* (1925). Munson's was the first serious overview and summation of Williams and, while it leaned heavily on Kenneth Burke's earlier statements and judgments, it lucidly summed up a growingly conservative view of Williams's achievement as it was understood by the late twenties. Many contemporary American writers, it was clear to Munson, had failed to develop in the years between 1913 and 1928; Sandburg, Lindsay, Sherwood Anderson, Masters, Dreiser, Mencken, Brooks had all fallen off or represented holding actions. But Williams had, if not exactly developed, "at least changed" in a "frantic effort to develop."

The Tempers, a conventional book with conventional metrics, rhymes, classical allusions, showed the heavy influence of Pound and Browning. It was an "Academy" book. But *Al Que Quiere!* showed a marked break with a conservative tradition. In the intervening four years Williams had found his subject in the particulars of his American background and his form in vers libre, a form necessitated by his life as a practicing physician, "writing poems in odd minutes between calls," for vers libre could concentrate on the distinctive weight of the single word rather than on "combinations of words." Munson summed up Williams's *ars poetica* as

follows: first, the cleansing of words, that is, removing their con-
notative drift; and second, the lyrical turn, that is, the exhilaration,
the sense of flight which accompanies the getting down of "an
exact perception of some object." Such a poetics allowed Williams
to include all sense experience, the rank as well as the pleasant.

Kora in Hell was, all things considered, a setback after *Al Que
Quiere!* So Burke, thus Munson. Williams, Munson felt, had been
wrong to listen to Pound's talk of his "praiseworthy opacity." The
trouble lay, really, in Williams's "association of ideas": a consolidation of "widely divergent glimpses of things for the sake of the
personal connection." It had turned out to be an "excessively subjective" methodology. Nor was Rimbaud really Williams's prede-
cessor, for the young Frenchman had been a skeptic who had
worked himself into *A Season in Hell* with no exit, but Williams
was more the optimist who had indeed tried to construct new
beginnings. Had not Williams himself admitted that the *Improvisations* suffered by "their dislocation of sense, often complete?"

Williams's *Contact* magazine laid down "a program for American writing" for its two hundred readers, a program which constituted "an artistic credo to which Williams had adhered with
ardor and fidelity" and a program which had, in large measure,
worked for him. Vachel Lindsay, Robert J. Coady's *Soil*, the
Seven Arts Group, Stieglitz—each had worked for a program of
national art and had failed. But Williams had shown in *Sour
Grapes* that his esthetic could work; it was an esthetic which recognized its own limits and which insisted on treating its subject
matter primarily as an object of the imagination.

The trouble with Williams, however, was that he was an American primitive, "lost in the unchartered American background,"
where the chaos of the New World threatened to overwhelm
him. Had not *The Great American Novel* demonstrated Williams's lack of pattern, his very inability to get the novel "under
way"? Williams's prose, Munson realized, was highly sophisticated
and could range from the associational complexity of Joyce to the
direct, simple idiom of the American backwoodsman. But an avant
garde sophistication borrowed from Europe did not seem to be the
best instrument with which to discover "the new terms" needed
for the American experience. *Spring and All* was still another
"thrashing about," with its "heavier stress upon novelty and the
imagination" than was evident even in *Kora in Hell*. Williams's
search for the new had degenerated into "a search for poetic conceits," with the fancy "forming unexpected, astonishing, novel

combinations." The book was neither a harmonious whole nor a "complete apprehension of actuality," but, rather, "an arbitrary composition characterized by independence."

In the American Grain, on the other hand, was a swing away from an avant garde cubist poetics to a viable American primitivism. Here was a history where the past was "made to put its weight directly and heavily upon the present." It was "American history with an emotional dimension." Munson detailed the three principal factors in Williams's history: (1) the New World with its "colossal forces"; (2) the white Europeans in America—Spaniards, French, and Puritans; (3) the Indian, rooted in the New World. In Daniel Boone, Sam Houston, and Aaron Burr, Munson saw that Williams had picked three of his own masters: Boone in letters, Houston in method, Burr in his "personal psychology" and insistence on preserving his own individualism against the pressures of society to conform. The prose itself was muscular, savage, a counterpointing of a "new eloquence" with Williams's "usual broken impatient hammering." But, Munson concluded, unless Williams reversed the psychological process of descent into the particulars of experience and ascended "into our unrealized potentials" towards the general, the patterned—towards, in short, a grand synthesis—Williams would have to remain a very good but minor figure.

A Voyage to Pagany

When Williams's first novel, *A Voyage to Pagany*, was published in September, 1928, it was dedicated "To the first of us all my old friend Ezra Pound." "You should have a copy the end of August," Williams had written to Pound in June, asking him to give the book "a little blurb," if Pound didn't "feel disgraced" by the thing. Pound generously responded with his brilliant and perceptive "Dr. Williams' Position," which appeared in the November number of the *Dial.* Pound began with an anecdote about Williams which revealed his habit of "unhurriedly" examining whatever was before him. It was this kind of minute attention to things, Pound said, which distinguished Williams from the "floral and unconscious minds" of most "murk'ns" who had the bad habit of taking an idea and serving it up in fifty different ways, "watered, diluted but still the same idea or notion, pale but not wholly denatured." Williams alone of American writers had refused to swallow ideas unexamined. Frost and Cummings were regionalists, "typical" New Englanders. But Williams, like that Greenwich Village character, Joe Gould, was a real artist with his "root in a given locality." He was an American artist, Pound conceded, but for complex reasons: if Williams had taken a stand counter to his English father, he was still the outsider looking in (a real "Dago immigrant," as Pound put it in one of his letters). He had been spared "the arid curse of our nation" by reason of his English-Puerto Rican birth, so that he did not have the desire, as Pound had, "to murder" those who had betrayed "the work of the national founders," Pound's great theme in the Adams *Cantos* he was then writing. Where Pound saw "scoundrels and vandals," Williams saw "a spectacle or an ineluctable process of nature." Even Williams's disgust never went beyond art.

Pound had learned that Williams's habit of "unhurried contemplation" irritated the British. However, there were a "small number of French critics"—such as Valery Larbaud, Eugene Jolas, and René Taupin—who admired the man's work, especially *In the American Grain*. And no wonder, Pound explained, for Williams started "where an European would start if an European were about to write of America: sic: America is a subject of interest, one must inspect it, analyse it, and treat it as subject." Williams's own critical tenets were summed up concisely for Pound in Williams's just published essay, "George Antheil and the Cantilene Critics": the critic's function was to say what a work of art "consisted of, what were its modes and procedures." But American criticism was still fifteen or twenty years "behind the times" and still "constitutionally unable to know when a creative act occurred."

Pound was ready to admit that there was an absence of major form in Williams, but this was really not very important. Williams was one of those writers who simply did not "conclude." The writing was often opaque, obscure, truncated, but Western thought was itself too tied up with monism and orthodoxy, with the received ideas of total form, and had too long censured the dissociation of ideas. Pound shrewdly observed that some "very important chunks of world-literature" lacked major form: the *Iliad*, *Prometheus Bound*, Montaigne, Rabelais, *Bouvard et Pécuchet*. What these works did have, and what was indispensable to them, was what Williams had—texture. If Williams did not seem to have a proper regard for the Flaubertian finish, still, there was "that other satisfactory effect . . . of a man hurling himself at an indomitable chaos, and yanking and hauling as much of it as possible into some sort of order (or beauty), aware of it both as chaos and as potential." Finally, if *A Voyage to Pagany* was Williams's "first long work" and probably his "worst" (how nicely Pound slipped this in!), it had passages "worth any one's while, . . . mental cud for any ruminant tooth." The novel had merely served, then, as an occasion for Pound to sum up Williams's achievement and to place him in the quite respectable tradition of processive, open-ended form.

Pound had liked *The Great American Novel* better because, if it was "more gnarled," it had the elements of a complex, intelligent form. And both books, different as they were, were in fact offsprings of *Ulysses*. Still, it was *In the American Grain* which held "the greater interest for the European reader." Williams was always at his best when he was least concerned with "form" and most concerned with the deeper, hidden consciousness of his characters; he only *seemed* to confine himself to presenting their "objective manifests." And, finally, there was the man's "integrity." Williams had shown through nearly two decades that he did possess staying power. "Dear Ezrie," Williams wrote Pound as soon as he had read the essay, "Nothing will ever be said of better understanding regarding my work than your article in the *Dial*. I must thank you for your great interest and discriminating defense of my position." Pound had, he realized, managed to "hit most of the trends" he was after; had, in fact, "clarified" Williams's own intentions to himself. As a result, Williams understood better where he himself was going.

An anonymous review (*Times*, Sept. 30, 1928) made an unintentionally ironic commentary on American sexual mores, one of the very things Williams had complained about in *A Voyage to Pagany*. "The artist who drew the jacket design" for the novel, the reviewer began, "may have come nearer the core of the novel than he intended or suspected, for in the idea of a serpent encircling the world, a serpent of evil eye and with forked tongue extended, there is expressed something of the evil which lurks behind this strange and sinister fiction." It was one way of viewing the *ourosbouros*—the serpent of time with its tail in its mouth—which Williams's brother had drawn.

Williams was made to sound like a cross between Oscar Wilde, bringing the gentle American reader insights into "regions of emotion and desire before which he will hesitate appalled," and Byron, in the "sinister" episode between Evans and his sister. The protagonist, the reviewer felt, must surely have been constructed from a cross section of pathological test cases (Williams, of course, was writing thinly veiled autobiography). Evans's search for happiness was illusory, defeatist, grounded as it was, finally, on the ascetic beauty of the "Continental scientific mind." Williams's women were only symbols, mere words "in the great scheme of the COSMOS made for the moment flesh."

Looking back at *In the American Grain*, Morley Callaghan (*Books*, Oct. 7, 1928) noted that it had been "so free from academic attitude" that few critics had known how to adequately handle it. Now Williams had extended his earlier theme in his new novel. Callaghan praised the Vienna section with its implied criticism of the American medical profession and the incestuous closing scenes between Evans and his sister. But he too was bewildered by Williams's unconcern with form, "as though he wrote the book without giving consideration to any such problem." If the prose was "unheroic" when compared to a piece like his earlier "The Destruction of Tenochtitlan," it was because Williams's expatriates deserved "a more casual treatment."

Williams's novel was "not a book that is likely to yield all its goodness to any but an American reader," the English reviewer for the *Times Literary Supplement* asserted in November. "To an European it is an interesting curiosity, rather enlightening and rather pathetic." Evans was "anything but the cultured New Englander," he noted, geographically misplacing Evans by several states, and "so ignorant that he forces Mr. Williams to spell every other French word he uses wrong, but not ashamed of his ignorance because aware of his force." And then, in a royal gesture of dismissal: "We cannot follow this record of spiritual growing-pains with anything but a slightly amused sympathy, and a certain incomprehension, while recognizing a rough, vigorous, sincere mind at work, which is determined to take nothing at second hand," (including, of course, the whole English tradition).

Louis Zukofsky's review in the *Symposium*, "Beginning Again with William Carlos Williams," was dated by Zukofsky October 8, 1928, although it did not appear until early 1931. The review forms a postscript to Zukofsky's long three-part essay on Henry Adams which had been appearing earlier in the same magazine. Drawing parallels between *Mont-Saint-Michel and Chartres* (1904) and *A Voyage to Pagany* along the lines of the American's instinctual quest for the mythical woman in Europe in the form of Adams's Virgin and Williams's Venus, Zukofsky pointed up the

basic difference between the two writers. In Adams there was a
tragic finality in his inability "to attain the ciborium" at the last;
but in Williams there was instead a constant regeneration, a moving "on to the Beginning." "There can be no lingering here for
what is final, for what resolves into unity," Zukofsky wrote. Instead, Williams went after beginnings and ever new beginnings,
which meant giving over the nostalgias of the past. Williams also
refused to settle for a "premature sentiment with regard to
America's peasantry—rare in recent fiction." He could see *through*
"incident," surrounding and fathoming things until they seemed to
live from within. Williams had pointed the way for other American writers to carefully consider their own beginnings precisely
and accurately; in short, to come into a sharp, unsentimental contact with their own place.

Two Critical Views, 1930

René Taupin's section on Williams in his *L'Influence du Sym-
bolisme Francaise sur la Poésie Américaine (1910–1920)* marks the
crest of critical attention, such as it was, devoted to Williams as a
poet before the trough of inattention which the next decade and
a half were to bring. In fact, Williams did not reemerge until the
publication of the first parts of *Paterson* in the mid-1940s. In the
Hound and Horn in 1931 Yvor Winters, in a review of Taupin's
study, noted: "I myself am especially grateful for the praise that
Mr. Taupin gives Dr. Williams, a writer who has seemed to me
for ten years or so one of the principle geniuses of our time, and
whose work has been stupidly neglected and ridiculed." And yet,
except for a passing comment noticing the similarity between
Hopkins's and Williams's metrics, Winters himself had nothing
more to say about Williams. (One suspects that for Winters the
term "genius" was about as welcome as a bout with St. Vitus's
dance.)

In 1929 Taupin, as an intelligent if not profound French observer of American poetry, saw Williams as few Americans were
to see him for at least another twenty years: as "probably among
the three best American poets," after, presumably, Pound and
Eliot. But, then, Taupin took much of his cue from Pound himself, whom he admired and with whom he was corresponding.
Much of Pound's 1928 estimate of Williams found its way into
Taupin's essay. So, for example, Taupin sounded like Pound when

he dismissed the "English" tradition of Edwin Arlington Robinson and Edna St. Vincent Millay, as well as the regionalist traditions of Masters, Sandburg, and Frost for being old and "hardly vital." If Williams had attempted an *American* art, Taupin meant by this not an art concerned "with American ideas and prejudices," as with Whitman, but one concerned with a "direct and full contact" between a man and his place. Despite Williams's own letter to Taupin that he hadn't read many of "the contemporary French writers or even the classics," Taupin was convinced that Williams's American art had indeed been shaped in large part by the French avant garde, and in particular by Rimbaud's *Illuminations*, as Pound himself had suggested. After the disciplined imagism of *Al Que Quiere!*, Taupin noted, Williams had "set up for himself the problem of a more faithful transcription of his emotions" in the *Improvisations*. Like Rimbaud, he had loosed the soul to dance. Both were realists, yet both possessed visionary imagination. Both showed a verbal drunkenness, a controlled dreamlike quality in their writings, and a marked opacity.

Unlike Pound and Eliot, however, Williams had not broken new ground in literature. Instead, he had extended or completed work begun by them. He had brought to American literature a greater emotional intensity than it characteristically showed, and he knew "more about the workings of the poetic imagination than any other" contemporary American poet. Most critics, Taupin noted, were not even aware of Williams's importance as a critical thinker, and only an unsophisticated reader would balk at Williams's pregnant obscurity. But if Williams was clearly an American in his whole sensitivity, he had nevertheless been unable to persuade his countrymen to accept his radical poetics. Henry James, too, had had the same problem, Taupin recalled: he also had "wanted to persuade the artists of his country to plunge in wholeheartedly 'up to the neck in all which their country and climate can give them.' Instead, James had found himself up to his own neck in Flaubert." Like Pound, then, Taupin viewed Williams as the outsider, informed by a continental sensibility, with a fresh vision of America, but a prophet unheeded in his own country.

Louis Zukofsky wrote a long sequel to Taupin's essay for the January, 1931, *Symposium*, in which he brought the latter's essay up to date. Zukofsky was interested primarily in showing Williams's importance for the American twenties. He had met Williams through Ezra Pound in 1928, the year he began his own epical *A* (still in progress as of this writing) and the two formed a long and important literary friendship which lasted till Williams's death. By 1931 Zukofsky's Objectivist platform was in full swing; in fact, the now famous "Objectivist" issue of *Poetry* magazine appeared a month after Zukofsky's sequel to Taupin, with Williams established among the Objectivists as grand old master of the movement. "He is of rare importance in the last decade," Zukofsky wrote. "The aesthetics of his material is a living one, a continual beginning, a vision amid pressure." Williams had managed to catch the actual life of things in his writing. *The Great American Novel*, for example, had caught "America, the shifting, as one hurriedly thinks of it or sees it perhaps as one charges from street car to street car." Williams had carefully avoided "sentimentalisms, extraneous comparisons, similes, overweening autobiographies of the heart, all of which permit factitious 'reflection about,' of sequence, of all but the full sight of the immediate." Those critics who saw Williams as only the poet of *The Tempers, Al Que Quiere!* and *Sour Grapes*—such as Munson and Burke—did not understand him, Zukofsky insisted, for Williams's own later criticism had invalidated much of his earlier poetry. Even the *Improvisations*, good as they were, were a kind of "Shakespearian verbalism." But the poetry since *Spring and All* was different in kind, for here Williams was using print not only as a guide to the voice but to the eye as well. "His line sense" was "not only a music heard, but seen, printed as bars." He was not a poet of the line but, like Pound, "of essential rhythm, each cadence emphasized, the rhythm breaking and beginning again, an action, each action deserving a line." Williams had caught his own moment in his poems, had managed to chronicle "the facts about us." A poem like "To Elsie" realized the very "social determinism of American suburbs in the first thirty years of the twentieth century." (Zukofsky's stress on Williams as a social critic, incidentally, was a new note in the Williams commentary which was to grow with the new concerns of the thirties.)

Williams welcomed Zukofsky's recognition, but he still had a long, lonely road to go. By 1930 he had gained some small but important recognition by American and French avant garde literary critics. (Pound had tried to get Williams a hearing in England and had failed, which did not surprise Pound as he packed up and left for Paris in 1920.) A small group of French intellectuals had been impressed by Williams's social commentary on America in *In the American Grain.* Valery Larbaud had given a favorable mention to

The Great American Novel when that book first appeared in Paris in late 1923, and Williams went out of his way to see Larbaud when he went to Paris in early 1924 (a visit which Williams re-created in the Rasles section of *In the American Grain*). In America, by dint of his own hard work and insistencies, Williams had managed by 1920 to find his way into most of the important anthologies. The response to him, such as it was, was heavily in favor of the classical, imagistic Williams of the teens, although a few admired the experimental Williams of *Kora in Hell* and *Spring and All*. Still, all of this activity was taking place in magazines with a circulation of a few hundred which ran for a few numbers and then went under. The large circulation trade magazines virtually ignored Williams and continued to do so for another twenty years. In the thirties, as the more forward-looking academics began to listen to critics of Frank Leavis's stature who were seriously attending to contemporary poets like Eliot and Pound and Yeats, American poets like Williams and Stevens were forgotten or left to the heated infighting and inbreeding of those important but largely unread little magazines.

These heated literary battles have about them a harsh angularity as one reads them now. Perhaps a single stray magnesium flare on the battlefield between the ancients and the moderns will serve to show fitfully something of the life going on in those little magazines. In the Fall 1929 number of the short-lived *Blues*, the twenty-four-year-old Kenneth Rexroth struck out against Yvor Winters's "neoclassic-neothomist-neodostoyefsky philosophy (if it merits the dignity of that term)," and pleaded for "a more explicit rebuttal," a "clarification of issues" about the nature of modernism. Jolas and his confreres at *transition* and *Blues* had "not shown that they were capable of this task and W. C. Williams' articles I think only make matters worse," Rexroth complained, pointing to the front line of the battle at that moment. Williams's critical essays were never "likely to become proverbial for their Aristotelian ludicity." Although Williams's theory was neither confusing nor confused, critics like Winters were wedded to classical formulas, and it was "with the greatest anguish that they see those formulas outraged or disregarded." There were no good critics in the field to defend the modernists, Rexroth felt, except, perhaps, Laura Riding and Allen Tate, with their pitiful "bathos of snobbery." Certainly neither of them was listening much to Williams.

References

Aiken, Conrad
  1919. *Scepticisms: Notes on Contemporary Poetry*. New York: Knopf, pp. 178–86.
Anonymous
  1909. "Verses by Dr. W. C. Williams: . . .," *Rutherford American*. May 6, p. 977.
  1925. "Back to the Indian," *Saturday Review of Literature*. Dec., pp. 425, 430.
  1926a. "American Pot-Pourri," *New York Times Book Review*. Feb. 7, p. 21.
  1926b. "Briefer Mention," *Dial*. Mar., p. 253.
  1926c. *Boston Evening Transcript*. Dec. 30, p. 6.
  1928a. "William Carlos Williams Explores the Evil of Life," *New York Times Book Review*. Sept. 30, p. 2.
  1928b. *Times Literary Supplement*. Nov. 29, p. 932.
Birch-Bartlett, Helen
  1921. "Koral Grisaille," *Poetry*. Mar., pp. 329–32.
Blum, W. C.
  1921. "American Letter," *Dial*. Apr., pp. 562–68.
Boyle, Kay
  1927. "In the American Grain," *transition*. Apr., pp. 139–41.
Burke, Kenneth
  1922. "Heaven's First Law," *Dial*. Feb., pp. 197–200.
  1926a. Review, *New York Times Book Review*. Feb. 7, p. 24.
  1926b. "Subjective History," *New York Herald Tribune Book Review*. Mar. 14, p. 7.
  1927. "William Carlos Williams, the Methods of," *Dial*. Feb., pp. 94–98.
Callaghan, Morley
  1928. "America Rediscovered," *New York Herald Tribune Book Review*. Oct. 7, p. 4.
Dudley, Dorothy
  1918. "To Whom It May Concern," *Poetry*. Apr., pp. 38–43.
Fletcher, John Gould
  1918. "Two American Poets," *Egoist*. Apr., p. 60.
  1921. "Review," *Freeman*. May, p. 238.
Freytag-Loringhoven, Elsa von
  1921. "Thee I call 'Hamlet of Wedding-Ring': Criticism of William Carlos Williams' 'Kora in Hell' and why . . .," *Little Review*. Jan.–Mar. and Autumn, pp. 48–55, 58–60, 108–11.
Jepson, Edgar
  1918. "The Western School," *Little Review*. Sept., pp. 4–9.

Jolas, Eugene
   1927. "On the Quest," *transition*. Dec., pp. 191–96.
Josephson, Matthew
   1923. "Great American Novels," *Broom*. Oct., pp. 178–79.
Katz, Adaline
   1922. Review, *Double Dealer*. Mar., pp. 163–64.
Kreymborg, Alfred
   1925. *Troubadour: An American Autobiography*. New York: Liveright, pp. 157, 186–93, 210, 242–44, 258.
   1929. *Our Singing Strength: An Outline of American Poetry (1620–1930)*. New York: Coward-McCann, pp. 504–10.
Lawrence, D. H.
   1926. "American Heroes," *Nation*. Apr. 4, pp. 413–14.
McAlmon, Robert
   1921. "Concerning 'Kora in Hell,' " *Poetry*. Apr., pp. 54–59.
   1938. *Being Geniuses Together*. New York: Doubleday.
Monroe, Harriet
   1920. "Others Again," *Poetry*. Dec., pp. 150–58.
   1924. "Poets the Self-Revealers," *Poetry*. Jan., pp. 206–10.
Moore, Marianne
   1921. "Kora in Hell, by William Carlos Williams," *Contact*. Summer, pp. 5–8.
   1927a. "Announcement," *Dial*. Jan., pp. 88–90.
   1927b. "A Poet of the Quattrocento," *Dial*. Mar., pp. 213–15.
Mount, Laura
   1926. "Thrilling Americana," *New York World*. Jan. 3, p. 6.
Munson, Gorham
   1922. "The Mechanics for a Literary 'Secession,' " *S.4 N*. Nov.
   1928. "William Carlos Williams, A United States Poet," in *Destinations: A Canvass of American Literature since 1900*. New York: J. H. Sears, pp. 101–35.
Pound, Ezra
   1912. "A Selection from The Tempers," *Poetry Review*. Oct., pp. 481–82.
   1913. "The Tempers," *New Freewoman*. Dec., p. 227.
   1918a. *Pavannes and Divisions*. New York: Knopf.
   1918b. "Books Current," *Future*. June, pp. 188–90.
   1928. "Dr. Williams' Position," *Dial*. Nov., pp. 395–404.
Rexroth, Kenneth
   1929. "Letter from San Francisco," *Blues*. Fall, pp. 42–43.
Riding, Laura
   1927a. (and Robert Graves) *A Survey of Modernist Poetry*. London: W. Heinemann, pp. 201–5, 216–17.
   1927b. "Jamais Plus," *transition*. Oct., pp. 139–56.

Ridge, Lola
    1926. "American Sagas," *New Republic*. Mar. 24, pp. 148–49.
Rodker, John
    1918. "List of Books," *Little Review*. Nov., p. 33.
Rosenfeld, Paul
    1924. *Port of New York*. New York: Harcourt, pp. 103–15.
Seiffert, Marjorie Allen
    1924. "Against the Middle-Aged Mind," *Poetry*. Apr., pp. 45–50.
Strobel, Marion
    1923. "Middle-Aged Adolescence," *Poetry*. Nov., pp. 103–5.
Taupin, René
    1929. *L'influence du Symbolisme Française sur la Poésie Américaine (1910–1920)*. Paris: H. Champion, pp. 278–86.
West, Rebecca
    1930. "A Letter from Abroad," *Bookman*. Feb., pp. 664–68.
Winters, Yvor
    1922. "Carlos Williams' New Book," *Poetry*. July, pp. 216–20.
    1924. "Notes," *Modern Review*. pp. 86–88.
    1931. "The Symbolist Influence," *Hound and Horn*. July–Sept., pp. 607–18.
Zukofsky, Louis
    1931a. "American Poetry, 1920–1930," *Symposium*. Jan., pp. 60–84.
    1931b. "Beginning Again with William Carlos Williams," *Hound and Horn*. Jan.–Mar., pp. 261–64.
    1931c. "Sincerity and Objectification: With Special Reference to the Work of Charles Reznikoff," *Poetry*. Feb., pp. 268–84.

CHAPTER 2

Holding Action: 1930-1945

Throughout the depression and the war years, Williams, like most other contemporary writers, was weighed in terms of his social and political worth; and in fact his writing came to place less emphasis on critical theory and a greater concern on witnessing to the socio-economic realities of the New Jersey industrial landscape which fed his roots. It was in the mid-thirties, too, that the judgment of Williams as the classical imagist broadened (thanks to Wallace Stevens) to include the view of Williams as "antipoetic" romantic. It was a category which subsequent critics pursued with unrelenting zeal for twenty years, as though the word somehow gave them a handy label for seeing, finally, into Williams's anti-Symbolist world. Williams's collections of short fiction and his two novels were duly noted and even sympathetically received. But though they were praised by a few discerning critics on the left as being equal to if not better than the fiction of writers like Farrell and Hemingway, they went largely unread. The publication of the *Collected Poems* in 1938 gave the establishment critics the chance to sum up Williams's career: Williams was regarded, and would continue to be regarded until the late forties, as one of many fine American lyric poets, a writer of no mean achievement, but of no great stature either. It would take *Paterson* to shake the critics into a major reassessment of the man's worth.

Writing about "Some Periodicals of the American Intelligentsia" in the *New English Weekly* in late 1932, the Englishman Austin Warren undertook to dismiss Williams as of no real consequence. It was true Williams had succeeded in getting himself into Louis Untermeyer's anthology and he had earned the respect of Munson and Burke. But no one, Warren quipped, could really say why they admired Williams. Their praise was undoubtedly "the product of loyalty to a veteran leader of the avante-garde who has never graduated out of the little magazines, never become a lecturer for the women's club." Williams was, like Amy Lowell and Ezra Pound, more important for "personal" rather than for "literary" reasons. True, Williams had been an instigator, an influence, but had he actually achieved anything of importance himself? His entire British reputation rested, in fact, on the Englishman's interest in what he thought was "distinctive" in American writing: "something violent and energetic and breezy and uncouth." Warren particularly deplored Williams's own flippant dismissal of contemporary English literature, a dismissal he found "impudently absurd." With both fists flailing, Williams replied to Warren in a letter published in the same magazine a month later. "One does not," he replied defensively, " 'graduate out of the small magazines' to success or failure in writing as Professor Warren would imply, though many writers have 'fallen' to the commercial magazines. . . . If I write poorly I write poorly, and if I write well I write well, no matter where my work appears. And it is far more likely that excellence will come of thought for the writing than from thought for the place into which such writing may advantageously fit."

In the meantime, Pound was still getting a word in for Williams wherever he could. Why, he complained in the June-July number of the *New Review* (Paris), hadn't anyone else besides Zukofsky "the sense to notice René Taupin's chapter on Carlos Williams?" Sure there were errors in such a pioneering book, as Winters, for example, had taken pains to point to, but they "cd. easily be corrected in a second edtn.," and, besides, they didn't flaw the section on Williams. "The logician never gets to the root," Pound commented incisely. "For orientation observe the growing strength of Bill Williams and the progressive dessication of logicists and the constructors of superficial sequence." It is that kind of comment, banged out on a typewriter impatiently, going straight to the problem—the necessary strategy, as Williams and Pound saw it, of eschewing logical sequence—which reads as crisply today as it did in 1931. If anyone saw it. Indeed, few did, but Williams was one. "I read what you said about me in . . . *The New Review*," he wrote Pound in December, "—and it embarrassed me—but I know you're right and it's to the point. It's just a tempermental job to feel anything but the force of what is being said, and still I felt embarrassed and still you're right." Perhaps, he explained, the revival of *Contact* would provide him with the forum he needed to get said what had to get said.

But *Contact* and the Objectivists and two *Collected Poems* and the fiction of a doctor and more poetry—the period from the early thirties up through *The Wedge*—were in fact to be a long hard holding action in terms of Williams's critical reputation. Williams at forty-eight could hardly be considered one of the bright young men. Even when he had begun to be noticed, he was hardly "young." Pound had made a British reputation for himself by the time he was twenty-five, Eliot before he was thirty. Eliot was only thirty-four when *The Waste Land* changed the literary landscape—changed, in fact, the literary fortunes of both the elder literary statesmen and of Williams's own contemporaries. Williams would remember the fact of *The Waste Land* as a bomb which had dropped on his own world. He himself would have to wait, wait longer even than Frost had waited, watch while Hart Crane's spectacular posthumous fame grew, watch the young Englishman Auden heralded by American audiences, watch Yeats canonized. And he would watch too even while his friend Wallace Stevens's reputation grew steadily, attended by an almost Byzantine respect and awe by a small, culturally elitist coterie of European and American critics.

Collected Poems 1921-1931

"Dear fat Stevens, thawing out so beautifully at forty," Williams had commented in his "Prologue" to *Kora in Hell* in 1918. Now it was Stevens's turn to be critical, and the banter had about it something of an October chill. "The slightly tobaccoy odor of autumn is perceptible in these pages," Stevens began his preface to Williams's *Collected Poems 1921–1931*, publication of which was delayed until January, 1934. Williams, Stevens insisted, would undoubtedly be horrified by being called a romantic. But romantic he was. Had he not "spent his life in rejecting the accepted sense of things," in itself a sign that he was a romantic? Williams was like the old philosopher, Diogenes the Cynic, who had insisted that happiness lie in rejecting conventional needs. For Williams had rejected all the conventions, the handbook grammars, of poetry. In another sense, Stevens playfully remarked, Williams was "Lessing's Laocoön: the realist struggling to escape from the serpents of the unreal." But what characterized Williams most centrally, perhaps, was his "passion for the anti-poetic," which he needed as a counterforce to his strongly sentimental side. "One might scan through these pages and point out how often the essential poetry is the result of the conjunction of the unreal and the real, the sentimental and the anti-poetic, the constant interaction of two opposites" which seemed to define Williams and his poetry.

Williams was, naturally, pleased that his old friend had consented to do the preface. But Stevens's talk about the "anti-poetic" —a phrase which subsequently became a handy touchstone for critics—not only bothered Williams; it enraged him. "I had never thought consciously of such a thing," he told Edith Heal twenty-five years later in *I Wanted to Write a Poem*. "As a poet I was using a means of getting an effect. It's all one to me—the anti-poetic is not something to enhance the poetic—it's all one piece. I didn't agree with Stevens that it was a conscious means I was using." But Stevens had not said it was a "conscious" means. In fact, Stevens was only gesturing, providing a series of interchangeable descriptive modifiers, lighthearted variants. But "antipoetic" was to crop up like a weed in review after review for the next twenty years while Williams kept kicking ineffectually at it.

Because of the delay in the publication of the *Collected Poems*, Carl Rakosi's review appeared before the book itself. One of the Objectivists, Rakosi had Williams's manuscript in his hands months before it was published, at a time when Williams was considering calling the thing *Script*. Writing in Zukofsky's *The Symposium* for October, 1933, Rakosi stressed Williams's "Objectivism." (For Williams, Objectivism was an extension of Imagism which included the mind as well as the eye, but Rakosi seemed to understand the term to mean a resurrection of the Imagist preoccupation with an isolated or pure perception of the object. Both, however, agreed in distrusting rhetoric.) "In Williams's clarifying limitation of style," Rakosi wrote, "the absence of overwhelming enthusiasms is a kind of virtue. . . . [Williams's] persistence and concentration on his object in the face of all kinds of contemporary rhetoric are a distinct service." The French Symbolists had been a negative influence on contemporary American writing, he asserted, because of their lexical and syntactic distortions, their studied deviations from prose. Pound had overcome this distorting influence by force of his critical energy, Eliot by mastering his tendency towards sentimentality, Cummings by "caper," Stevens by pattern. Modern society, however, "with its unconscious physical aversion to the poetic process," expressed itself by none of these, but rather by a vernacular "in which objects are presented *in situ.*" It was Williams who had most clearly recognized the specific temper of his own moment. Since *Al Que Quiere!* he had delineated a "solidarity of atmosphere . . . comparable to Hardy" which expressed his own world with "a consistence and a simplification, a character." He could isolate and present the objects around him—his world—with the clarity and enlargement of a microscope. Rakosi saw that Williams's success in creating that world was due in part to the particular way in which he worked symbols: Williams's symbols needed no special labor, no special "collaboration" by the reader. Williams's images usually made their impact on the reader with "the speed of the inscription," as in the description of a dead baby as

> a white model of our lives
> a curiosity
> surrounded by fresh flowers.

Marianne Moore's poetry relied too heavily on an "exclusive selection and the fineries of the lexicon," a regimentation about the order of her images, a hard logic, a distant frozen contact with the subject, a too rigid academicism. But Williams eschewed such rigidities. There was the sense in reading him of watching a mind in the very process of looking for the adequate comparison, a strategy which kept a poem by Williams "graceful and light," but which in the hands of a lesser artist also increased the risk of dullness and banality. Williams's effects were of two kinds. First, those that worked by accretion, by the expansion of the prosaic; and second, those that worked by surprise and "a telescoping of jocularity." When, in the spring of 1969, L. S. Dembo asked Rakosi about Williams's part in the Objectivist movement, Rakosi had come round to a different view: "Williams had not come together with Zukofsky, Charles Reznikoff, George Oppen, and Basil Bunting to found the Objectivist movement." In fact, he had "had very little to do with it. He was included, but it didn't come from his initiative." Such is the frailty of Mnemosyne. But even after thirty-five years, Rakosi still felt that in Williams's poetry one had the sense of "a man there talking." With Stevens, on the other hand, one sensed a poet who had "killed all subject-matter," in the process transforming himself into "something wonderful and beautiful."

Williams "has written some of the most obscure poetry of our time," C. G. Poore commented in his review of the *Collected*

Poems (*Times*, Feb. 18, 1934), "just as Einstein has written some of the most obscure equations." And, despite the support and admiration of "many of the most distinguished critics of contemporary poetry," the public had (understandably) never taken to him. The problem was this: if some of his poems had at least a "superficial intelligibility," how was the reader to thread his way through the "clueless profundities" of the poetry into the bright simplicity of a poem like "The Red Wheelbarrow"? Williams had provided a program note for that piece, and Poore urged him to do the same for all of his poems to make them accessible to a larger audience. On the other hand, he was also willing to admit that Williams's special salvation as a poet resided in his very intransigency, his integrity, his sticking to his guns. It was an old problem familiar to Williams, who had once written that, if he addressed himself to illiterate old women, they too had to listen hard if they were going to understand him.

Blair Rice commented in *Nation* (Mar. 28, 1934) that Williams's poetic strategy had been the same strategy Williams had described for Poe: a movement to clear the ground. This had also been the task Pound had set himself: to hack away the dead timber "of withered words, stock responses, overripe images, and [the] decayed rhythms" of the language. Williams's painterly eye had resulted in a poetry "that is clean and spare and that transmits all the light." Like his own pioneers and Indians, Williams had emphasized a life of "immediacy" and sensuousness, a life of "pure observation," without pretense, "open," gay, unconstrained. But Williams's Objectivist poetics also suffered from having excluded too much; he had given up too "many useful techniques," including metaphor. As a case in point, Rice compared Williams's treatment of old men in a passage from *The Descent of Winter* ("What chance have the old?") with Eliot's treatment of the same subject in "Gerontion," opting for the latter on grounds that it caught the "more essential facts of senility, . . . the tepid inner drama of reminiscence."

In her review of Williams's *Collected Poems*, "Heirs of the Imagists," (*Books*, Apr. 1, 1934), Babette Deutsch stressed Williams's link with the old Imagists. The truth was, she wrote, that Williams was one of the few whose performance had justified the existence of the group. Still, this newer Objectivist movement was little more than a "cult of lyric nudism." "People," she noted, "accustomed to the passionate imagery of Yeats, to Eliot's suggestive music, to the panoplied mysticism of Hart Crane or the rich allusiveness of Pound . . . will find themselves at a loss before this stark and unashamed simplicity of statement." His work was abrupt and frank, antipoetic, closer to the French rather than the English tradition. It was marked by "clarity, incisiveness, the swift contrast, the pleasure in the grotesque." But the methodology of the photographic instant was finally, she insisted, a limitation, a meagerness. One missed "the exaltation that comes of a myth-making power" and "the profound excitement . . . produced by poetry in the tradition of the metaphysical."

Conrad Aiken (*NR*, Apr. 18, 1934) lamented Williams's insistency on throwing "in his lot with the 'little' magazines, avoiding the organized ballyhoo of Big Time publishing." The result was that both his own reputation and his influence had been severely restricted. The best of Williams—*Al Que Quiere!* and *Kora in Hell*—had been altogether omitted from this new collection without ever having been made widely available. Aiken saw that Williams, like Eliot ("in other respects his antithesis") had a "very individual style and a formidable critical awareness with which to defend it." He had to agree with Stevens that there was indeed in Williams a strong "sentimental" side underlying the "antipoetic": "one has always the feeling about Williams that he *wants* to be more 'poetic' than he is," Aiken commented. Williams had a keen sense, a passionate love for things in all their common physicalness, but he kept "checking himself," rubbing out the color, stripping the image, reducing his rhythms to those of prose. In fact, Williams consciously avoided completeness, either of statement or of form. Instead, he sought the effect of a rapid succession of sensory images caught in a broken rhythm, without order or "luxurious elaboration," without "any literary 'calculation.' " Happily, he had departed from this theory in practice, and particularly in such early long poems as "History" and "The Wanderer." He was, then, "a poet in spite of himself," who kept beginning again, dealing with emotions only on the behavioristic level. He was better taken in large doses, and, at fifty, was still the "promising poet."

Marianne Moore's review, "Things Others Never Notice" (*Poetry*, May 1934), considered Williams in the light of Stevens's prefatory remarks. Williams, she wrote, was "drugged with romance"; he was a bee after its opposite representation, the exact likeness of the object, reality. Tension or struggle had been "a main force" in Williams's poetry; it had created a "breathless budding of thought from thought" which insisted on lopping finished patterns "at the acutely right point." Williams's struggle had taken the form of "a dissatisfied expanding energy" which could make a poem urgent for us because it was "urgent for him."

Geoffrey Grigson, pontificating in the British *New Verse* magazine for April, 1934, admitted that he was puzzled by Williams's "pips." Williams wasn't even a "useful simpleton," he quipped, for "the simple, very small, unrhythmical, anti-poetic pips which he prints as poems . . . are not poems, but little knock off bits of unmade poems." In fact, Williams wasn't even capable of a truly imagist poem—a pip—because he kept staining his poems with his own emotions. Anticipating tiresome responses like Grigson's, and thinking perhaps of *The Faerie Queene*, Williams had written in his 1933 review of Zukofsky's "An Objectivist Anthology" that "the difficulty in facing a 'new' work, critically, [was] first to see then to say something that will be at least of an equal freshness with the work itself. But most often we set in motion an antiquated machine whose enormous creaking and heavy and complicated motions frighten the birds, flatten the grass and fill the whole countryside with smoke." In the July, 1934, issue of *Poetry*, he wrote that it was unfortunate that the English critical temperament, while "far more scholarly . . . than that of most Americans," had been "lamed" by "a national prejudice in favor of respectability and conservatism." It was nothing short of insulting to a reader to have a reviewer force "his opinion upon him without giving any indication from the book reviewed of how this opinion came to be formed. The point is that a reader has a right to expect from a reviewer a view of the direct quality of what is being reviewed." When a critic treated a "book in the vein of something ridiculous," Williams pointed out, that critic offended not only the author, but, more importantly, "his own English readers whose possible interest he has ignored in a manner which cannot be spoken of as anything but ill-bred." Williams was speaking primarily of F. R. Leavis's cavalier treatment of Pound's *Active Anthology*, but the timing and force suggest that the image of Grigson's face as a typical English reviewer must have come into view as he wrote his comment.

Prose and Poetry, Mid-Thirties

"Dr. Williams is, in this reviewer's opinion, one of the three or four finest poets now writing in English. [His work] in its integrity of purpose and its profound sincerity, offers an inspiration we would do well to heed." Thus T. C. Wilson—poet, fiction writer, and contributor to *Contact II*—wrote in a January, 1934, review of pamphlets for *Poetry*, three months before Grigson's summary dismissal of Williams. But Wilson's was a lone voice whistling in the wind. Williams's *A Novelette and Other Prose (1921–1931)*, published by Zukofsky's To Publishers in January, 1932, went unnoticed. And there was only passing mention of his book of short stories about New Jersey during the depression, *The Knife of the Times and Other Stories*, published two months later by Angel Flores's Dragon Press in Ithaca, New York. "Few books were sold," Williams recalled later, "and I never heard of Angel Flores again." A friend picked up a batch of the books on the boardwalk in Atlantic City for fifteen cents apiece and sent them back to Williams—a gesture which served as a critical commentary in itself.

Williams had a "limited" but "interesting talent," one reviewer commented (*Sat R*, May 7, 1932). He had a physician's eye and a hard objectivity, but, in reducing his stories to the human interest level, he had missed the dimensions of revelation. The stories were, in fact, simply "no more important" than if they "had happened to his next-door neighbor." It was a comment which failed completely to understand that that was exactly the most important thing for Williams. Another reviewer (*Books*, June 19, 1932) observed, with more attention to Williams's own strategy, that the stories were in the same vein as his imagistic poetry: "clipped, terse fragments, situations which promise more often than they relate dramatic action." If some of the stories owed something to the Hemingway school for their "tempo," Williams also demonstrated a clinical calm, an even-colored tone, an objectivity which set the best of those stories off from the "feverishness of our more subjective writers of fiction."

Williams, now in his fifties and still hampered by his failure to find a big press, found himself forced to publish in small editions. His two volumes of verse, *An Early Martyr and Other Poems* (1935) and *Adam and Eve and The City* (1936), were limited to 150 copies each. Elaborate and expensive editions, these were published by Ronald Lane Latimer's Alcestis press, the same press that also was publishing Wallace Stevens's *Ideas of Order* (1935) and *Owl's Clover* (1936). In spite of the fact that the books were difficult to come by, and in spite of the incongruity of a democratic poet writing proletariat verse for those who could afford expensive

editions, both volumes received wide and favorable notice. It was
Williams's social sensitivity which many critics stressed. They
sensed a growing social consciousness coupled with a sharper,
clearer, more economical, less rhetorical style than they found in
the new leftists, including the young Auden. "Williams has
gone too long without honor in critical circles because he has been
rebel enough to choose his own subjects and method instead of
following (to use his own phrase) the rules of 'the bought
courts,' " wrote Ruth Lechlitner (*Books*, Jan. 19, 1936). His
spareness and strict discipline, gained from his association with the
Imagists, had given him a marked superiority over the "intellectual verbosity and shock-the-reader method of so many young
left-wingers." Williams could link "clear observation" with an
"unconfused, sympathetic understanding" to create such perfect
forms as "To a Poor Old Woman," "The Dead Baby," and "Proletarian Portrait." She praised especially "An Elegy for D. H.
Lawrence" for its psychological understanding of Lawrence, and
noted that both poets had much in common, including their eschewal of the all-embracing Whitman, their dislike of certain
kinds of "social, emotional and intellectual uncleanliness," and
their advocacy of sense-intelligence.

T. C. Wilson (*Poetry*, May 1936) also praised Williams's new
social consciousness—his "assertion of the human and social values
of his material" over his earlier "mere sensory impressionism."
With few exceptions, Williams's earlier work had lacked a "center
of reference" around which his facts might magnetize. But now
he had wedded his social concerns to his "exemplary sobriety" and
"his close contact with the actual world," blessedly devoid of that
subjective "tendency to hysteria or attitudinizing or self-justifica-
tion" one saw in so many of his contemporaries. Williams's human
figures, too, had replaced his earlier concern with still lifes and had
about them "a certain essential rightness." In fact, with its social
commentary, "The Yachts" was probably "the finest poem" the
man had ever written.

Robert Lann (*NR*, July 15, 1936) noticed in Williams, on the
other hand, "a profound pessimism." Flying in the face of most
critical opinion, Lann saw Williams as primarily concerned with
"the static and defined moment rather than with the dynamic flux"
and took it as a sign that Williams found life "unpleasant and fu-
tile." Moreover, whenever Williams tried to argue in his poetry,
thus abandoning his own objectivist strategy, he fell flat on his
face. Williams's forte was "the single sharp concept," and he

fumbled when he tried his hand "at the complex succession of concepts that life usually involves." Here Lann did strike the right chord, for the problem of the long sequence, given the strategy of the focused moment with its refusal of rhetorical solace and rhetorical continuities, did present Williams—and other modernist poets—with a real problem. For Williams's long poems of the thirties seem now in retrospect a groping towards the cubist mural of *Paterson*. Still, Lann, caught up too much in his own moment, that long afternoon of the depression, miscalculated when he insisted that Williams was not "part of the continuing line of social development" in literature.

"The Yachts" came up for special attention again in Robert Fitzgerald's review of *Adam and Eve and The City* in the November, 1936, issue of *Poetry*. Williams had shown signs of development in both volumes of poetry, Fitzgerald noted; he had added new scope and coherent form to his "freshness." "The Yachts," the Lawrence elegy, and some other poems showed "a formal and human density" lacking in most of his earlier poetry. And "The Crimson Cyclamen," Williams's elegy for his painter-friend Charles Demuth, was nothing less than "a complete exercise in the contemplation of a natural, rather than a human, order." All of these developments had sprung out of Williams's Objectivism.

Eda Lou Walton collapsed the distinctions between Williams's Imagism and his Objectivism in her review in the *New York Times Book Review* in November, 1936, simply calling Williams the best writer in both modes. Williams had surmounted the inherent limitation of Imagism—the focusing of the poem on a single object—by widening the description of the object to "indicate a more and more intensive or evolving significance," a moving from the thing to the idea. Ruth Lechlitner (*Books*, Nov. 22, 1936) thought *Adam and Eve* a lapse over *An Early Martyr*, partly because Williams's Objectivist technique was not suited to his new subject matter. "Adam" and "Eve" and "The City" were "blurred," "cryptic," and Williams's method of "stripping" his descriptions to "skeleton words and phrases" had been pushed to such an extreme in "The City" that the whole poem moved "jerkily." But "The Crimson Cyclamen" exhibited a "mathematical beauty" and a "consummate mastery of structure" where color itself had been transformed from a sensory mode into "a thought process." It was, in fact, one of the best poems Williams had ever written.

White Mule

Williams's two volumes of poetry were followed by a long prose interlude. "Tired, for the moment, of writing poetry," he explained in the August, 1937, number of the *Writer*, "I turned for relief to prose to make use of a material of which I was full, knowing full well that the problems I had to face would be no different from those I was used to." So he had turned his attention to the writing of *White Mule*. It was language Williams was after, the language all around him, and he saw that prose was simply another mode of that language. Since poetry demanded an "intense application for its best effects," it tended to exhaust one. He needed a temporary break away from poetry if he was to get the language fresh and alive and give it to the young as free of lies as possible. For an old, tired language could kill the "composition" called man as surely as *White Mule*'s hero, Joe Stecher, had drifted into the living death of the "arthritic" social theories of a past age. Williams was, in fact, after a clinical diagnosis of those socio-linguistic forces, wrongly labeled American idealism, which had shaped not only the Stechers but in fact every single child Williams had ever brought into the world. Here was, then, the single great theme which was to run through all of Williams's fiction: the effect of America on his people. In the space of three years Williams published *White Mule* (1937) and *In the Money* (1940) —Parts I and II of the Stecher trilogy—as well as a new volume of nineteen short stories, *Life Along the Passaic* (1938). He also saw *In the American Grain* reprinted. "That it [White Mule] was a hit of a day with the critics was at least a compliment to us both," Williams remarked twenty years later in *I Wanted to Write a Poem*. It was his "first real success." Certainly a good part of the book's success was due to Williams's finally having found a good publisher in James Laughlin's new venture, New Directions. From 1937 on, Laughlin was to publish most of Williams's writing. It was not always an untroubled relationship, but it worked out in the long run for both men.

Most critics of *White Mule* naturally continued to view Williams as a poet who had turned his Objectivist tools and strategies to building a novel. Many of them held back, refusing to take Williams as a novelist with any more final seriousness than he seemed to have allowed himself in his offhanded remarks about his own work in the *Writer*. But several critics clarified a number of Williams's methods, at the same time revealing his impact on other contemporary writers. Alfred Kazin (*Times*, June 20, 1937) seems to have come closest to Williams's real intention. Commenting on the "peculiar transformation" which occurs when poets, including Williams, turn to the novel, where people became "creatures of light . . . oppressed by the pathos or tragedy of the norm," Kazin noted that Williams had managed to give fiction a new "texture." (That, incidentally, had been Pound's touchstone in judging *A Voyage to Pagany* nine years earlier.) There was in Williams a "new world of sound," similar in some respects to what one found in Joyce. Williams had caught the accent of real speech, its "rough, gravely ironic rhythmn." Williams's characters even talked with a native unobtrusive freshness. Here was speech "deeper" and "more meaningful" than "the violent accuracy of naturalism."

Kazin saw Joe and Gurlie Stecher as immigrants looking back nostalgically to Old Europe, but "determined to follow the promise of a new life," to follow, in fact, the American dream. They had had to pay for that "dream" "in pride, in security, in tenderness." Yet, if they could not "go back," America, on the other hand, had not become their home. It was simply that "loud stranger" whom "they would like to know better." Life for Joe reduced itself to a struggle to earn a living; it was his only "moral law," informing his whole life. Even a Fourth of July doubleheader was reduced to its work-ethic significance. In this, Joe was like most American men, for whom life became, tragically, little more than "a cycle of sleep, work and dinner," a "stasis and the ebb and flow around it," with somewhere an undefined "gleam in the darkness."

White Mule moved out from its first chapter like spokes from a hub, Philip Rahv commented perceptively in his review (*N*, June 26, 1937). In fact, the first chapter formed a microcosm of Williams's "creative credo." For his distinctive strength lay not in a vision of endings, as in so much modernist writing, but in the beginnings of things. *White Mule* was a continuation of that "intense search for America" which had informed the very conception of *In the American Grain*. The Stechers were, really, "instruments to register with unwonted sensitiveness the American scene." Rahv saw that Joe was Williams's own counterpart in his intense desire to be free of interference in order to get his work done, for Williams had insisted on keeping free of the ideological rhetoric of the class conflict which would have muddied his clean words.

In the title for his review, "If Joyce Wrote 'Studs Lonigan' . . ."
(*Sat R*, June 26, 1937), N. L. Rothman focused on the two genres
of fiction he found interwoven throughout *White Mule*. Williams, he saw, had brought to bear on the New York of the 1890s
stylistic concerns of James Joyce, even though that mode was
"not best calculated to bring out the full pattern of this scene,
veering as it does away from steady detail and circling about the
eddies of personality." The personalities themselves were "perfectly realized": Joe was "an idealist out of an ancient mould";
Gurlie, "proud and exultant, New York's Mrs. Bloom"; Flossie, a
"peerless account of an infant alive." Rothman noted too the shortcomings of using an Objectivist spareness for a scenario which
seemed to be the naturalist's sprawling domain by right. Here was
the trained miniaturist undertaking a mural.

Williams's old friend, Fred Miller, editor of the by then de-
funct leftist magazine *Blast* (which had published most of the
early "proletariat" fiction collected by Williams in his *The Knife
of the Times*), threw off a review for the *New Republic* (July 7,
1937) with a real kick to it. Williams had first met Miller in the
early thirties in an apartment over a garage on Staten Island frying
Japanese beetles in coal oil to stay alive; he was in many ways like
Williams's close friend of the twenties, Robert McAlmon. And it
was Miller with whom Williams collaborated on the *Man Orchid*
fragment in the mid-forties. Only a friend like Miller could have
talked about *White Mule* in the offhand, familiar tone of a Pound
doing his best circus barker imitation: "Williams is hot after the
secret of the verisimilitude they got into writing when it was new
(the sagas, etc.), before poetry had turned away from the 'anti-
poetic' facts of life." The novel was blessedly without the "jerry-
built framework of dramatic clichés" critics usually called plot.
Only someone like Miller, who knew firsthand how unions, scabs,
plutes, blackballs, and hunger worked, could end on a note like
this: "Don't think I want to carp at a book of such excellence. . . .
But a one-time union organizer [like Joe Stecher] gone completely open-shop needs the explaining he doesn't get here." Miller
seems to have forgotten that Williams had a tendency to write in
narcissistic parables and that, in Joe, Williams saw much of his
own independent spirit.

In a considered, sensitive review, entitled "Everyday America,"
for the *New Masses* (Sept. 21, 1937), a review largely free of
ideological cliché (if not bias), the young Stalinist poet, Sol Funaroff, approached *White Mule* from a Marxist perspective. Both

Imagism and Objectivism, Funaroff argued, were finally attempts "to present an empirical view of phenomena" free of any ideology. Both modes could be reduced, finally, to Williams's adaptation of an American pragmatism. And this "detached, empirical outlook of the pragmatist," Funaroff argued, was "the typical *Weltan-schauung* of the middle-class individual, trained to embrace an objective, impartial viewpoint concomitant with the liberal-democratic tradition." But this was clearly not a viable attitude for Funaroff, and he was sure that Williams himself was unsatisfied with it. The fact was, as Funaroff saw it, that Williams had been more than a craftsman or technician. For Williams's very use of the "antipoetic" and the commonplace was itself "an attitude toward reality," a primary concern with the "lower levels of American life," in fact, the proletariat. Funaroff praised Williams's use of language, not for its "linguistic" experimentation but rather for its "ontological" underpinnings. What Williams had done was to unhook "the grammatical apostrophes of literary dialogue" and create in its place "the bare movements of reality." This he had done through his "flexible conversational patterns," as well as "individual forms of speech, contrasts in dialect, and the simultaneity of speech and movement." Joe Stecher represented the type of the immigrant in search of new roots; he was essentially a "moral man" trapped in an immoral America "at the height of its expansion," and caught between the laziness of his fellow workers and the corruption of a trade-union bureaucracy. Gurlie was the shrewd, aggressive wife out to make it in America, an insistent cicada crying after "the philosophy of success." It was too early in the trilogy to finally judge Stecher, but his direction, Funaroff warned, would depend, finally, on "Williams' own understanding and resolution" of his great theme.

James T. Farrell, author of the *Studs Lonigan* trilogy and a socialist critic, took Funaroff to task in his own review of *White Mule* (*So R*, Winter, 1938). It was not pragmatism, Farrell insisted, that Funaroff should have identified with empiricism, but Objectivism, which was "empiricism applied to the field of poetry." Objectivism considered things in themselves, without recourse to a larger framework. Williams himself was so far removed from pragmatism that he could not even create a viable relationship between characters, let alone construct a social world. Even so, Williams could write with "precision of perception" in "a distinguished prose." With a little unacknowledged help from Rahv's review, he noted that the best parts of *White Mule* were in the finely wrought surfaces of its beginning. The entire novel, in fact, unfolded "from this introductory chapter." Farrell was, in effect, quarrelling with Funaroff's view that Williams had moved beyond Objectivism (which Farrell reduced to Imagism). As he saw it, Williams had really not budged at all from his old Imagist stand: he was still the recorder of the isolated moment.

In the Money

When Clifton Fadiman noted offhandedly the existence of *In the Money*, the sequel to *White Mule*, in the *New Yorker* (Nov. 2, 1940), America was in a new decade, almost in another world, and the concerns of the late thirties were no longer the concerns of a country moving inexorably closer to war. Fadiman dismissed *In the Money* as not "a very exciting show," whose style was "transparently simple, almost to the point of monotony." Most of Fadiman's column went instead to a review of that memorable novel, *The Voyage*, by Charles Morgan. R. A. Cordell (*Sat R*, Nov. 9, 1940) merely commented with relief that Williams had "no axe to grind, no economic, social, or political prejudices to dictate scene or character." Fred Marsh (*Times*, Nov. 17, 1940) noted Williams's "rigorous" and "rarefied" realism, comparing it to Farrell's "heavy, powerful, muggy naturalism," except that it was "slighter and lighter."

Ruth Lechlitner (*Books*, Nov. 17, 1940) noted that few writers possessed "the courage and psychological insight to take a scalpel to the Gurlies of America," because they knew that "Glorified American Motherhood (as it likes to see itself in the women's magazines) would rise up with holy indignation." Joe himself lay exposed in his own mixture of kindliness and laissez-faire ignorance in family matters. One weakness of the novel was that the minor characters, in fact the "complete social and economic background," were not sketched in sufficiently. Williams's Objectivism made him too detached an observer (a criticism leveled, incidentally, at Flaubert and Joyce a hundred times).

White Mule had been "a somewhat overelaborated version of a conventional plebian story," Frank W. Dupee noted (*NR*, Nov. 18, 1940). In fact, Williams was "merely rewriting Dos Passos according to Imagist principles." But *In the Money* was a "tense, finely written little novel," even if Williams's rehabilitation of the "commonplace" involved, really, "no challenge to our intellectual patterns." And if his literary program was not "quite the Great Mission that his most fanatic admirers represent it to be," still, his "precise realism" was "a relief after the big murals of John Steinbeck and other belated workers in the American folk-epic tradition."

"Williams' object steadily has been that still imperfectly charted new world, the essential America," Rosenfeld noted in the *Nation* (Nov. 23, 1940), emphasizing what he had said of Williams fifteen years before. Williams took his symbols not only "from history," as he had in *In the American Grain*, "but more frequently from the life and landscape of . . . industrialized northern New Jersey." That world had been realized "in a swift, lean style." In the clash between Gurlie and the other characters, Rosenfeld read the forces which had transformed many of the immigrants who had washed up against the American dream. Williams's weaknesses were still with him: a dramatic tension which continually went slack, the overuse of bare dialogue, the medical moralizing. Still, the book was Williams's best fiction to date.

"On his subtle, flexible, non-literary monotone, Dr. Williams seems to carry, without gasp or gesture, the whole load of daily living in the U.S.," the anonymous reviewer for *Time* (Dec. 2, 1940) summarized. *In the Money* was, in fact, "a broad advance on the naturalist front." "Judged even by the flattest traditions of Naturalism," Williams's subject matter could scarcely be said to exist. Nevertheless, the book was "as fully fleshed, as complex, and as curiously beautiful as daily life" itself. Williams had, in fact, managed to demonstrate "social significances" which even trained sociologists could "only bumble over."

Life Along the Passaic River

Between these two novels, Williams's second collection of short stories, *Life Along the Passaic River*, had appeared (Feb. 1938). Rosenfeld (*Books*, Feb. 27, 1938) regretted the collection's over-reliance on dialogue—at times awkwardly rendered—and its noticeable vagueness of sense impressions. Still, Williams had presented "a true, sympathetic comprehension of the ways, beings and deep effects of earthy, inarticulate members of the immigrant stocks," particularly the "poor Poles, Italians and Jews of the North Jersey industrial area." Williams characteristically wrote "little dramas" in an "incisive, homely, brusquely rhythmical prose" reflecting "a raw and earthy life."

Philip Rahv (PR, Mar. 1938) noted Williams's "alienation of design," his direct approach to the naked object. Williams's perception of things "intimately involved" the meaning of those things as well. As a result, "the cohabitation of language and object" was so harmonious that rhetorical forms were not only "superfluous," they actually tended to "nullify the incentive to creation" in Williams. Williams, he felt, began and ended his stories without deliberation and "simply as the spirit moved him"; he was interested in writing rather than in "literature." But if his subjects were circumscribed by his own experience and by the local, there was an exceptional "authenticity" about them. It was "pain which is the source of values here," Rahv commented. Here were some of the "pure products of America" gone crazy, yet treated with genuine sympathy. In place of an objectively realizable form, Williams had opted for a "phenomenology." But without a major form the novel's details lacked any significance beyond themselves. Unfortunately, Williams did not seem interested in those "social and historic" relationships which could "unify" and "significate" facts "on a place beyond sensation or nostalgia." It was this absence of what Williams himself might have called an "ideological presumptuousness" which, if "admirable in its stoicism," also constituted Williams's defeat. Still, Williams did "think about America, if only to sketch it in psychic outline." And one could ferret out a real "interaction" between Williams's "phenomenological principle" and his "American mysticism," present at least as a direction in *White Mule*, and fully informing the best story in this collection of short stories, "The Venus." (Ironically, Williams—because of space limitations—had detached that story from *A Voyage to Pagany* ten years before.)

Rothman too stressed Williams's lack of formal design (*Sat R*, Mar. 19, 1938). The book was a collection of sketches, "stabs, brilliant and inspired, at truth." As in his "expressionist poetry," Williams had sought in these stories "to catch in mid-air the gleaming, immediate spark of life and hold it in the gleaming, immediate word." When he succeeded, as in "The Use of Force" or "A Face of Stone," his was "the best kind of literature"; when he miscalculated, the results were simply prose fragments.

Williams was a realist, Eda Lou Walton noted (*N*, Mar. 19, 1938), who used "realism with the precision of a surgeon exposing the vital organs," or, alternately, with the "skill as of x-ray in penetration and analysis." Like Hemingway, he used a clipped prose, but he was not "a sentimentalist, or a romanticist," nor was he "disillusioned." Williams's realism also had its larger significance, since all of his stories dealt with "the comedy and tragedy, and always the human dignity, of birth and death." If there was evidence in them that Williams favored the political left, it was also clear that he had arrived at that position through "practical experience." He did not have to serve as propagandist; the squalid reality of life lived along the Passaic River spoke for itself.

Fred Miller (*NR*, Apr. 20, 1938), who had originally published six of these stories in *Blast* between 1933–35, stressed Williams's search for character "in these mongrel isolated Americans along the Passaic." Williams's "social awareness," he noted, had grown "considerably" since his first collection of short stories and "every suggestion of the preciousness that, here and there, tinged 'A Voyage to Pagany' (1928)" had been obliterated. Williams had learned to harmonize style and realism, had once more demonstrated "that the more truly localized the art, the more it is universal."

In the American Grain, 1939

When New Directions reissued *In the American Grain* in 1939, Horace Gregory consented to write an introduction for it which has been used in nearly all subsequent reprintings of the book. It is an essay very close in spirit to the views and even the polemics of Williams himself. While Gregory was writing the introduction, Williams sent him whatever information about the genesis of the book he could recall. It was faulty information, as Williams's wife showed him, but he sent it anyway with his characteristic gesture of enthusiasm and shrugging apology.

Gregory's introduction is valuable for several reasons, not the least of them being his strong defense of Williams's impressionistic strategy and Gregory's recapitulation of the book's fortunes in the fifteen years since its initial publication. *In the American Grain* had first appeared, Gregory noted, at a moment when the New Humanism and the disciples of Parrington had pointed to Impressionism as the common enemy. As a result, Williams's book, together with others like it, including Sherwood Anderson's notebooks and D. H. Lawrence's *Studies in Classic American Literature*, were suspect from the first. Impressionistic studies were either "publicly ignored or attacked as heresy." Since then, how-

ever, the critical climate had changed and Williams's book had
weathered the storm, growing steadily in popularity. Williams
was one of the few writers who could be called sincere without
irony or apology; nor was his sincerity merely a mask. His very
theme—"America as a new world to be rediscovered at every
turn"—was a dangerous one and full of contradictions. But it was
intimately linked with the voice speaking it, a voice able to ad-
just itself to the cadences and imageries of the various historical
moments under investigation. Only in his attack on Puritanism did
Williams "betray the moment" in which he had written the book.
True, he had caught the "destructive element" in Puritanism, but
he had failed to do justice to Cotton Mather's wit and imagination. Gregory had high praise for the book's lyricism, and he
thought the one-page Lincoln section had managed to give "a new
and vivid semblance of reality" to that "unwieldy myth." Williams had presented a picture of America in its "signs and signa-
tures, its backward glances and, by implication, its warnings for
the future." He had produced a "source book of highly individual and radical discoveries . . . as one might say that a river is a
source." Even as the book had fallen out of print, it had exerted
"an influence that rose from the subsoil of the time in which it
was written," helping to shape no less a poem than *The Bridge*
itself.

The Ebbing of Williams's
Poetic Reputation

"We have nothing but Arnold's touchstone to guide us in this
difficulty [of establishing traditional literary norms], and our own
hard work to make us worthy of guidance; that, and the Grace
of God." So hymned Yvor Winters in his 1937 study, *Primitivism
and Decadence: A Study of American Experimental Poetry*. To
follow Winters's critical pronunciamentos on the late nineteenth-
and twentieth-century Romantics, and on Williams in particular,
is to watch the steady deterioration of Williams's (and Winters's)
literary reputation, together with the steady growth of a stiff, ar-
rogant righteousness of tone in this grand dismissor. Before he
came to suspect even his own poetry, Winters had had mostly
praise for Williams, as in his review of *Sour Grapes*. And even in
his 1937 study he could still praise Williams for his technical sophistication in the area of free verse, even though he thought Wil-

liams's poetry suffered by an excessive intensity of tone coupled
with "conventional" language. He also found Williams limited
by his characteristic eschewal of ideas in his poetry.

Then, in his review of Williams's *Complete Collected Poems*
(*KR*, Winter 1939), Winters came down heavily with a moral-
ist's had against Williams's so-called anti-intellectualism. He mis-
read Williams's dictum that there are "no ideas but in things," and
charged him with being "in no position to distinguish good ideas
from bad" or "sound feelings from false." Williams, he insisted,
distrusted "traditional form as a kind of restraint or inhibition:
since he fails to grasp its significance, it appears to him another mechanical sentimentalism." Williams's ideas were bad in themselves,
so his poetry was best when he followed "his favorite formula"
and left ideas alone. A Williams poem was typically "composed
of perfectly unrelated items," and, if they were "amusing," they
were also "empty," as Williams, he felt, had himself confessed in
"This Florida: 1924." Williams could handle "the simpler events
of human relationship, chiefly love," with some skill, and he could
handle "symbols of elemental forces and instincts" in isolation,
especially if such forces could be translated into images of "power"
and "terror," because his "rapid and muscular rhetoric" were best
suited for such themes. Still, if Williams was more limited in scope
than either Hardy or Bridges, he was also as indestructible as Herrick, so that by the year 2000 Williams would surely be established, along with Stevens, as "one of the two best poets of his
generation." Critical opinion by then would have seen that Williams's free verse far surpassed either Eliot's or Pound's. This was,
indeed, to be placed amidst a pygmy pantheon, to be the best of a
truncated lot.

In 1965 J. Hillis Miller wrote to Winters asking him if his
opinion had changed in the intervening twenty-five years. Yes,
Winters replied in a postscript, except that now he would restrict
even "more narrowly" his choice of Williams's successful poems to
three from *Sour Grapes* and two from *Spring and All*, all "minor
poems," but "close to perfection in execution." Then he offered
his final dismissal: "To say that Williams was anti-intellectual
would be almost an exaggeration: he did not know what the intellect was." Williams, he had come to see, finally, "was a foolish
and ignorant man, but at moments a fine stylist."

We ought not to suppose, really, that Winters's attitudes had
undergone a radical transformation. Only his insensitivity of tone
had been perfected. Even in 1937 Winters could write that Wil-

liams was "wholly incapable of coherent thought," had not, in
fact, had "the fortune to receive a coherent system as his birth-
right," which was like saying that Williams had not had the good
fortune to have Paul Elmer More stand as his godfather. As for the
prose, Winters found it "largely incomprehensible," *A Voyage
to Pagany*, displaying an "almost ludicrous inability to motivate a
long narrative." Somehow, almost as if by chance, Williams had
written *The Destruction of Tenochtitlan*, manifesting "one of the
few great prose styles of our time." It was one of Winters's characteristic tricks, this old give-and-take, to first give praise and then
to qualify, until one was left with a constricted center moving
towards a cipher, the critic's ability to make the poet vanish.

There were other summaries and other dismissals of Williams in
the late thirties besides Winters's. So, for example, the September-
October, 1938, issue of the British *Twentieth Century Verse*,
given over to a discussion of what was American about American
poetry, considered Williams among others. The magazine's editor,
Julian Symonds, judged American poets to be "individual and
American" only to "the degree in which English writers find them
both valuable and unsympathetic." He divided American poets
into those with "a markedly European habit of mind" (Eliot,
Pound, Aiken, Ransom), and those with a "markedly American
habit of mind" (Tate, Winters, Marianne Moore, Williams). The
"European" group, he felt, had taken "their several ways of escape
from this world through one or another tunnel of 'tradition.' "
But with the markedly American poets, Symonds admitted that
he was on unsure ground, that in fact, he could not understand
them at all. He could "appreciate" in Williams, for example, "a
certain ironic simplicity of language." But he did not know what
his poems were *about*, or, alternatively, *why* the poem had *this*
particular text. Like most Englishmen, he was simply at a loss to
explain Williams. Yvor Winters had done a two-page analysis of
"By the road to the contagious hospital" in his *Primitivism and
Decadence*, calling it one of the few "perfect" poems of Williams's. But Winters's analysis left Symonds bewildered. Familiarity with the text showed it to be "such a piece of secondhand and
commonplace observation as might be turned out by any good
poet on an off day." If Williams's poems had "good qualities,"
Symonds prophesied correctly, they were "not likely to be shared
by poets writing in England now or for some while to come."
Symonds was not unsympathetic. He honestly seems to have felt
sheer incomprehension about what Williams was after; this Amer-

ican search for new rhythms and habits of speech was not only "surprising" to an Englishman, it was often simply regrettable.

Symonds had also sent out an inquiry to a number of poets, and Williams was one of the few to answer. To the question, "Do you regard yourself as part of the 'American tradition?,' " Williams had answered, modestly, "Yes, of course, I am the fountain head!" And to the question whether or not "poetry written by Americans during the last ten years shows any line of development," he answered that there had "been a great progression" from Whitman and Poe and Freneau in the "selection and elaboration of formal design." And then, frustrated by the nature of the questions, he added, "Good God what is the matter with people? Do they take us for albinos? Red eyes and white wooly hair or something?"

Collected Poems, 1938

When the *Complete Collected Poems of William Carlos Williams* was published in November, 1938, by New Directions in an edition of fifteen hundred copies, it was a time for looking hard at Williams's achievement once again. Babette Deutsch (*N*, Nov. 19, 1938) stressed Williams's all-pervasive vitality. If he was too spare in his descriptions and sometimes too obscure, he also had a "keen sensibility open to the least and meanest, as well as to the lovely and superb, impressions of his own place and time." In spite of Pound's early influence, Williams was primarily interested in American subjects—the provinces and small towns along the Passaic—and in American rhythms, that mixture of the colloquial and the real which had "the bright staccato of electric signs flashing and winking." Deutsch had already made many of the same points about Williams in her 1936 *This Modern Poetry*, stressing there the "unexampled nakedness" of his poems. Williams was an Objectivist, for whom "the object seen, the clear line, the pure color, is enough." But his reliance on the brief moment, however keen, and his view of America, with its exhilaration and appropriation of the commonplace, were too restrictive. What his poetry lacked was a central, all-informing myth.

Philip Horton, who had published his *Hart Crane: The Life of an American Poet* the year before, attempted in his review of the *Collected Poems* (*NR*, Dec. 21, 1938) to sum up Williams's achievement. "One cannot feel that he is an important poet, and

one knows that he is not an insignificant one," he began. He rejected both Funaroff's and Farrell's attempts to define Williams's
Objectivism, considering the poetry as simply "the experience of
a highly individual mind." Williams's style, taken to its logical
end, was self-destructive, an "exercise in spiritual hygiene," tending as it did to the ultimate starkness of a poem like "The Locust
Tree in Flower." Such a poetics not only eliminated the visionary,
it did away with more human staples like humor and pathos as
well. Had not Wallace Stevens himself already pointed clearly to
this difficulty in emphasizing the conflict between Williams's
"sentimental" and "anti-poetic" selves? The best Williams's
poetics could accomplish was to create a tension between the
objective and the subjective which functioned as "a physical law
of the poet's universe." Essentially, however, the poetry was
merely a "public record of a private conflict that happens also to
be common to most poets."

"I'm not important but I'm not insignificant. Boy! that's pretty
cagey shootin.' I wish I could split 'em that fine. I guess a fella
has to write a biography before he gets that good! Big-shot stuff.
I better watch my step from now on." Every reviewer's terror:
that the living figure whom he dispassionately analyzes will, in his
turn, turn on him. Williams's vinegary retort appeared in the
January 11, 1939, letters section of the *New Republic.* Here was
yet another one of those pontificators using Stevens's antipoetic
dictum as a cudgel. Why hadn't Horton "paid the least attention
to the book as a thesis on the conception of form which it attempts to realize—if failingly," Williams asked, at the same time
directing attention to the central critical concern he himself had
been after. "To hell with him," Williams ended. "If he hadn't
had Stevens to teach him how to look crookedly he wouldn't
have had anything at all to say. Tell him to go wipe his nose."

"Despite the recent painful efforts of reviewers to classify
Dr. Williams, to call him one thing or another, and attempt to
determine his 'importance,' " Horace Gregory said in his review
(*Books,* Feb. 5, 1939), "I think the poems themselves escape all
facile definitions. They have lived through 'imagism' and 'objectivism' and much disfavor, and now seem as fresh and impudent
as ever." Perhaps Williams's outburst helped to clear the air, for
Gregory's was not only a good review; it helped to further define
and elucidate categories for Williams criticism. It suggested placing Stevens's preface in its proper historical context and so provided a wider, less constricting view of the poet. For Gregory,

Williams's real importance and direction lay in the unity of his speech with his images, images which were presented through an essential American idiom, eye and ear poised together. This was much harder to do than to merely render slang, dialect, or jargon. Written from what seemed "the very center of a spoken language," many of the poems had come "to possess a classic purity of utterance." Williams's characteristic short lines did not indicate staccato rhythms; rather they emphasized "the flexible, brilliant, and at times austere sound of American voices" heard aslant in daily conversation.

Still, this "sharp-eared, sharp-eyed, KINEMATIC" poetry was but one side of Williams, a side culminating in a piece like "The Cod Head." There was also another Williams, closer to D. H. Lawrence in his "epigrammatic wit" and "insight into the essential nature of humanity." Like Lawrence, Williams also favored the "poetic intelligence" over the mere intellect. And like Lawrence he too was fully conscious of his own imaginative and authentic uniqueness. Gregory also cautioned against reading the *Complete Collected Poems* as a summation of a poet's life; it was only a halfway house. Even at fifty-five Williams showed "promise of a vitality to be extended into the future."

In his review (*Sat R*, Feb. 11, 1939), Paul Rosenfeld called Williams one of the "five or six writers who justify the world's reference to a contemporary American literature of high quality." Williams was still, essentially, an Imagist, following an esthetic of ascesis "headed by Pound," an esthetic concise, restricted to intense observation, indifferent "to the beauty of sound and periodic arrangement." But Williams was "more profoundly related to American life," with its "fierce, nervous, and emotional tension," than the expatriates. His very style was "high-tensioned, extremely energetic, with plenty of dynamic punch, ascending cadences, and irregular rhythms of short and stabbing lines." And if the poetry was not all satisfactory, it did undoubtedly have "texture," "truthfulness," a "subtle consciousness of life."

It had been a disservice, really, to praise Williams "for the steadfastness of his 'anti-poetic' attitude," Louis Untermeyer wrote (*YR*, Spring 1939), for Williams's range and development were "much greater" than even his admirers claimed for him. After the early "escapism of the Imagist," Williams's characteristic idiom had developed, followed by his "continual striving for an inflection expressing himself and his immediate scene." If Williams did not always succeed, he did often enough to present a stripped utterance at once powerful and native, and in some of his longer poems he had made "a new verse out of broken and syncopated rhythms." Now he was even beginning to create his own poetic tradition.

R. P. Blackmur, comparing John Wheelwright's *Mirrors of Venus* and Williams's *Collected Poems* (*PR*, Winter 1939), saw Wheelwright as one "who insists upon his inheritance and attempts to make the most of it" and Williams as one "who, looking at the batch of the half-inherited, denies that here is anything to inherit." Williams was all for "the flatness of the general," one who took "every object, uninspected, as fresh." He had created "an extra-ordinarily solid and flexible species" of free verse not by using a conscious free verse form, as Winters had said in *Primitivism and Decadence*, but rather by instinct and hard work. It was a medium which had been successful for himself, but which had failed with his imitators. And no wonder: Williams had reduced his style to a highly personal voice expressing his personal concerns. It was "a remarkable, but sterile, sport." Williams's was a poetry of "unexpanded notation," which had the advantage of drawing our attention to "the unrelenting significance of the banal." If the poetry seemed to be written for that abstraction called the average man, it had overlooked that other equally viable abstraction, the normal man. The difference came down to this: that the tragic element and the deeper significations of human experience were simply not part of Williams's poetry.

If Gregory saw the *Collected Poems* as a kind of halfway house leading forward, Mason Wade (*Times*, July 23, 1939) thought he saw the volume as an "epitaph" for the period from the Imagists up through the thirties, years which had "seen poetic progress as well as the disintegration of the word and a widening of the gap between the poet . . . and his audience." Williams was "the lyricist of everyday life," closer to the American earth than Pound, Eliot, Cummings, Stevens, or Marianne Moore. He was the singer of the "wretched" and of the "Passaic, that filthy river." But his final place, Wade judged, would be "just below the first." "I'm just short of being one of the best, it seems," Williams mused nervously in a letter written to Gregory the same day he saw Wade's review. It was "too bad."

"Imagist, Objectivist, Proletarian—all of these merely signify convenient directions rather than accurate descriptive titles for his achievement," wrote Vivien Koch (*Voices*, Dec. 1939). What one did find in Williams was "a line of steady simplification of poetic energy" and a "gain in social awareness," an esthetic, in fact, "of poverty." And *Poetry* (Sept. 1939), which had watched Williams from the beginning, featured a ten-page overview by Ruth Lechlitner of Williams's thirty-year poetic career. The volume demonstrated Williams's "close and consistent . . . contact with the natural, the human, the heterogeneous but strongly individual facets of American life," and she praised him especially for his "delicate and understanding and cruel and true portraits of children . . . frankly based on sex reactions"—poems like "The Ogre" and "Sympathetic Portrait of a Child." She, too, saw the pervasive influence of D. H. Lawrence on Williams. Lawrence was less disciplined than Williams, but both showed "an exuberance, a sheer physical delight in discovery." Williams's poems about flowers and landscapes were not really still lifes, for they showed a constant "tension, the pull of mass against mass: action, struggle, growth . . . always the acid dip of motion." *An Early Martyr* was a "passionate indictment . . . of the social order responsible" for the early martyrdom of the poem's hero. Williams's psychological portraits, on the other hand, his "Adam," his "Eve," and the "City," were failures, mere "separate notations," rambling impressions lacking fusion. But *Elegy for D. H. Lawrence*, with its interweaving complex central symbol of the serpent, worked; and "The Crimson Cyclamen" was probably "the most perfect example of Objectivism," for in "this almost mystical apotheosis of perfection all separatenesses are united, 'merging into one flower.' "

Lechlitner ended her review with a look towards the future and towards *Paterson*, Williams's work in progress. Could the method of "The Crimson Cyclamen" be the nascent method for that long poem? Could Williams fuse the multifaceted American scene into "an ordered pattern as inevitable in growth, meaning and fulfillment as the cyclamen in flower?" Could Williams find a way "to present the human order through one man who is all men, one city that is all cities. Could there be found a sustaining and unifying symbol for such a presentation?" Her final question in effect asked whether Williams was going to continue to develop. It was, really, the underlying question of so many of the commentators watching Williams moving towards his sixtieth year, waiting for the culmination towards which his work was tending but which it had not yet reached. If he failed to find "a further course of development," she judged, it would be "because he lacks a conscious, clear-cut focal point." Because his own polarized culture worked steadily against his finding the kind of focal unity he

needed, he might be absolved as a human being. But if he remained "content with isolated perceptions and arbitrary composi-
tions," she warned, he would "not be absolved as an artist."

Williams's Poetry during the War Years

World War II had its own preoccupations, and few first-rate
volumes of poetry were published in America during those years.
Williams published only two books during that period, one a
slight pamphlet and the other a volume printed by a small press
in a limited edition. In the meantime, he was thinking about and
writing his first drafts of *Paterson*. The reviews of Williams's
The Broken Span, eighteen pages of poems published in January,
1941, in New Direction's new "The Poet of the Month" series,
recapitulated the old chestnuts. One reviewer (*N*, Feb. 22, 1941)
praised Williams's "sharp and undeflected gaze," and his "insatiable
curiosity for the common concerns of mankind" as well as his
"anti-poetic observations." John Sweeney (*YR*, Summer 1941)
praised Williams's "fugitive suggestions of tenderness or irony,"
as well as his controlled sentimentality and economy, while re-
gretting that the "dab method did not permit the complex intellectual textures which compose particulars into densely wrought
argument." *The Broken Span* added nothing to the *Collected
Poems*, wrote Oscar Williams (*NR*, Sept. 29, 1941), dismissing it
with a sharp, "I cannot imagine what else than an idling indul-
gence, dyed-in-the-wool-of-having-arrived, could have allowed
the publishing of this anticlimax, this unexciting selection." And
another reviewer, Peter Munro Jack, looking over eleven volumes
for the *New York Times Book Review* (Dec. 14, 1941) a week
after Pearl Harbor, dismissed Williams's poetics as nothing more
than "the absence of rhetoric," itself an affectation. Possibly the
details from *Paterson* might "be built into something resembling
architecture," but that was all.

With the war on and paper rationed, Laughlin at New Directions could not publish Williams, and so Williams had to look elsewhere. "I've been trying everywhere to find a publisher for my
next book of verse, probably the best yet," he wrote Robert
McAlmon on September 4, 1943. "They all say they're so sorry
but that they have no paper. I've tried about all. Jim Laughlin,
who promised me that he would print anything I wrote, merely

said he'd like to do the book but that he also could not get the paper for it." But Williams did finally manage to find a printer and his own binder and 380 copies of *The Wedge* were printed by the Cummington Press in September, 1944.

At first, no one even noticed the book. Then Horace Gregory complained of this neglect in a review of Auden, Cummings, and Williams (*Sat R*, Dec. 2, 1944). The reason for neglecting such an important poet, Gregory thought, might have been that people saw the 1938 *Collected Poems* as "definitive and final." But *The Wedge* was, in fact, "probably the best of Dr. Williams' single books of poetry" yet. He realized that it had "the currently unfashionable character of being without rhymes," but there was "more firmness and more control" in Williams's lines than in most conventional poems. His lines were "closer to the sources of life itself and of poetry" than either Auden's or Cummings's were. "I appreciated what you said of *The Wedge*," Williams wrote Gregory on New Year's Day, 1945. "How lost a book of poems can seem to its author! This one of mine is as though it had been dropped down a rat hole."

But in February the reviews finally began coming in. Weldon Kees used much of his review (*Times*, Feb. 11, 1945) to "reintroduce" Williams to the public. He could understand Williams's being neglected as a poet, and he expected modernist poetry to be "neglected." But Williams's short stories were certainly accessible to anyone who liked Hemingway or Sherwood Anderson, and their neglect was "merely puzzling." Commercial publishers had never been attracted to Williams, and anthologists usually managed to represent him "badly." To make matters worse, Williams's "continued devotion to imagist doctrines" was unfashionable in the formalist forties. In spite of all this, Kees insisted, Williams's best work, while resisting such "compulsions of fashion," managed the American language "with a strictness Sandburg for one could not touch." Williams kept finding, "in areas that many poets might dismiss as unrewarding, values and distinctions that only his methods of observation reveal." Williams no doubt had his faults. He could be "indiscriminate" in choosing his subjects, and he did not seem able to focus his ideas. "His unsynchronized leaps into the arenas of formal ideas have always caused his admirers embarrassed dismay," Kees wrote, lamenting that Williams had taken it upon himself to attack the whole metaphysical tradition in his introduction to *The Wedge*. But Williams could

write poetry; there was something "magically intense" about
poems like "Burning the Christmas Greens" which redeemed the
man.

F. O. Matthiessen (*NR*, Feb. 12, 1945) stressed the Whitman
and Thoreau tradition of an "organic" poetics in Williams, at the
same time pointing to the dangers of such a poetics. For there was
even less "formal necessity" in the poems in this volume than there
had been in such earlier pieces as "The Yachts" and "The Catholic
Bells." Still, there was here an "intimate knowledge of humanity,"
a Laurentian mixture of love's gentleness and violence, and always,
as in "The Dance," there was Williams's characteristic gusto.
Elizabeth Drew (*Books*, Mar. 11, 1945) stressed the habitual
juxtaposition of violence and gentleness in Williams. It was true
that Williams could link an intrinsic formal rhythm to an emotional pitch, especially in his short lyrics, but his rhythms often
went "flat and slack," degenerating into prose, when he tried the
longer poem. But perhaps, she was at least willing to concede, this
was an intentional strategy on Williams's part.

In his review for the April, 1945, number of *Poetry*, Marshall
Stearns proceeded to dismantle a representative selection of Williams's poetry in order to exhibit its lack of a discoverable syntax,
its confusion of meaning, and its formlessness. His analysis of the
first two problems was to set up an imaginary straw man and then
proceed to knock it down. Williams's poetry, he said, showed no
signs of having progressed or even of having changed significantly in *The Wedge*. The man was still a "latter-day Imagist."
In spite of his rejection of Stevens's formula, Williams's poetry did
in fact turn on the "conflict between the sentimental" and the
"anti-poetic." In attempting to "correct" Williams's line breaks,
especially lines which broke at a "function-word" ("that," "at,"
"of," "but,"), Stearns only demonstrated his own obtuseness.
Williams at sixty-one was probably too old now to compose his
projected magnum opus, Stearns suggested, but he could still offer
readers more fine lyrics like "The Yellow Chimney."

"The poetry of William Carlos Williams is no longer as exciting as it was once," chimed in F. W. Dupee (*N*, Apr. 14,
1945). In fact, his best poems had been written fifteen years before. Williams had simply stalled into a "monotony of springtime
ecstasies, suburban glimpses, and sketchy anecdotes." In a piece
like "Burning the Christmas Greens," for example, Williams had
concentrated "so much on describing the *thing* (the fire of greens)
that the *idea* is left to smuggle its way into the poem by virtue of

hints and asides." Moreover, Williams had doggedly refused to allow the language to carry anything like a "literary resonance" which might have assisted "in the fusion of thought and symbol." In fact, he had established "a tyranny of objects under which ideas must lead a rather furtive existence." Williams still stood on "the threshold of poetry," Denis Devlin wrote (*SR*, Summer 1945), refusing to "face the transformation that might take place inside." His "poems" were really a "pre-art," justified in his case from a personal and social standpoint, for his obsession with "aesthetic scruples" had created a remarkably "bare texture and rough rhythm." But it was "the rhetoric one missed" in Williams; the poems were simply unfinished. True, his precise images had a "geometrical clarity," reflecting a "quotidian" consciousness, but they refused "to lapse into the dark unconscious where imagery is fertilized." Devlin missed, too, that philosophical attitude one discovered in Stevens or the rhetoric of grand passion one found in Yeats. Apparently, Devlin failed to sense the nervous tensions informing the rhythmic surfaces of even Williams's still lifes. Nor did he see that for Williams the only valid philosophy was one grounded fully on a psychology of sensory apprehension.

Williams, R. P. Blackmur wrote in his "Notes on Seven Poets" (1945), was "just as limited as H. D." (Williams had been compared with H. D. [Hilda Doolittle] as a fellow Imagist for nearly thirty years by then.) But where H. D. was "cold, 'Greek,' fast, and enclosed, Williams is warm, 'primitive,' of varying speed, and open to every wind." Williams ignored "the sense of order that goes with the long history of the craft of verse." Instead, he had insisted on "an organic theory, that each poem has an intimate order of its own, which it is the business of the poet to make out of the ardor of his direct perception." But the reader, Blackmur quipped, could no more be expected to find a special, "intimate form"—an inner shaping necessity—in a poem than he could expect to find radically new forms in every woman he met. In fact, he insisted, Williams was really more conventional than he let on, using both conventional themes and slightly disguised conventional forms. What Blackmur did not ask, however, was whether or not Williams himself might not have known this: that, really, if one spoke, one spoke of subjects and themes used in some tradition, and that the older rhythms had their place and ought to be impressed when they were of use.

"The philosophers are trying to label the arts," Williams complained to Norman MacLeod in July, 1945, "to pigeonhole one's works without realizing that—they'll burn their fingers off in the end, if they are not careful—somewhere, in some piece of art resides a radioactive force beyond anything but their copying in their static spheres. I fight with Blackmur, I feel resentments against them all, and all I can do (growing old) is to compose. It is the only recourse, the only intellectual recourse for an artist, to make, to make, to make and to go on making—*never* to reply in *kind* to their strictures."

By 1945 he had learned to let the older critics go their own way. Perhaps his sorry encounter with the *Partisan Review* crowd had taught him that he could not hope for impartial treatment. In the summer of 1940, for example, he had flailed out against the aristocratic hauteur of the *Partisan Review's* critical strategies, and against, in particular, the negative criticism leveled against the young poet Kenneth Patchen by another young poet bred in the Formalist tradition, Randall Jarrell. Williams went after the editors for allowing their Mr. Jarrell to air "such a wastebasket full of . . . trite flippancies." A man with a reputation behind him, he wrote, was entitled to make a few "unsupported critical remarks, even silly ones," but Jarrell was "just another of those professional literary sophomores who turn up from the universities every now and then to instruct us out of the book in our errors," critics whom he detested as he did "plant-lice."

"William Carlos Williams is almost too much of a fact to be criticized," Jarrell wrote one war and five years later in the Winter 1945 issue of the *Partisan Review*. There was a charm, an honesty, and "rather astonishing limitations" to his work, limitations of an "intellectual" sort, as if Williams's critical remarks "had been made by Henry Ford." The criticism was "kinaesthetic, only intermittently conscious." His poems, on the other hand, had caught "for good" Nature at "the edge of the American city"; caught too, "one of the great mythological attitudes of our country: Brooklyn, the truck-driver looking shyly at the flower." But Jarrell was not willing to lock horns with a tough stag like Williams. He ended, therefore, by praising the older poet's eternal youth. If such "optimism of ability and courage" was "touchingly wrong in the old Hercules, dying in his shirt of fire," it was somehow "precariously right for the young one." In short, Williams was the very "America of poets."

It was a truce of sorts, and Jarrell tried, in his nervous, distant way, to make things right with Williams without compromising himself. So, when he reviewed the first book of *Paterson* the following year, Williams was so pleased that he had Jarrell and his wife out to 9 Ridge Road for dinner and found Jarrell "very pleasant." Then Williams didn't hear from him again. "We had not been particularly friendly before that and can only presume that he had reverted to his old instinctive antagonism. I may be mistaken," he wrote Babette Deutsch in July, 1947. Williams was mistaken, but only by half.

Academics and Avant-Garde: Two Camps

In her *Directions in Modern Poetry* (1940), Elizabeth Drew devoted some seventy-five pages in whole or in part to Eliot, forty to Yeats, twenty-five to Pound, twenty to Hart Crane, twenty to Auden, ten to Stevens, and two full pages plus passing references to Williams. This will serve as an example of just how high Williams's reputation stood among academic critics thirty-five years ago. Using "The Red Wheelbarrow" as an example, Drew conceded that there was "nothing whatever superfluous in the poem." The question was, rather, "whether there is enough there to make a poem at all." Williams was a Wordsworthian of sorts, a purist afraid that his transparent medium might be "filmed or crusted" and so "distract attention from the truth." Such poets were "afraid that words may lead them astray, seducing them into irresponsibilities and irrelevance." Because Williams had deliberately inhibited his language, had not allowed it to function freely, he could be summarily dismissed as of no real consequence.

Against the judgment of the academies can be placed the judgment of one of the minor avant garde writers, Robert McAlmon. In his memoir, *Being Geniuses Together* (1938), McAlmon wrote that his old friend Williams had been "one of the most interesting 'sensibilities'" America had produced. If he was "over-impressionable," lost "in a species of life wonder" so that he often failed to adequately "clarify his observations," he had undoubtedly written many fine poems and short stories. Still, McAlmon had noticed that Williams was reluctant to publish his best material because it had "come straight from a direct and stark impulse." Of course, McAlmon noted testily, one could not expect the *boobus Americanus* to see what some of the best minds had seen. "That Larbaud, Valery, Gide, and a quantity of other continental and

English writers" had found "Bill's work unique among . . . American writers" was "more interesting" to him than anything a writer like H. L. Mencken "could have to say." Williams, he summed up, was indeed "a force, an influence, a direction, and a sensibility in American literature rather than the mere author of 'books.' " In the years after World War II, that force would finally gather its strength and come rolling in, and the voices of the critics would accordingly rise louder and more insistently like some great "thrust and recoil, a great clatter," all rolling in towards that late wonder: *Paterson*.

References

Aiken, Conrad
    1934. "The Well-Worn Spirit," *New Republic*. Apr. 18, pp. 289–91.
Aldington, Richard
    1941. *Life for Life's Sake: A Book of Reminiscences*. New York: Viking, pp. 136, 143.
Anonymous
    1932a. *Saturday Review of Literature*. May 7, p. 719.
    1932b. *New York Herald Tribune Book Review*. June 19, p. 7.
    1940. *Time*. Dec. 2, p. 83.
    1941. "In Brief," *Nation*. Feb. 22, p. 152.
Blackmur, R. P.
    1939. "John Wheelwright and Dr. Williams," *Partisan Review*. Winter, pp. 112–15.
    1945. "Notes on Seven Poets" in *Language as Gesture*, pp. 352–63. New York: Doubleday.
Cordell, R. A.
    1940. "The Stetchers Again," *Saturday Review of Literature*. Nov. 9, p. 5.
Dembo, L. S.
    1969. "The Objectivist Poet: Four Interviews," *Contemporary Literature*. Spring, pp. 155–219.
Deutsch, Babette
    1934. "Heirs of the Imagists," *New York Herald Tribune Book Review*. Apr. 1, p. 16.
    1936. *This Modern Poetry*. New York: W. W. Norton, pp. 69–72, 263.
    1938. "Poet in a Barrel," *Nation*. Nov. 19, pp. 542–43.
Devlin, Denis
    1945. "Book Reviews," *Sewanee Review*. Summer, pp. 456–66.

Drew, Elizabeth

1940. (and John L. Sweeney) *Directions in Modern Poetry*. New York: Gordian Pr., pp. 187–88.

1945. "Provocative Poetics," *New York Herald Tribune Book Review*. Mar. 11, p. 23.

Dupee, Frank W.

1940. "W. C. Williams as Novelist," *New Republic*. Nov. 18, p. 700.

1945. "Imagists and Ex-Imagists," *Nation*. Apr. 14, pp. 421–22.

Fadiman, Clifton

1940. "A New Novel . . . W. C. Williams," *New Yorker*. Nov. 2, pp. 68–69.

Farrell, James T.

1938. "Shorter Reviews," *Southern Review*. Winter, pp. 615–18.

Fitzgerald, Robert

1936. "Actual and Archaic," *Poetry*. Nov. 1936, pp. 94–96.

Funaroff, Sol

1937. "Everyday America," *New Masses*. Sept. 21, pp. 25, 27.

Gierasch, Walter

1945. "Williams' 'Tract'," *Explicator*. Mar., p. 35.

Gregory, Horace

1939a. "Fresh, Impudent Poems," *New York Herald Tribune Book Review*. Feb. 5, p. 10.

1939b. "Introduction" to *In the American Grain*. New York: New Directions.

1944. "Brilliance and Unconvention," *Saturday Review of Literature*. Dec. 2, p. 50.

Grigson, Geoffrey

1934. "Two Poets," *New Verse*. Apr., pp. 18–19.

Horton, Philip

1938. "Anthology of a Mind," *New Republic*. Dec. 21, p. 208.

Jack, Peter Munro

1941. "The New Books of Poetry," *New York Times Book Review*. Dec. 14, p. 5.

Jarrell, Randall

1945. "Poetry in War and Peace," *Partisan Review*. Winter, pp. 120–26.

Kazin, Alfred

1937. "William Carlos Williams Applies the Insight of a Poet to a Novel of Unusual Quality," *New York Times Book Review*. June 20, p. 7.

Kees, Weldon

1945. "William Carlos Williams," *New York Times Book Review*. Feb. 11, p. 5.

Koch, Vivienne
  1939. "All the Differences . . .," *Voices*. Dec., pp. 47–49.
Lann, Robert
  1936. "Some Poetry in Review," *New Republic*. July 15, p. 304.
Larsson, Raymond
  1935. "Recent Verse," *Commonweal*. Jan. 18, p. 350.
Lechlitner, Ruth
  1936a. "Ahead of His Time," *New York Herald Tribune Book Review*. Jan. 19, p. 13.
  1936b. "To the Mind as to the Eye," *New York Herald Tribune Book Review*. Nov. 22, p. 14.
  1939. "The Poetry of William Carlos Williams," *Poetry*. Sept., pp. 326–35.
  1940. "In the Money," *New York Herald Tribune Book Review*. Nov. 17, p. 18.
Maas, Willard
  1937. "A Novel in the American Grain," *New York Herald Tribune Book Review*. July 11, p. 4.
McAlmon, Robert
  1938. *Being Geniuses Together*. New York: Doubleday.
Marsh, Fred T.
  1940. "William Carlos Williams' New Novel," *New York Times Book Review*. Nov. 17, p. 7.
Matthiessen, F. O.
  1945. "Fragmentary and Whole," *New Republic*. Feb. 12, pp. 232–33.
Miller, Fred P.
  1935. "*The New Masses* and Who Else?" *Blue Pencil*. Feb., p. 5.
  1937. "With a Kick to It," *New Republic*. July 7, p. 257.
  1938. "Passaic River Stories," *New Republic*. Apr. 20, p. 341.
Moore, Marianne
  1934. "Things Others Never Notice," *Poetry*. May, pp. 103–6.
Poore, C. G.
  1934. "The Poetry of William Carlos Williams," *New York Times Book Review*. Feb. 18, p. 2.
Pound, Ezra
  1931. "Our Contemporaries and Others," *New Review: An International Notebook for the Arts Published from Paris*. June-July, pp. 149–54, 164–65.
  1933. "Prefatio Aut Cimicium Tumulus" in *Active Anthology*. London: Faber & Faber, Ltd.
Rahv, Philip
  1937. "Torrents of Spring," *Nation*. June 26, p. 733.
  1938. "Hard History," *Partisan Review*. Mar., pp. 48–50.
Rakosi, Carl
  1933. "William Carlos Williams," *Symposium*. Oct., pp. 439–47.

Rice, Philip Blair
1934. "William Carlos Williams," *Nation*. Mar. 28, pp. 365–66.
Rosenfeld, Paul
1938. "A Doctor in New Jersey," *New York Herald Tribune Book Review*. Feb. 27, p. 6.
1939. "Williams the Stylist," *Saturday Review of Literature*. Feb. 11, p. 16.
1940. "Williams the Conqueror," *Nation*. Nov. 23, pp. 507–8.
Rothman, N. L.
1937. "If Joyce Wrote 'Studs Lonigan . . .'," *Saturday Review of Literature*. June 26, p. 5.
1938. "Brilliant Stabs at Truth," *Saturday Review of Literature*. Mar. 19, p. 16.
Stearns, Marshall W.
1945. "Syntax, Sense, Sound, and Dr. Williams," *Poetry*. Apr., pp. 35–40.
Stevens, Wallace
1934. "Preface" to Williams's *Collected Poems 1921–1931*. New York: Objectivist Pr. Reprinted in *Opus Posthumous*. New York: Knopf, 1969.
1946. "Rubbings of Reality," *Briarcliff Quarterly*. Oct., pp. 201–2; reprinted in *Opus Posthumous*. New York: Knopf, 1969.
Sweeney, John L.
1941. "New Poetry," *Yale Review*. Summer, pp. 817–27.
Symonds, Julian
1938. "How Wide Is the Atlantic? or Do You Believe in America?" *Twentieth Century Verse*. Sept.-Oct., pp. 80–84.
Untermeyer, Louis
1939. "Experiment and Tradition," *Yale Review*. Spring, pp. 608–13.
Wade, Mason
1939. "The Poems of William Carlos Williams," *New York Times Book Review*. July 23, p. 12.
Walton, Eda Lou
1936. "New Poems by William Carlos Williams," *New York Times Book Review*. Nov. 15, p. 3.
1938. "X-Ray Realism," *Nation*. Mar. 19, pp. 334–35.
Warren, Austin
1932. "Some Periodicals of the American Intelligentsia," *New English Weekly*. Oct. 6, pp. 595–97.
Williams, Oscar
1941. "The Poet of the Month," *New Republic*. Sept. 29, pp. 410–11.
Wilson, T. C.
1934. "The Pamphlet Poets," *Poetry*. Jan., pp. 225–29.

1936. "The Example of Dr. Williams," *Poetry*. May, pp. 105–7.
Winters, Yvor
   1937. *Primitivism and Decadence: A Study of American Experimental Poetry*. New York: Swallow Pr.
   1939. "Poetry of Feeling," *Kenyon Review*. Winter, pp. 104–7.

CHAPTER 3

Putting Paterson on the Map: 1946-1961

Paterson is Williams's magnum opus, his contribution to the epic literature of America, his most sustained work. It is the major pronouncement towards which he was working in one form or another for over thirty years. It was this work which forced the reviewers and critics to overhaul their estimates of the man's achievement. This chapter is an attempt to separate the *initial* critical response to the four, then five, parts of the poem. The early debate both for and against the poem was heated and sustained, but the most characteristic gesture on the part of its first critics was a puzzling hesitancy over how to talk intelligently about a long poem which refused to fit into any of the traditional categories or, indeed, even generic forms. In fact, it would take the critics more than twenty years to begin to find even an adequate vocabulary with which to treat the poem's lexical density and radical poetics. In the years between 1946 and 1961, then, we can see the critics making their initial adjustments to a major poem in the process of its five-part unfolding.

Paterson I

At first, *Paterson* was virtually ignored. And when it was mentioned, it was misunderstood. Part of that misunderstanding lay, of course, in the difficulty of talking with any finality about only the first part of a longer poem. Randall Jarrell's review of Book I stands head and shoulders above the rest, as his friend Robert Lowell noted in his own review of the book. Reviewing a three-month batch of poetry (*PR*, Sept.-Oct. 1946), Jarrell stated sim-

ply and unequivocally that Book I was "the best thing William
Carlos Williams has ever written." It was hard to quote from such
a poem, because that was "like humming a theme and expecting a
hearer to guess from that its effect upon its third repetition in a
movement." The truth of the matter was that *Paterson* was an
orchestration of themes: "Dr. Williams introduces a theme that
stands for an idea, repeats it over and over in varied forms, devel-
ops it side by side with two or three more themes that are being
developed, recurs to it time and time again throughout the poem,
and echoes it for ironic or grotesque effects in thoroughly incon-
gruous contexts." Jarrell devoted most of his space to a summariza-
tion of the poem's argument, seeing its subject as the search for "a
language so close to the world that the world can be represented
and understood in it."

"How wonderful and unlikely that this extraordinary mixture
of the most delicate lyricism of perception and feeling with the
hardest and homeliest actuality should ever have come into being,"
Jarrell summed up with a note of atypical enthusiasm. If "the next
three books are as good as this one, . . . the whole poem will be
the best very long poem that any American has written." But
Jarrell's enthusiasm for *Paterson* was never to stand so high again,
and even his view of the first book would yellow with time.

Most of the early reviews of Book I overlap in their critical
perspectives, taking their clues from Williams's own fragmentary
prose introduction, as one grasps at anything solid in a river which
threatens to pull one under. Isaac Rosenfeld (*N*, Aug. 24, 1946)
stressed the various levels of meaning in *Paterson:* the level of
theme; the level of language and communication between man and
the city, the self, and others. He noted too the levels of language—
the prose collage of "local history, newspaper clippings, expense
accounts, letters and reminiscences"; and the "deceptively . . .
simple poetry." He admired Williams's clean idiomatic prose, mis-
takingly assuming, as many critics after him were to do, that
Williams had written it all himself. He saw the prose, here "moved
into the poetic foreground," as fixing the meanings upon which
the poetry would draw in a strategy analogous to T. S. Eliot's
notes in *The Waste Land*. It was an analogue Williams himself
was to borrow to defend his insertion of the long eight-page letter which ended the second book. The prose also allowed for "a
sociological or historical distillate of the city" which the lyrics by
their nature could not do. But the poetry, he felt, would have to
be able to detach itself "from the prose conveyor belt" and work

out its own design, as the section on the *National Geographic* snapshot of the native chief and his wives had developed into the theme of marriage and "communication between lovers." Finally, the mood of summary and wisdom would have to continue its centrifugal force outward to include more than Williams's pre-occupation with his own *ars poetica*, his world where only words grow. It would have to reach out to include Williams's world of childbirth, women, life along the Passaic. Rosenfeld was asking, essentially, for the social esthetic of the thirties.

In her short review of the book (*Books*, Sept. 22, 1946), Ruth Lechlitner began by quoting the lyric passage about the Passaic ("From above, higher than the spires . . .") as prose, further breaking down formal distinctions, and then cataloguing the "Patersonia" which made up "the water-woven texture of the poem." It was the river which determined the environment of the city and the poem. Williams had achieved a surface in which discrete objects maintained their distinctiveness yet managed to be interconnected "through the sensual texture of word and phrase, figure and image." It was something like what Joyce had achieved in the "Anna Livia Plurabelle."

In the Autumn issue of *Voices* (1946), William Gram found *Paterson* "unprepossessing" and "a singularly difficult and trying manuscript." Williams had tried, Gram felt, to "quite consciously" draw up "a pattern of universal values," somewhat as Auden had done in *For the Time Being*. But where Auden had succeeded in instinctively drawing disparate materials into a major form "along every plane of knowledge and experience," Williams's self-consciousness had resulted in a failure. Still, there were "individual accomplishments within the larger frame," even if the frame was unsuitable for the long poem.

In the February, 1947, issue of *Poetry*, Edwin Honig, after extending all of the usual caveats about the tenuous nature of evaluating an unfinished poem, set out to plot the projected curve of *Paterson*. He read Williams as trying to make the city "the focal myth wound out of the poet's consciousness," or, as Joyce had done in *Finnegan's Wake*, to make the myth coextensive with consciousness itself. In place of a conventional pattern tying the poem together, there were prose sections threading the scattered facts of history. The scheme of the poem as Honig saw it was this: "for the philosophy: 'no ideas but in things'; for the poetic logic: 'to make a start,/ out of particulars/ and make them general'; for the guiding symbol: man as a city; for the referents: . . .

'my sources . . . / the secret of that form/ interknit with the unfathomable ground/ where we walk daily'; for the central images: the river, the falls, the rocks, the green things separately growing; and for the artiface: a language, . . . of 'deformed verse . . . suited to deformed morality.' "

Williams's "personal problem," like Eliot's, was to be constantly rediscovering a language which would "embody" the flux and "rescue something of the waste of moment-to-moment reality." Forever "absorbed and rejected" by his place, Williams was trying "to maintain the balance" between the surface illusion of the thing and a psychic penetration to its core, often failing to find what "laughs at the names/ by which they think to trap it," but also succeeding in capturing at moments that secret in the self-distracted, nervous tension of the poem's very texture. The prose was, finally, superfluous. Williams's love of the human seemed "fixed, alien, and cold" to him—a clinical, even mathematical diagnosis of the ways in which men tried to communicate, through "the language of sex," their curiosity and knowledge. And Williams's solution to the problem of language had been a personal one; he had in effect bypassed the enormous problem of discovering a universally valid epistemology. What Book I moved towards was a "personal faith" that only in a "penetration to the sources of being" did language become real.

In the summer of 1947, a year after the book had been published, Robert Lowell noted in *Sewanee Review* that "Paterson has made no stir either in the little magazines or in the commercial press." And yet there was "no living English or American poet who has written anything better or more important." Eliot, Frost, Pound, and Stevens were among those still quite active when Lowell said this. And, having said it, he added a footnote that it was "a defect perhaps that the human beings exist almost entirely in the prose passages." ("That's something to think about," Williams wrote Lowell that August, thanking him for the review.) Lowell also noted that Williams was more like Wordsworth than any of his contemporaries, for *Paterson* was "comparable to *The Prelude* and the opening of *The Excursion.*" By identifying himself with the city, every detail of Williams's life became "an experience, a memory, or a symbol." Whether he moved outward into the world or inward, personifying nature, Williams could fit his observations to the right rhythms. Part of Williams's achievement was that, while there was nothing in the nature of the short poems "to indicate that they could carry the major theme of the poem (the city, the mountain and the river: a man, a woman, and the man's thought)," still Williams had achieved a musical organization, as his friend Jarrell had noted. *Paterson* was "a sort of anti-*Cantos* rooted in America, in one city, and in what Williams had known long and seen often." In its very rootedness and in its dramatic unity, *Paterson* possessed what the *Cantos* lacked. By comparison, *The Bridge* was "relatively inexperienced, chaotic and verbal." In fact, *Paterson* made most contemporary poetry "look a little secondhand."

Two overviews of Williams's development, which took into consideration the radical departure signalled by the arrival of *Paterson* I, appeared in 1946 and 1947, the first by Parker Tyler and the second by Frederick Morgan. The essay by Tyler, an old friend of Williams's and the editor of several smart little magazines with expensive formats, appeared in the special issue of the *Briarcliff Quarterly* (Oct. 1946) which honored Williams. Tyler reviewed Williams's progress from the days of the Imagists thirty years before to *Paterson* itself. Williams's primary concern had been with "the concrete, the data of experience," the "quiddity" or "whatness" of "the American environment." This was different in basic intention from Crane on the one hand, who was looking for rhetorical formulas, and from Eliot on the other, because the underlying emotional strata which is the *donneé* of objective correlatives simply did not exist in the elusive and unformed environment which Williams had chosen as his world. Europe had been formulated as America had not, and Eliot's objective correlative, taken to its extreme, had already ended in the hollow, effete cry of Swinburne and the memory mechanisms of Mallarmé. Williams stood over against the tendencies of the Frenchman in this way: where Mallarmé transformed the local into "a formula of sensation," Williams's local, his "poetic evidence," purposely remained "brutally *untransformed*."

The significance of what Williams was attempting in *Paterson* could be understood by looking at *Leaves of Grass* and then at *Finnegan's Wake*. There was no typical action in Whitman, Tyler pointed out, only passivity. And one of the basic requirements for both myth and epic was the sense of struggle towards the individual forms of destiny. Whitman was no more than a "barbaric yawp" echoing hollowly in the wilderness of an America without a dominant myth against which to measure or check the occasion of that cry. Joyce's dominant myth, on the other hand, was the dream, in which contemplation or *dreamed* action substitutes for epic action. Like Whitman and Joyce, Williams too was in search of the universal, but one checked against himself and his experience. He too was looking for the dominant myth, "the fugitive forms of behavior not accepted as ritual." What Tyler heard as the essential music of the quest in *Paterson* was a "materialistic sadness, a distinctive celebration of the Blossom of Life whose final seed is Death." *Paterson* was filled with the dream speech of the river; its "prose quotations of the river legends" formed "a *sibylline enunciation* of the city's dream rather than its interpretation." It was this language, then, which formed a kind of new objective correlative based on the dream-consciousness of Williams's Paterson and, indeed, of all men. Since, as Tyler saw, the subject matter of *Paterson* centered on Williams's own psyche, and since the poem was in fact an autobiographical confession verging on neurosis, much of the poem was inaccessible to the reader. At the heart of *Paterson* was a central myth which the first book had not disclosed, although there were whisperings. There was a real danger, however, that while the thread of the poem seemed strong enough, the poet might still lose himself in the labyrinth of his created city.

Frederick Morgan (*SR*, Autumn 1947) attempted to pinpoint "some of the difficulties which an Imagist and vers-librist technique must encounter in attempting to solve [the] large problems of form" in a poem like *Paterson*. It was a problem which many of the critics had touched on, but Morgan set out to do so by presenting a historical overview of Williams as a good but limited lyric voice. Williams's was "a poetry of direct observation of individual objects" employing three techniques: (1) color contrast, (2) a spare presentation of concrete detail, and (3) a "special" use of rhythm. Williams's Imagistic presentation of the object meant the "atomization of experience into images . . . sufficient unto themselves," without benefit of the speaker's own attitude towards his material. Scraps of dialogue, mimetic sounds, even visual reproductions like the soda sign in "The Attic which is Desire" were all logical extensions of the Imagistic mode. This technique could be expanded somewhat crudely by simply accumulating details, but this did not alter the strategy. The thought behind the process still remained minimal.

Morgan saw Williams's rhythms as characterized by "a continuous movement and adroit timing of the beats." He had avoided the inherent monotony of free verse by using the short line with its varying terminal pauses, "the irregular indentation of lines," and "the breaking off of stanzas." He took issue with Winters's analysis of Williams's meter as being grounded in a modified accentual base (really a kind of ersatz sprung rhythm). There were no metric rules in Williams. If Williams's poetry were written as prose, Morgan maintained, it "would never be recognized as a poem." But written as poetry, there was "an intensified perception of the contours of the rhythm." On the other hand, metrical verse, with its multiple grades of tension between meter and rhythm, was capable of a greater range of effects than was free verse, which had to rely solely on variations in speed from line to line. Free verse was also incapable of carrying much thought or emotion. Because Williams had, therefore, "deprived himself of all the poetic means which might sustain prolonged meditation," he was forced to rely on commentary, on the statement of an emotion or the use of anecdote. When he tried to reason in his poems, he simply failed, often giving the impression of desperately floundering in trying to give an adequate description of the object. His poetry was, really, a formless "pre-poetry."

Having thus established the limitations of Williams's poetics, Morgan turned to *Paterson*. Williams had tried "to merge consciousness with environment," but had failed to control the form of his consciousness. He was too self-conscious, his landscape and rhythms weary and flabby, his prose a device "to pass off his raw material as the finished product." If his concern with the American place and a native idiom was a worthwhile topic, Williams had not demonstrated that he was an adequate spokesman for those ideas. Nor was Williams's "short stabbing line" and "powerful, broken rhythm" any more "directly related to the tempo of American life" than any other line. Crane had at least created a partial success in "The Bridge" by writing some great poetry, and Eliot, for all his "traditional" language, was perhaps more truly American than Williams. In the final analysis, Morgan wrote, Williams had done some good early work; he had opened a landscape and he had taught us to look more closely. But his forms were restrictive, a dead end, and he could only wish the man "would get back to doing what he can do well": writing imagistic lyrics.

Paterson II

Williams finished Part II of *Paterson* by the summer of 1947, expected to see it appear that fall, and found he had to wait until the following April. Therefore, it was not until mid-June, 1948, that the reviews finally began to trickle in. Robert Lowell's appreciation (*N*, June 19, 1948) was the first. Book II, he said, was an interior monologue by "Williams, anyone living in *Paterson*, the American, the masculine principle—a sort of Everyman." The park where Williams walked was "Everywoman, any woman, the feminine principle, America." The whole poem was, like Hart Crane's "For the Marriage of Faustus and Helen," about marriage, about the straining towards marriage, and about divorce. There were the worlds of the preacher—"ineffective, pathetic, and a little phony," Alexander Hamilton, and the great industrialists, and, alongside them, "the humorous"—dogs, children, and natural objects.

Paterson, Lowell commented, was "an attempt to write the American Poem," to incorporate "the American myth." If that myth was in many ways "hollow, windy, and inert," still, it was a serious matter for Americans, who simply had to face the fact that their country was "immense, crass, and Roman." The trouble was that the myth swallowed up so much of the poetic landscape that it seemed to leave no room to populate the poem with people. In none of the best long American poems, and this included *Leaves of Grass*, the *Cantos*, *The Waste Land*, *Four Quartets*, *The Bridge*, did the characters take on a developed dramatic dimension; instead they simply melted into voices. *Paterson* too was without fully developed people. But comparing *Paterson* with *Leaves of Grass*, Lowell found that Whitman's language had "less variety, sureness, and verve than Williams's"—that Whitman's was the softer, more formless, imagination. *Paterson*, he summed up, was "Whitman's America, grown pathetic and tragic, brutalized by inequality, disorganized by industrial chaos, and faced with annihilation." No poet had written of the country "with such a combination of brilliance, sympathy, and experience."

Like so many of the front-line reviewers of an epic promised piecemeal over the years, Richard Eberhart (*Times*, June 20, 1948) resorted to the burden of repeating the argument of the whole before attending to his own coordinates for plotting this particular part. Williams, he insisted, was not a philosophical or meditative poet; he was, rather, "realistic," "objective," immediate. If *Paterson* owed something to Pound's *Cantos*, still, Williams's was the "more limited" field, less contrived, less dense, more easily accessible, the cinematographic scene shifts reinforcing the integrity of the isolated moments of perception. The prose sequences reflected the prosaic quality of life itself; integrated with the lyric moments, they swung in the direction of a new genre. Cress's long eight-page letter which ended the book Eberhart wrongly attributed to Williams himself. In fact, the letter had come from a young poet named Marcia Nardi and was real enough, as was the neurosis and frustration of the type of American woman Eberhart thought the letter so clearly represented.

If Eberhart saw the letter as an honest portrait of "a woman not content with woman's position in the world," Ruth Lechlitner (*Books*, June 27, 1948) saw with a woman's intuition that the letter was "too painfully real to have been wholly 'invented' by Dr. Williams himself." It was, in fact, "probably the most naked revelation to date of the problem of the modern woman whose creative capacities are . . . blocked . . . by her need for love as a woman, and what happens when she is drawn to the intellectual-creative male." As such, Cress was as much a victim as was Hamilton's "great beast" (the people), and an integral part of the theme of the "coming night-time for love," which in America was reflected in its "shallow women, . . . refusing men."

Leslie Fiedler (*PR*, Aug. 1948) quickly attended to new volumes by three younger poets—Everson's *The Residual Years*, Jarrell's *Losses*, Berryman's *The Dispossessed*. Then he focused on the "Grand Old Man's" second installment of *Paterson*, which suffered, Fiedler thought, from several of Williams's chronic shortcomings: the "polar failures" of his flat realism and his unswerving sentimentality; his inability to work with philosophical questions or a discursive frame; and his sole reliance on the visual to the exclusion of sound, rhythm, and song. Williams's debt to Pound had, Fiedler implied, driven him onto the wrong track. First, the myth of the ideograph in which sound and drawn shape were pressed into a unity was in fact a nostalgia, and worse, a fallacy, which had led Williams to neglect the world of sound. (Williams, incidentally, had already taken Pound to task in print for his ideographic theories as early as 1940.) Second, the form of *Paterson* was clearly a lineal descendant of the *Cantos*—a "collage of fragments whose architecture is a continuing irony of disjunction." The form was so established by the mid-forties that Fiedler could speak of *Paterson's* form as conservative, already imbued with a "classic" air. *Paterson* had "candor," a "freshness of vision," and the "charm" of Williams's created personality with his "radical vagueness of ideas" joined to his "sensual precision"; it had the marks of Williams's "respect for language," and his "ironic and tender regionalism." But Williams was too self-indulgent (as in quoting at such length from Marcia Nardi), clumsy in his use of

transitions and in his irrelevant additions. Fiedler closed by acknowledging Williams's already historic position in modernism,
but asserted defensively that the old man might best be served by
the kind of "impious" discrimination he had presented.

William Van O'Connor (*Sat R*, Sept. 25, 1948) was as ambivalent, and as apologetic for being so, as Fiedler had been. Williams
had drawn a "sentient America, gross and directionless," in which
"symbols function loosely" and tangentially to his "shrewd and
sometimes oversimplified comments." *Paterson* fell below *The
Waste Land;* like *The Bridge*, it was too close to its material and
lacked a "sufficient historical and philosophical perspective on contemporary America," lacked too the "fulness" and "interrelatedness" necessary to any long poem. Frederick Eckman (*GG*, Autumn 1948) noted *Paterson*'s complex, uneven mosaic structure
which was neither narrative nor epic, but rather a "highly-charged
long poem," lyric and meditative in nature. It was a form loose
enough to contain whatever "might be expected to occupy [an]
agile, questioning mind." There was also a new kind of lyric in
Paterson, characterized by a longer line and a more subdued intensity than one usually found in Williams.

Robert Fitzgerald (*SR*, Autumn 1948) took Williams to task
on several accounts. First off, there were too many prose interruptions in *Paterson*. If some created ironically effective juxtapositions,
others were frivolous, and still others were disproportionately
long, such as the distraught excerpt which closed the book. Moreover, Williams's intellectual position seemed confused, reducing
itself at best to "a half-baked romantic naturalism." Despite its fine
passages, its sense of having caught the common life of *Paterson* in
its pages, a world "bright, raw, bitter-tasting, full of smoky sun-
light and suburban underbrush and grit blowing from vacant lots,"
despite its honesty and vigor, *Paterson* was, finally, "too cranky,
too leaky, to be considered a whole work of art in any sense" that
Fitzgerald could understand.

Louis Martz (*YR*, Autumn 1948), after praising Pound's
achievement in the Pisan sequence following the dry middle period
of that long poem, turned to *Paterson*, "a poem cast in the form of
Pound's best cantos." But it was different from the *Cantos* in being firmer and more limited and far less bookish, since Williams
had focused primarily on what he had seen "directly, immediately" in and around *Paterson*. Book II picked up, clarified, and
expanded the "complex of analogies" initiated in Book I: the
dwarf had become "the poet defeated and crushed by his environ-

ment," the minister's wife "some vital principle" fleeing from a tired language, crying out to be seen not as material for literature but as a human being. Here was love in all of its manifestations, and at the heart of it was the lonely evangelist-hero, "a last, faded, apostle of charity." *Paterson* might well be "one of the most important works yet written by an American poet."

Edwin Honig (*Poetry*, Apr. 1949) saw *Paterson* now as extending along two fronts: as testament and as confession. Paterson himself had developed from mere observer to actor in the drama. If *Paterson* was not a master work, still, Honig felt, "the prescription for one" was inherent in the poem. The trouble with Williams lay in his way of communicating: he could write about the people who inhabited his world, but not to them. Williams had smashed hard against the "staleness of old forms, old language, old styles," telling the truth without falsity. And Dr. Paterson had identified himself with his codified, brutalized, dehumanized people "exploited by the mythical divorce" created by Pound's statisticians—bankers, legislators, industrialists, educators. It was this theme of divorce which finally justified the inclusion of Nardi's long letter, Honig felt, for it was an actual "replica" of that theme, its "depressive weight" finally obliterating "the poetry itself." But he counted this as a weakness disrupting the more "objective symbolic relationships set up in Book One," rather than as a way of coming closer to the fiction of a phenomenological reality containing within itself the real and not the "literary" divorce of which Williams had despaired. Like Lucretius, Williams adhered to a Heraclitean vision of the eternal flux of all things. But where Lucretius had stabilized that ocean of flux in the ideal island of "Venus the procreator, the repository of all earthly beauty," Williams had only "the beauty of honesty" to rely on, which became in fact an "anarchic resentment of things as they are and a valve for emitting steam concerning things they should be." Honig did not see that Williams also had his (momentary) "island of rest" in the core figure of the ever young virgin, radiant and fresh in a world of detritus: Kora in Hell. But he did see that Paterson/Williams was both "the longing, dispassionate recreator of the everyday world of the senses, . . . and the besieged expositor of poetic values, striking out at a devaluating world."

Vivienne Koch's *William Carlos Williams* (1950) presented a thirty-page reading of *Paterson* I and II, all that had appeared at the time she gave the manuscript to *New Directions*. Her reading is mainly New Critical, a seriatim glossing of the text—some of it good, much of it obvious. The language of *Paterson*, she pointed out, was "neither prose nor common speech," but an assimilation of both. The prose passages and the poetry were not distinct levels of discourse, but formed "a continual structural and thematic interlacing." *Paterson* was a flowing, and the figure of Paterson himself contained the myth-generating (and generated) giant—the poet, the citizens of Paterson, in fact, the city itself. He was also the thoughts of the poet, father *and* son. Complementing Paterson were the many women. The poem's central concern was the language which, like the old families of Jersey, had become vitiated, degraded, incestuous with the passage of time. It had, therefore, to be renewed, as suggested by the contrast between the Jackson whites and the African chief's nine fertile wives, or the divorce between Mrs. Cumming and Sam Patch and the language. Koch touched too on Williams's echoic devices, his strategy of establishing a beautiful visual and sound pattern only to undercut it by letting the impoverished American language speak for itself. Following Jarrell, she saw Book I as having established the major themes "as in a symphonic overture."

Book II, then, was "the first movement" in that symphony. The elemental character of the place—Garret Mountain on a Sunday afternoon in May—was a replica of our deformed, reduced world. The Evangelist, a figure of "superb vigor" ringing out against the dullness around him, was "a bit obviously" contrasted with the figure of Hamilton and the complex associations of Pound's sense of usury. In the final part of II, Williams's steady evocation of love moving towards sure consummation had been checked hard by the hysterical letter of the rejected beloved. Koch's understanding of the significance of that letter was perceptive, sensitive. It served a "curious double agency," part of the "anti-poetic 'historical' prose-threads," cutting not only against the woman but against Williams himself, exposing the poet's own "mean inadequacies of conduct" even as he searched for beauty and communion.

Paterson documented in its very form "*how* ideas come from things." If it seemed to arise out of an "uncompromising materialism," it had arrived "at an almost classical humanism," for it was self-knowledge (including a knowledge of evil) which led to the possession of the human whole. "It is clear now," Koch concluded tentatively, "that in *Paterson* Williams is attempting one of the most adventurous and passionate assaults upon the moral structure of the American grain which the poetic imagination in this country has yet conceived."

When, however, Koch came to review *Paterson* IV two years
later (*KR*, Summer 1952), her acceptance of the poem was
quieter, more qualified. "I must now add that the whole poem falls
short of my expectations," she wrote. There were "too many flat
and diverse prose passages from sources ranging from inventories
to technical journals" which were simply not assimilated to the
poetic force field. Nor was there "the surface 'pay-back' of [an]
immediately memorable texture" such as one found in Stevens,
Eliot, or Dylan Thomas. And the poem's assimilation of Pound's
usury and Social Credit theory had been a serious mistake, as a
number of critics were to insist. The sense one had of the poem,
finally, was of man's "humanly circumscribed power."

Paterson III

Reviewing the third part of *Paterson* seven weeks after it appeared (*Times*, Feb. 12, 1950), Richard Eberhart spoke admir-
ingly of Williams's sense of immediacy, of his ability to present
the gritty "particulars of reality." What he lamented was the
poem's self-conscious form which barred it from all but the specialist. Selden Rodman (*Books*, Mar. 5, 1950) felt, with the appearance of *Paterson* III and Koch's study, that Williams had
finally demonstrated his majority, that "the body of his work, in
its seriousness, its humanity, and its indefatigable straining after
perfection, entitles him to rank among the few men of letters we
have produced whose essential 'Americanism' goes deep enough to
elude national boundaries." *Paterson*, he felt, would "have no rival
among American poems of comparable length."

"More than ever," Hayden Carruth maintained (*N*, Apr. 8,
1950), "it becomes apparent that Dr. Williams has in mind a
whole, inseverable poem, not a discrete tetralogy." Carruth enu-
merated the stock of symbols, whose meanings were "drawn from
a common fund of romantic ideas": first, Paterson the hero-city-
man-giant, whose dreams were citizens, whose history "is roughly
coterminous with, and equal to, the history of America," and,
second, the woman-mountain. These two were "activated by the
four elements," both benign and malevolent: water—the river, the
falls, by extension the flow of time, the flow of a "pre-mental language"; earth, the chatterer; fire, "the creative act, in love or art";
and wind, "inspiration, the integrator, the carrier of sounds and
smells." Book III centered on "a search for a language" and the

rejection of all dead abstractions, a search with its analogue in the sound of the falls themselves. The language, grounded on the present, was discovered or invented "by writing instantaneously, even carelessly." The "meaning" and the hundreds of hidden allusions in *Paterson* would, he felt, be eventually tracked down. What did trouble him—and he addressed himself directly to Williams— was Williams's line; not the meter and not the rhythm, for which Williams clearly had an "astonishingly pure feeling," but the *line*. "These lines are not run over, in the Elizabethan sense; nor are they rove over, in the Hopkinsian sense; they are hung over, like a Dali watch. They break in the most extraordinary places, with no textual, metrical, or syntactical tension to help us over." Williams was to spend the rest of his life defending his line to poets and critics and he seldom satisfied any of them, regardless of which tack he tried.

Monroe Spears (*Poetry*, Apr. 1950) rejected Williams as "very limited" and "very minor," a poet who had "been praised far beyond his deserts." Enumerating *Paterson*'s major symbols, Spears rejected them as mechanical and willful counters. Williams really had "no coherent pattern of ideas," except old throwbacks to the twenties: "shocking the bourgeois, revolting against Suburbia, preaching the gospel of Beauty . . . and poetry as the only salvation." Placed against Eliot, Williams's development had ceased years before; he had hardly progressed beyond Imagism. *Paterson* was "not only *about* the failure of language"; it *was* "a failure of language." If some critics had praised *Paterson* highly, that was due more to the ingenuity and subtlety of the critic who could, "if he wants to, discover complexity and unity in almost anything," than to anything really present in the poem itself.

William Van O'Connor also came down hard on the poem (*Sat R*, May 20, 1950), arguing that there was still "a terrifying chasm between the inarticulate, sensate world Williams presents and the redeemed world he seems to believe possible through the grace of beautiful language." Richard Ellmann (*YR*, Spring 1950) disliked *Paterson*'s way of viewing "everything from the point of view of language." The poem had a "loose but insistent" structure and an irregular verse pattern, "often based on a short line of three or four accents." Contrary to what Stevens had proclaimed about Williams's poetry, *Paterson* was "the most pro-poetic of poems," if by poetry one meant "a form of creation which is more dependent upon observed data than most poets would allow."

In his careful, considered review of Williams's *Paterson* III, *A*

Dream of Love, and *The Clouds,* as well as of Koch's study, F. W. Flint addressed himself first to the phenomenon of Williams (*KR,* Summer 1950). Here was "the scientifically trained, experimental, romantic-idealist mind in *extremis*" whose writing undermined the very "premises on which this mind was originally constituted." If Williams was far less glamorous than Whitman, he was far more contemporary "than any poet before him has ever been." Academic critics like Winters and Blackmur had treated Williams with condescension, and Williams had repaid them by heaping scorn upon them in *Paterson,* where they had become "clerks/got out of hand." Williams, by his own admission, Flint pointed out, had pleaded "his inability to handle traditional coin traditionally," and so had issued "a fluid currency of his own: a set of protean, imagist-symbolist centers of force which polarize his loose, fragmentary material." Still, like so many other critics, Flint noted that *Paterson* III was a falling off from the first two books. It seemed, perhaps, too philosophical, even too "old-fashioned arty." Overall, then, the initial commentary on *Paterson* III, what there was of it, was negative or at best qualified. The critics were waiting, naturally, for the whole poem before reaching their verdicts.

Paterson IV

The bulk of the critical comments on *Paterson* for the decade after the publication of its first part often share a kind of abstract immensity and a general inutility where they do not demonstrate a sense of confusion or condescension. Even Jarrell's remarks, for all their witty readability, are more concerned with themselves than with listening hard to Williams. Williams himself expected this and (more or less) patiently bided his time, as forty years of general inattention or benign incomprehensibility had taught him to do. It is no wonder, then, that he should have become excited when, finally, a competent academic critic like Louis Martz—poet, editor of the *Yale Review,* and professor at Yale—published his essay on *Paterson* which, twenty years later, can still serve as a model for clarity and understanding. "On the Road to Paterson" initially appeared in *Poetry New York* early in 1951, months before *Paterson* IV appeared, which makes the essay all the more remarkable for its findings.

"During the years 1946–51," Martz wrote, "we had the privilege of watching one of the most exhilarating sights in recent literature. A writer over sixty, whose work for nearly forty years had seemed only a series of new starts, burst in a fury of creation that suddenly lifted him to a major place among American writers." There were (and are) many critics who would refuse Williams that place, but the fact of *Paterson* and so many other works, written between 1946 and 1951, was against them. Threading Williams's career, Martz saw "an order, a reason, a firm and central purpose to be discerned." He had to agree with Blackmur that Williams's poems lacked "culmination." There had been only one period of "settled achievement": when Williams wrote *Spring and All* with such poems as "To Elsie" and "By the road to the contagious hospital." Later pieces, like "Burning the Christmas Greens" and "Perpetuum Mobile," were extensions of this style: a style of "concrete details, presented with spare, terse commentary, in short lines, brief stanzas, clipped, rigorously designed." Williams had continued throughout the forties to find "a more inclusive and flexible style," as in *The Clouds, The Pink Church*, and in the prosaic, "rippling, colloquial rumination" of "The Forgotten City."

But Williams's real successes after *Spring and All* had been prose successes. The short stories of the thirties and forties demonstrated a "mature mastery of a narrow range continued in the best of the later stories." But here too there was a lack of culmination. Williams had reached his peak in the 1938 collection, *Life Along the Passaic River*, with a bare, frank, incisive style which paralleled but had not gone beyond his poetic style in *Spring and All*. The longer fiction lacked the sense of development which would have raised them to "a major achievement."

Martz, then, saw all of Williams's work leading up to *Paterson* as "by-products, preliminary steps, to that splendid achievement." There were markers in the earlier volumes of poetry pointing towards *Paterson:* "The Wanderer," "Paterson: Episode 17," "Paterson: the Falls," "For the Poem, Patterson" [sic]. But the masterful fusion of *Paterson*'s prose and poetry into a single major achievement could not have occurred without the prior achievement of *In the American Grain*. This was not a history, but rather an exploration of "the nature of man's fate" which presented "an attitude toward life," and conveyed, "through historical symbols," Williams's ethical and aesthetic ideals. Like *Paterson, In the American Grain* considered two ways of treating "achieved and dying forms amid the active flux of the new and unachieved": the way of the Puritan and the way of those men filled with "wonder" at the

New World. Dr. Paterson was, in fact, doing what Williams's Poe had done before him, searching and pointing out the fineness of the "Beautiful Thing" in, as Williams had said, the "hard, sardonic, truculent mass of the New World." *Paterson* was the fusion of the kind of prose and the kind of lyric which Williams had perfected, a prose "imbedded in and held together by a matrix of poetry that 'catches aslant' the significance which 'prose (journalism)' misses." The relationship between the two forms varied. Sometimes the poetry extended the meaning of a prose passage, transforming it into a symbol. Sometimes the prose stood in ironical contrast to the poetry. Where the significance of the prose was not always clear, it still served its function "in terms of the big, encompassing symbol of the poem: the roar of the Passaic Falls," the incessant hum of the quotidian in the dream-like consciousness of the complex figure of Paterson, "city, man, and poet." The "Beautiful Thing" was manifold and yet unitive. It was for Martz "the human spirit . . . finding pleasure in the strength of its own perceptions, in its sympathies, its loves, its ability to mold a world."

Martz demonstrated that Williams knew exactly what he had been doing all along, how he had taken Eliot's and Pound's measure and had consciously chosen another path. Quoting from Williams's own "Letter to an Australian Editor" (1946), he showed that, whereas Eliot's and Pound's creative imaginations had been fertilized androgynetically by "a direct descent of great minds" (the great tradition) in which the younger poet used or deviated from the older forms in order to assert his originality, Williams's own fertilization had been fed, rather, by the forms of the present, by the fertility of his own place.

"I had not anticipated such attention," an astonished Williams wrote Martz in late May, "such a reading of my slowly developing viewpoint until after, at long last, I had myself been able to bring myself into focus, not until perhaps I should long have been dead. I cannot enough thank you for having made the effort to gather up a meaning from my piecemeal and often rambling work. I realize fully that I have not been able to state clearly enough, articulately enough, what I have to say and that it is a duty which everyone (who reads me) has a right to expect of me. . . . I must gather together the stray ends of what I have been thinking and make my full statement as to their meaning or quit." Martz's attention had shown Williams that others could detect a significant pattern in his work, and this gave him the confidence to continue.

That pattern lay, essentially, in his continuing search for the "new measure" which was to occupy him in his last years. The position establishing the need for such a new measure had been made; now it was more a matter of listening to those concerned with what he was after, rather than waging his old war with his old enemies. "You have thought it worth your while to take pains to study my texts. No one has done that. Most have put me down for a rough sort of blindsman, who out of resentment against certain practices of the accepted schools of thoughts has gone wild with resentment and nothing more. At least I survived. You have been studious enough, attentive enough to see under that the real drive —something I myself have often lost sight of—and brought it into the light." This was the true function of the critic: to explain the poet's work. It was an oasis for Williams before the general run of dull, ornamental reviews began to flow in with the publication of *Paterson* IV in June.

When *Paterson* IV did appear, it signalled the completion of Williams's original design for his poem. The critics, understandably uneasy and apologetic in writing about an unfinished poem, could breathe more easily now that they had the whole thing before them. They could, by virtue of hindsight, explain that they knew all along that Williams knew what he was about; or they could, with all the evidence in, show the thing to be a failure. "Dr. Williams does not leap to Cathay and he places no improbable strain on our imagination, no such strain as that which broke Crane's 'Bridge' and made it finally unusable," Eberhart wrote a scant week after the book was published (*Times*, June 17, 1951). By stepping away from the sea and back to Paterson, Williams had given us "a philosophy of probability and use." He had taken a big chance in attempting "to define a new context" and had "mastered a very large area of experience."

Ruth Lechlitner (*Books*, July 1, 1951) saw *Paterson* as "the contemporary poet's search for an identity with, and for a language indigenous to, his industrial-social environment, through which he may escape—as man and artist—a 'premature death.'" The "key" to that escape lay in song, which she saw as synonymous with the "radiant gist that resists the final crystallization." But had Williams discovered that song? He seemed to stand in grave "danger of self-defeat in his linguistic efforts to 'escape' his environment," largely because the song too often failed to communicate to his contemporaries, "including the representative Sunday-holiday crowd." His "experimental and imitative form" effectively and unfortunately reduced his audience to the few, to the poet and the critic equipped to deal with a modernist esthetic.

Time magazine, too, lingered on the lyric Williams in its short review of *Paterson* IV in mid-July (1951). Obviously uneasy with the poem's "dull, prosy flats," *Time* conceded that the epic as a whole "makes a bold bid for attention as one of the few important poems written in the 20th Century U.S." And in the October, 1951, issue of *Harper's*, Lloyd Frankenberg, admitting that he was baffled by the poem's thematic connections, also admitted that he had come only by degrees to appreciate Williams's best poems, "looking so hard for what wasn't in them that I missed what was." Dudley Fitts (*Sat R*, July 21, 1951) wavered between praise for the poem's "more or less triumphant conclusion," with its "startling vitality," "audacious sexuality," and "poetic credo" and uneasiness before a confusion of undigested materials which struck him like so many "colorful noise-shapes in a dream."

But Hayden Carruth saw the impact *Paterson* would have from the beginning (*N*, Aug. 25, 1951). "There can be no question that in the years ahead 'Paterson' will receive the close attention of the critics, whatever may be the outcome of their deliberations," he wrote. *Paterson*'s symbols, or better, objects, would in due time be interpreted: "it will be neither an easy job nor a job that one man can hope to accomplish by himself." In the meantime, the major theme of *Paterson* stood clear: "Modern society has been divorced from its healthy and natural sources by the corruptions of church, state, commerce, and education; we can be saved only through . . . a newly *invented* language, which will be free from the traditions of intellectual society and will constitute an act of marriage with nature as it appears in the earth, in men and women, and in ourselves."

To those who denied the validity of the theme that the poet can save his people, Carruth answered that it was "a valid subject for a work of art" proved by the presence of the work itself. To those who found the theme worn out, outmoded, he answered that it had so far been worked unskillfully and by young poets, and that *Paterson* was the work of a mature man whose thoughts, complex though they were, were "instinctive" with him.

Some other questions were raised by what Carruth called Williams's "lyrical meditation": could a new poetic language be based solely on contemporary American speech patterns? Could a poem with so much documentary prose material survive in the public mind? And what was one to make of Williams's willful destruc-

tion of "the convenient fiction that the poet and the man are sep-
arable," of the constant intrusion into the mesh of his poems of a
"real" self rather than a fictive, larger-than-life, public self?

"Dr. Williams' immediacies (and he is our master of the spontaneous effect) are so often colored by his unpretentious humanity that he seems almost to be improvising, as if he were not one
of the very few really accomplished poets in English today,"
wrote M. L. Rosenthal (*NR*, Aug. 27, 1951). *Paterson*, he insisted,
was "a unit—humane, passionate, self-humbling, assertive of a minimum value," as free as possible from "sentimental and purely literary assumptions," itself a "product of as rigorous a discipline" as
Eliot had demonstrated in *The Waste Land*. There was a "family
resemblance," too, to the *Cantos* in *Paterson*'s surface multiplicity
and even in some of its attitudes, but the personalities of both
poems clearly belonged to different orders.

With all the evidence in, Jarrell offered his findings (*PR*, Nov.-
Dec. 1951). Since his first high praise of *Paterson* I in the pages
of the same magazine five years before, he had executed his brilliant "Introduction" to the *Selected Poems* in 1949, praising and
discriminating, always with his peculiar élan. With only the
slightest hesitancy, he reiterated his admiration for the first part of
Paterson—"I do not see how anyone could do better using only
those rather mosaic organizational techniques"—before he let go
with the "cruncher": "I waited for [those books] more or less as
you wait for someone who has gone to break the bank at Monte
Carlo for the second, third, and fourth times; I was afraid that I
knew what was going to happen, but I kept wishing as hard as I
could that it wouldn't." Jarrell found "a scrappy inconsequence,
an arbitrary irrelevance" about the whole poem, and there were
sections in the final part that sounded "exactly like the stuff you
produce when you are demonstrating to a class that any prose
whatsoever can be converted into four-stress accentual verse simply by inserting line-endings every four stresses."

Jarrell came down hard, too, on several of Williams's organizational strategies: there was too much of the evangelist and his ser-
mon, and what was somebody else's eight-page letter doing in the
poem? Williams ought to have avoided not only Pound's credit
and usury themes, but the organizational principle he had employed in the middle and later *Cantos*. Jarrell condemned it as an
"Organization of Irrelevence," that "if something is somewhere,
one can always find Some Good Reason for its being there." Williams, was, finally, "a *very* good but *very* limited poet, particularly in vertical range," who had even further limited himself "by

volunteering for and organizing a long dreary imaginary war in which America and the Present are fighting against Europe and the Past." Placed against his old enemy, Eliot, and by implication, the cosmopolitan European tradition, Williams seemed parochial. Coming as it did, after Martz's essay, Jarrell's review strikes one as too self-conscious, too brittle. To Williams, it constituted a betrayal.

When, in the summer of 1957, Edith Heal, interviewing Williams, picked up the *Selected Poems* with Jarrell's introduction, Williams squirmed under the sting of Jarrell's dismissal of *Paterson*, putting it down to Jarrell's distaste for the characters of the fourth book (even though Jarrell had admitted he could not bring himself to talk about what would not "satisfactorily conclude even a quite mediocre poem"). Williams tried to keep his remarks general, to aim them at the hydra-headed critic. But one of those heads bore a startling resemblance to Jarrell, as another looked suspiciously like Marianne Moore, who had criticized *Paterson*'s foulness in her letters to Williams. "If you are going to write realistically of the conception of the filth in the world, it can't be pretty. . . . The poem in Book Four," Williams insisted, was "the same poem as it was in Book One."

In his overview of *Paterson* I–IV, which appeared in the August, 1952, number of *Poetry*, Hugh Kenner honed in on what he saw to be Williams's characteristic and unique strategy in the poem. Even the most willingly appreciative critics of the poem had been rendered inarticulate because they did not have the critical tools to deal with the poem. *Paterson* was not a metaphor for something else about which the critics could then expound; it was about itself, about a dense phenomenological reality, a *coming at* the still inarticulate, still provincial sense of the American experience, an eschewal of Pound's and Eliot's concern with creating a new artifact out of the fragments of the past. Williams was the first poet, Kenner insisted, who was out to discover "the core of America that is itself, new, and so far unvocal." In the *Autobiography*'s own phrasing, the American artist had to "recover underlying meaning as realistically as we recover metal out of ore."

The meaning of *Paterson* did not localize itself; it was inherent, caught, in the fabric of the whole poem. As "controlling image," there was the roar of the falls, the confused, dense language. And there was the "complex image" of the burning of the library: "part impatience with books, part purgation of them, part an image of live reading, a lending of blood and heat to the past," as

Pound's Nekuian Odysseus had blooded the ghosts of the past at the beginning of the *Cantos*. But Williams, unlike Pound, saw a poem as a "solid surface, hollow, ringing," in which all depth was an illusion which the reader had come to expect. Kenner ended by focusing on a singularly apt image for Williams's poetics (and, one might add, for the writing habits imposed on a poet by the confluence of his literary and medical professions) in the image of Williams as obstetrician, "devoting in a few critical moments his every wile, his concentration, so far as his capacity allows, of the entire tradition of medical science since Hippocrates, to the deliverance, with his bare hands, into independent life of something he did not make, the identity of which he unshakeably respects, and which but for his ministrations would die voiceless."

In October, 1952, *Golden Goose*, which had published Williams's "The Pink Church" in 1949, devoted twelve pages to Williams, including two letters on prosody which Williams had earlier written to Robert Beum, one of the magazine's editors, and a long review by Beum and Richard Wirtz Emerson on a number of Williams's recent books. Emerson insisted on the necessity of all the sprawling details of *Paterson;* if the progression was not orderly, it was "also *not* confusion." And Book IV was particularly successful as a culmination to the poem. There were dull stretches, but there were dull stretches in the life of any city, any man. Williams, he concluded, was "a craftsman without parallel and with few peers" whose "emphasis on the spoken language was enough to insure his rank as a major writer."

Williams's "personal epic" was, Edwin Honig wrote in *Voices* (May–Aug. 1952), "the first poem of considerable magnitude since Pound's *Cantos* or Eliot's *Four Quartets*." He noted that critics like Jarrell, "whose original ardor was dampened by a superficial reading of the later parts," had missed the integrity of the whole. The prose passages had their own "intrinsic interest, together creating a polyphonic tonal scale," a "dramatic projection on all levels of the living language," much as the best Elizabethan dramatic writing had done. Williams had succeeded, in fact, in writing a language without literary archaism, "a language we can understand," something no American poet had achieved since *Leaves of Grass*.

The structural methodology of *Paterson*, Robert Hazel wrote in the Fall 1952 issue of the *Hopkins Review*, was disparateness, its form a collage: "There is in Williams the element of radical nihilism (attack on rhetorical patterns, even the structure of the sentence itself) which one finds in the 20's particularly in Cummings and Pound." But Hazel's most interesting comments dealt with an evaluation of Williams's linguistic methodology. *Paterson*, he said, used a language which consciously eschewed the comforts of eloquence, which moved "away from the absolute monarchy of metaphor and symbol, towards prose." There was the continual skirting of eloquence and then the stubborn refusal to use it or any absolute. His thinning out of the language of poetry made Williams "more usable to young American poets" than Eliot was. Williams's language had a high incidence of "very pure tone"; had, in fact, an organic inclusiveness which allowed the poet to "say almost anything without seeming wrong."

But there were also those critics who meant to stamp out Williams's poem as if it were a virus. By far the most vehement of these was Joseph Bennett's essay in the *Hudson Review* (Summer 1952). Ostensibly undertaking an umbrella review of a large number of Williams's works which had appeared in the late forties and early fifties, Bennett focused on the later poetry and in particular on *Paterson*. Williams's real gift, as he saw it, was for the imagist lyric, which he had "perfected . . . beyond any of the group who were working with it before 1914." But in attempting the long poem he had failed miserably. Bennett spent ten pages cataloguing Williams's faults with an invectiveness unmatched by any critic writing on Williams before or since. He summarized his remarks with the general condemnation that Williams sidestepped poetry, "substituting for it sentimentality, pathos, self-revelation, self-pity, surrealism, raw emotion, gruesome anecdotes, and hammering repetition of grandsounding phrases." He "demonstrated" each charge by going to Williams's less successful experiments or by quoting out of context. But for the poems in *Paterson* he reserved a special metaphor: "His 'poems' are headless and footless. Cut them anywhere . . . and like amoebas, the jelly flows back together and the animal is the same. . . . Any part of *Paterson* can be taken out and put elsewhere in the poem." Finally, *Paterson* failed because the long poem, unlike the imagistic lyric, required "intelligence, rational discrimination, dramatic skill, psychological acuity, . . . emotional subtlety" and "patience and care," none of which Williams possessed. So the river of critical opinion could still flow in two widely separate channels. Insensitivity to what Williams was about was one thing, but the stridency of Bennett's review was inexcusable. It was as if he had actually tried to pound Williams himself into accepting his demoralizing verdict.

The editors of *Perspective*, published by Washington University, devoted their Autumn-Winter (1953) number to a multi-faceted investigation of the seventy-year-old Williams. Among those who contributed articles were Hugh Kenner, George Zabriskie, Guy Davenport, and Ralph Nash, the last three on aspects of *Paterson*. George Zabriskie's article, "The Geography of 'Paterson'," with maps of the Passaic River and of Paterson, is not a critical study but rather a reading of Paterson's local geography and history written by one "who was born below the falls, and spent most of his first twenty years on the upper reaches of the river." Zabriskie described the course of the Passaic from those upper reaches; located "lovely Ringwood," the locale of the Jackson whites; and described the history of Hamilton's Society for the Establishment of Useful Manufacturers (SUM), the falls themselves, the mills, the lock-outs and strikes of Paterson, the Jersey Dutch influence, Garrett Mountain, and Lambert's Castle. He discussed, too, the fire, flood, and tornado of 1902 and 1903 which together devastated much of old Paterson, including the old library, events which governed much of Book III. It was a handy *vade mecum* for getting at the landscape in forming Williams's own background and his world of Paterson.

Davenport evaluated Williams's original use of Pound's usura theme in a piece called "The Nuclear Venus: Dr. Williams' Attack Upon Usura." The economic hortatory theme was clearly related to Williams's "sympathy for and disapprobation of 'the amnesic crowd (the scattered)' " in the second part of "Sunday in the Park." Davenport listed the kinds of sources available to Williams, largely assimilated from Pound: Del Mar's *Barbara Villiers, or a History of Monetary Crimes*; Eustace Mullins's *A Study of the Federal Reserve*; and Pound's *Cantos* and his money pamphlets. The people of *Paterson* (read America), caught in an "aimless pursuit of pleasure and denied beauty because of its costliness," were blocked by usury, by church officials, by government leaders, and the bomb. Since, for Williams, moral beauty and physical beauty were at their centers one, physical beauty suffered by the corruption of the moral fabric. Davenport noted Williams's emphasis on circulation, dynamic energy, kinesis to create new beauty. For this reason the eternal unchanging sea was "NOT our home." The journey to the sea symbolized an all-encompassing breakdown of all distinctiveness, all difference melding into the world of eternal abstraction, as radium moved towards inert lead, or money stagnated in banks, or knowledge (the classics) became dead artifact, nostalgic ornament.

In "The Use of Prose in 'Paterson'," Ralph Nash attempted to systematically demonstrate how the various kinds of prose functioned in the poem. There were essentially three kinds of prose extracts which had either been borrowed from other sources and inserted into the text, or invented by Williams himself: personal letters, newspaper clippings, excerpts from books—especially local histories—and authorial summaries of such materials. After demonstrating in some detail where and why Williams placed many of his prose passages, Nash summed up by saying that the prose passages contributed "a sense of immediacy" as well as "a sense of distance and objectivity." They also documented Williams's search for a language, showing the "continuity of that problem" both in the world of the poem and the world from which the poem was created. There was, too, the strategy of counterpointing the prose with the lyric aspects of the poem, "the intrusion of flat prose rhythms, . . . the ironic juxtapositions of lyric affirmations and unpleasant 'facts', . . . the contrast of the urban and the pastoral, [the] outright examples of the failure of language," and the prose insistence "on the here and now and then of Paterson as place." Williams's refusal to find solace in the fictive, his insistence on using the real as he found it, was "a positive, novel contribution to the meaning and the technique" of *Paterson*.

"No one to the present moment has so looked within me," a surprised Williams wrote Nash in January, 1954. He admitted he had often used prose instinctively, without clearly articulating the reasons *why* he had used it. But Nash had gone to the heart of the problem by focusing on Williams's stylistics; for years Williams had had to fight against established canons of taste in order to arrive at "a world which breaks through to the actual." It was this emphasis on the function of the prosaic which had always "stood between" Pound and himself, and in fact, constituted one of the main loci of a modern poetics.

Confessing to a keen interest in the music of poetry, James G. Southworth, writing in *More Modern American Poets*, wondered "whether a more traditional form"—rhyme, rhythm, stanza —might not have made *Paterson* a better poem. But he was convinced, from manuscript evidence and by tinkering with the poems themselves, that "Williams knew what he was about," at least often enough. When he came to deal with the metaphoric structure of *Paterson*, however, Southworth fell particularly flat. He provided a dull prose glossing, a confusion covered by large, well-meaning generalities such as: "Interspersed among the passages of poetry are prose passages that at first glance seem irrelevant. Careful reading, however, reveals that they are integrated with the preceding verses, but provide details that would be inappropriate as verse, usually because of their undue length." It was a kind of generalization unpardonable even in 1954.

But there was worse to come. The Summer 1955 issue of the *Western Review* provides one of the most inaccurate readings of *Paterson* ever printed. In a nine-page piece entitled "The Symbolic Structure of Paterson," Frank Thompson set out to show logically and systematically why *Paterson* had to fail. The logical development of the essay reads like a parody of *Alice in Wonderland* in places. Concentrating on the poem's symbolic structure, Thompson "showed" how the male–female symbols moved from the concrete to the abstract at a third and fourth remove. (One suspects that Thompson was really hitting at Williams for bringing in the theme of usury, Pound's pet: "We know quite well where this theme comes from, and this knowledge only strengthens our rejection of its use.") *Paterson* failed as a poem, finally, because Williams was "not a conceptual thinker." Still, Williams had at least pointed to a way of writing "the extended poem on American themes." Such commentaries, gratefully, die of their own inanition.

There were, in the meantime, new overviews of Williams, such as Sr. Bernetta Quinn's essay on Williams in *The Metamorphic Tradition in Modern Poetry*, published in 1955. Williams wrote Sr. Quinn early in 1956 that her essay was "the most searching analysis of my purpose and style that I have ever encountered." One can only repeat what Williams said of the critical mind that could freeze the processive methodology of a poem as complex and as dynamic as *Paterson:* that here was a "phenomenal reader" with a generosity, a religious sensibility, an intelligence, and an understanding all brought to bear on the narrow area of modern poetics.

"Before judging the total merit of *Paterson*," Sr. Quinn had written, "one must weather a preliminary season of understanding, . . . of giving the poem the creative reading that such an undertaking deserves." She had herself weathered just such a time, reading through old histories, such as Nelson and Shriner's *History of Paterson and Its Environs* in three volumes; Jenny Marsh Parker's history of Rochester; and a dusty tome, *History of the Old Dutch Church at Totowa, Paterson, New Jersey, 1755–1827.* She had read the criticism, such as it was, on Williams, and Williams's own critical commentaries scattered about in the little magazines. *Pat-*

erson's prose provided "a study in sources, an ignorance of which is one of the main causes why citizens of Paterson walk around asleep." Among these sources were the early "wonders" of the area: the history of strikes, the Indians and their persecution, the 1902 disasters, the witch-hunting Puritans (Van Giesen), Revolutionary politicians (Hamilton), the blacks, the immigrants who settled the area. She unravelled and then synthesized in detail the intricate, complex, metamorphosing symbols and themes of *Paterson:* the river, the poet, the giant, the city, the man, the woman, the mountain, the flower, the rock, the falls, the language, blockage, divorce, marriage, cancer, usury, murder, the radiant gist, the cure, the father, the son. She controlled the multiple strands of the poem with skill and dexterity, virtues which—among critics of the poem before and since—have proven rare.

Williams's whole life, she summed up, had been devoted to releasing "the radiations of being from common objects," of letting "man's earthly garden shine forth." Williams had spent a lifetime preparing the world for "a future generation." But Williams told Sr. Quinn that he himself needed a stronger faith in his own achievement. He did not believe, really, that the pantheon of poets, of whom he was one, were finally "as important as you think us or as we think ourselves. . . . Are the underlying principles you speak or write of forward-looking enough and solid enough to stand the test of time? Will future generations think of us as good poets?" At seventy-two even Williams, assured of some measure of fame, was inclined to worry about the process of canonization.

Glauco Cambon's long essay on Williams, "William Carlos Williams' 'Paterson' as the Drama of Integrity," first appeared in Italian in *Paragone,* a Florentine magazine, in early 1955, and then as part of his *Tematica e sviluppo della poesia americana* in the following year. In 1963 Cambon presented a translation of his study called *The Inclusive Flame,* a phrase lifted reverentially from *Paterson* III. The chapter on Williams remained unchanged, and so deals only with the first four books of *Paterson*. If its beginning has something unintentionally humorous about it, it remains an illuminating study that rises, at moments, to brilliance. And it complements vividly Sr. Bernetta Quinn's exactly contemporary study.

As Cambon saw it, *Paterson* was "the supreme endeavor of the poet at self-integration," the enterprise long-pledged in the early poems. *Paterson*'s great theme was "America as a civilization in the making," especially concerned with the mythical origins of the place, its degeneration, its multiple-single characters, the search for a redemptive language, and "the shock of brute chronicle forever rehearsing man's fall." The American artist, continually searching for an adequate language, found himself distrusting the very words he used. Earth, air, fire, and water were symbols not only of "man's perennial fate" but of "the phenomena of language" itself: (earth) "dark, solid, and seminal"; (water) "fluid, confused"; (air) "thin and unstable or quickening"; (fire) "intensive and destructive, or purifying." The styles of *Paterson* constituted a "music of ideas," a unification of themes effected by verbal iteration, words echoed, altered, syncopated, "alternately distended in effusive spells and contracted into jumpy contretemps." Williams echoed other American artists, too, particularly *The Bridge* and *The Waste Land*. Because *Paterson* had succumbed "partly to the disintegrating process," a victim of its own boldness, and because it was, by its own definition, unfinished and open-ended, the poem had to be considered a partial failure, fluctuating between "polemical realism" and a "tenuous impressionism." Still, one kept coming back to *Paterson*, for its very processive state, its flux, was a vital reflection of Williams's world and his people. By rejecting "any decadent complacency" he had faced "reality wholesale" and had possibly even "mastered" it.

Paterson V

All during the forties, Williams had talked of *Paterson* as a poem in four books, the last of which arrived in mid-1951. But by early 1952 he was already telling Allen Ginsberg and Robert Lowell that he was toying with the idea of a fifth book with Ginsberg as its center. In fact, anyone reading the 1957 *Selected Letters* carefully could see that Williams was seriously contemplating just such an extension. The publication of Book V coincided with Williams's seventy-fifth birthday, September 17, 1958. An artist's seventy-fifth birthday is a big event, and the *Nation* delivered its own salvo in its May 31 issue, with four prepublication excerpts from the poem, together with tributes from Louis Zukofsky and Richard Eberhart (who, in a fifteen-line poem, took the occasion to argue gently with Williams's antitraditionalist poetics), and with M. L. Rosenthal as presiding speaker.

In the American Grain, Rosenthal said, was "an attempt to sum

up the materials of an informing American myth; it is one of the
truly germinative American prose-works of this century," a judgment which by the late fifties seems to have gone unchallenged.
Paterson had been "a devastating comment on every phase of our
life . . . relieved by momentary oases of perceived or envisioned
beauty." Now, in *Paterson* V, Williams had given the poem another "much needed dimension," an aesthetic refocusing of the
large cultural questions he had raised in the first four books, but
with an archetypal and symbolic emphasis new to the poem. It
was "a mellowing without loss of energy," a stepping away from
the "roar of the present" into the measured world of the imagination.

In the very decision of Williams to write a fifth part to *Paterson*, Eberhart noted (*Times*, Sept. 14, 1958) that there was a
comic "denial of the work of art as inevitable," and "an insistence
on its flowing, protean, ever-changing nature." Whether Book V
was an organic part of *Paterson* or really another, separate poem
was a question which continues to be asked by nearly every reviewer and critic of the poem up to the present. Babette Deutsch
(*Books*, Sept. 28, 1958) saw *Paterson* V as organically related to
the earlier parts, growing "as naturally as a green branch stemming
from a sturdy old tree." *Paterson* V also moved easily from prose
to verse and extended some of the earlier motifs, allusions, images:
the locust tree, the eagle, the sparrow, the snake, flowers, the unicorn tapestries—bringing these into a new prominence. If the
poem dwelt on the past—on Toulouse Lautrec and Chaucer and
Sappho—it also stood "firmly in the present," with Pound and
Ginsberg sharing the same space. On its radical differences from
the original parts she was silent.

John Ciardi (*Sat R*, Oct. 11, 1958) defined *Paterson* as a modern epic—"symphonic in its development, the themes touching,
developing, dissolving, its hero an intellectual Ulysses . . . seeking
to evoke and to enter the meaning of the landscape of his life"—
whereas *Paterson* V was a search not for one's place but for oneself. What struck Ciardi was the developing musical metamorphosis of the woman and the imagination into the figures of the
virgin and the whore, reconciled, finally, in the "whole woman
with whom he (the poet) has experienced that enduring human
communication which is a lifetime of love."

W. D. Snodgrass (*HR*, Spring 1959), thought the addition "a
weaker performance" than such other late poems as "Of Asphodel" or "To Daphne and Virginia," but still impressive, with

"many passages of clear, clean writing which anyone might envy."
Moreover, Williams had undergone "a tremendous change in
style" in the direction of "conventional English poetry." In "Asphodel," for example, Williams had finally "stopped being a
rather academic theorizer on the nature of poetic language" to
say "what he had to get said, in whatever way he could get it
said"; by which Snodgrass probably meant that Williams had returned to the neural itch of the old iamb. And, in one of those
left-handed salutes, he could speak of Williams's insistence on
being "wrong, pigheaded, pompous, even loud-mouthed—anything
but correct and half-dead." Against this we can place Hugh
Kenner, among the handful of mandarin critics since World War
II. The movement of *Paterson* V, he noted in the May (1959)
number of *Poetry*, was "unknotted by Williams' characteristic
musculature of diction," where "nothing impedes the rapidity of
declaration." Williams escaped the verdict of a naive transparency,
a flirting with "a dozen clichés of feeling: sentimentalities about old
age and harlots, birds and flowers," by paying such conventions
"no heed" and instead uncovering "what was in the sentiment before convention overtook it."

Charles Olson's review of *Paterson* V in the *Evergreen Review*
(Summer 1959) commented perceptively on the real strength of
the poem. Williams was not, finally, offering the Cloisters tapestry
or any other "fussy, cute" replica "(flowers and all that, and at the
feet of the beloved)," as the answer, as a kind of aesthetic salvation
for the reader. What the poem was offering was "quite exactly . . .
the path of itself," the trajectory force created by the lines moving across a field. *Paterson* V was, in Thom Gunn's estimation
(*YR*, Winter 1959), "the very minor work of a major poet."
Williams, in fact, had been made "unfit to write poetry of con-
secutive discourse" by his imagist discipline and ought never to
have undertaken a poem of the scope of *Paterson* in the first place.
He reiterated Jarrell's argument about an organization of irrelevance; the poem really was random. Whole sequences "could be re-
arranged and still mean as much and as little as they now do." But
in time Gunn came to reappraise Williams's achievement. First in
the *Yale Review* in the fall of 1962 and then in his introduction
of Williams to an English audience in the pages of *Encounter* in
1965. In this way Gunn offered a tacit apology for his earlier offhanded dismissal, showing he had been won over, at least in part, to
Williams's poetics.

Two textual readings of *Paterson* V appeared in 1960, only two years after the publication of the poem, a sure sign of Williams's acceptance by the academy. These were Walter Sutton's "Dr. Williams' 'Paterson' and the Quest for Form" in *Criticism*, and Louis Martz's much anthologized piece, "The Unicorn in Paterson: William Carlos Williams," in *Thought*. Most of Sutton's eighteen pages were a redaction of points which Sr. Bernetta Quinn had made five years earlier in *The Metamorphic Tradition*, together with a cursory reading of the major themes of Book V. Sutton's main argument was that the open-ended form and relative unity of *Paterson* I–IV allowed for the addition of any number of new books. And yet, while there was "a continuity of image and theme and metrical form" with the earlier books, Williams's attitudes towards and treatment of his new material were also different. Williams's poetics, in fact, stressed "the incompleteness and lack of self-sufficiency of the individual organism." It ran counter, therefore, to the Coleridgean—and New Critical—notion of the unity of a work of art.

Martz's piece (revised and retitled "Inventions for the Loom" for inclusion in his *The Poem of the Mind*) reads as if it were two essays. The first part is a brief reading of *Paterson* I–IV, ferreting out, in particular, Pound's presence in the poem. Pound was there in Williams's line: "the mold is Pound's, combining verse and prose; the line is Pound's, with its flexible cadences, breaking the pentameter; but everything is altered through Williams' invention, his conviction that bold exploration of the local will result in the discovery of a new world blossoming all about him." And Pound was obviously present in the usury theme. But there was also Williams's exorcism of Pound's spirit, in his refusal to be pulled out to sea, towards "a lost culture, a pull outward from the source," and his turning instead inland at the end of *Paterson* IV, as his Poe had "faced inland, to originality" in *In the American Grain*. Martz read Williams's own account of Poe's poetics as "perhaps the best account of *Paterson* that we have yet received":

the significance and the secret is: authentic particles, a thousand of which spring to the mind for quotation, taken apart and reknit with a view to emphasize, enforce and make evident, the *method*. Their quality of skill in observation, their heat, local verity, being *overshadowed* only by the detached, the abstract, the cold philosophy of their joining together; a method springing so freshly from the local conditions which determine it, by their emphasis of firm crudity and lack of coordinated structure, as to be worthy of most painstaking study.

The second part of Martz's essay was a reading of the central organizing symbol of Book V: the Unicorn tapestries housed at The Cloisters on the northern tip of Manhattan. For Martz the tapestries were like *Paterson* in their "peculiar combination of the local and the mythical"—the mythical king-self, Paterson, the unicorn, the force of the imagination surrounded by a stunning array of 101 realistically rendered flowers, trees, shrubs and herbs (one thinks of Marianne Moore's real toad in an imaginary garden). Book V suggested, then, "a kind of tapestry, woven out of memories and observations, composed by one man's imagination, but written in part . . . by all the milling populace of Paterson, past and present, including that unicorn in the center of the field."

In "Poetry and the Behaviour of Speech" (*HR*, Winter 1961–62), Denis Donoghue attacked the symbolist tenets of Paul Valéry's *ars poetique*, translated as *The Art of Poetry* by Denise Foliot and published by Routledge and Kegan Paul in 1958, the year *Paterson* V was also published. (The introduction to Valéry's poetics was, ironically enough, by the enemy himself: T. S. Eliot.) Donoghue's main contention, expressed with great subtlety and fine precision, was that Valéry's divorce of the poetic artifact from the raw stuff of living, vulgar, importunate prose was not only bankrupt; it was, finally, without specific reference to "credible human speech." Taken to its extreme, the poem, which moved inevitably towards an abstraction where words were manipulated like musical counters, became "a purely sonal absolute for the life of the poem," where "the connexions between speaker, listener, and fictive 'situations' " became tenuous.

Against Valéry, Donoghue placed Williams. "No poet in our time has placed a higher value upon the flavour of convincing speech," he wrote. Williams valued "speech as sign of individual existence, as proof that there is something *there;* speech issuing from a man in a particular place at a particular time and incorporating that place and that time in its tonality." *Paterson* V had demonstrated clearly what "poetry as fair speech" could mean, for here the translucency of the lines defined "with remarkable exactitude a movement of feeling which comes into full being for the first time in the words themselves." Williams had caught in the mesh of his lines "a human situation acknowledged as real and, if not our own, continuous with our own." In a real sense, then, Eliot's lifelong European desire to purify the dialect of the tribe had been answered by Williams's successes with the new measure, everywhere present in "the lithe speech" of *Paterson* V.

In 1961 John Thirlwall's sixty-page essay, "William Carlos Williams' 'Paterson': The Search for the Redeeming Language—A Personal Epic in Five Parts," appeared in *New Directions* 17. Thirlwall, a professor of English at the City College of New York, had access not only to the then uncatalogued collections of Williams's papers at Buffalo and Yale, but, from 1953 on, to Williams himself. If Sr. Bernetta Quinn and Louis Martz give more sensitive readings of Williams, Thirlwall simply had access to information which no one else had. Thirlwall will be—indeed has been—superceded in many of his readings, but his essay must, by its very nature, remain a primary document for all future scholars, commentators, and critics. For several years, Thirlwall took down, in weekly meetings, Williams's own thoughts about his poetry either by ersatz shorthand or by dictaphone. His essay is studded with transcriptions of these interviews, which often jut angularly into the essay without benefit of critical shaping. Thirlwall is weakest in his own five-page commentary on *Paterson*, given as Appendix I. He is strongest in presenting the long genesis of the poem: "The Wanderer" (1914); "Paterson" (1926); the fiction of the thirties, the influence of *Aucassin and Nicolette* on the prose-poetry form; and the notes for a novel, *Fairfield*, written in the late twenties, with its heroine Dolores Marie Pischak. Thirlwall was also the first to make explicit Williams's social concerns throughout his various *Patersons*: the Paterson silk strike of 1913 (when twenty-seven thousand workers under the Industrial Workers of the World struck for six months, until they were finally broken by Billy Sunday and the police), and the working class pathetically enjoying a Sunday afternoon on Garrett Mountain.

Thirlwall found five central strategies operating in *Paterson:* (1) the use of techniques Williams had mastered in his short fiction, such as the juxtaposed vignette; (2) short, intense, isolated lyrics; (3) the use of "factual" material—letters, artesian well charts, advertisements; (4) the eschewal of the "poetic," of "romantic slush"; and (5) the use of the fantastic, frequently violent, unexpected, but omnipresent: the fire, tornado, and flood; the dwarfs and giants; Sam Patch; the fantastic possibilities inherent in atomic fission.

There were two passages in *Paterson* which Williams particularly liked, Thirlwall noted. The first occurred in *Paterson* II, in the passage about the lovers in the park, with its contrast between the meanness of the situation and "the aristocracy of the metrical arrangement of the verse." The second was the famous "The descent beckons" passage, which, Williams later saw, included all the implications of his variable foot. (In fact, if one reads the two passages, it is clear that the variable foot is also lodged in the triadic structure of the earlier piece. We can see Williams working towards the discovery of the variable foot in the process of creating this poem.)

Thirlwall plotted the changes which had occurred in Williams after his strokes: a quietness, relief from worry, a new religious sensitivity (this last particularly fascinated Thirlwall). In several talks with Williams, he charted the genesis of *Paterson* V, with its new interests, new perspectives, and its celebration of all those artists who had meant so much to Williams. In the late poems, love was clearly Williams's major theme, and had had a "calming, steadying" influence on the poet. Williams had come to accept life and old age. "*He* has learned," Thirlwall added by way of *moralitas*. "He has made peace with the world, with his wife, with himself." When Thirlwall wrote this, many of the critics had also made their peace with the old man. Williams had finally arrived.

References

Anonymous
  1948. "Verse," *New Yorker*. Sept. 4, pp. 75–76.
  1951. "A Poem of America," *Time*. July 16, pp. 94, 96.
  1964. Review, *Times Literary Supplement*. Sept. 10, p. 842.
Bennett, Joseph
  1952. "The Lyre and the Sledgehammer," *Hudson Review*. Summer, pp. 295–307.
Berryman, John ,
  1959. "From the Middle and Senior Generations," *American Scholar*. Summer, p. 390.
Cambon, Glauco
  1961. "William Carlos Williams and Ezra Pound: Two Examples of Open Poetry," *College English*. Mar., pp. 387–89.
  1963. "William Carlos Williams' 'Paterson' as the Drama of Integrity," in *The Inclusive Flame*. Bloomington: Indiana Univ. Pr.
Carruth, Hayden
  1950. "Dr. Williams' *Paterson*," *Nation*. Apr. 8, pp. 331–32.

1951. "The Run to the Sea," *Nation*. Aug. 25, pp. 155–56.
Ciardi, John
1958. "The Epic of a Place," *Saturday Review of Literature*. Oct. 11, pp. 37–39.
Corman, Cid
1960. "Double Take: Another Response (see *Paterson V*, Mike Wallace Interview)," *Folio*. pp. 29–30.
Davenport, Guy
1953. "The Nuclear Venus: Dr. Williams' Attack upon Usura," *Perspective*. Autumn-Winter, pp. 183–90.
Deutsch, Babette
1958. "The Roar of the Present," *New York Herald Tribune Book Review*. Sept. 28, p. 11.
Donoghue, Denis
1961. "Poetry and the Behaviour of Speech," *Hudson Review*. Winter, pp. 537–49.
Eberhart, Richard
1948. "Energy, Movement and Reality," *New York Times Book Review*. June 20, p. 4.
1950. "The Image of Ourselves," *New York Times Book Review*. Feb. 12, p. 5.
1951. "A Vision Welded to the World," *New York Times Book Review*. June 17, pp. 5, 18.
1958. "A Vision of Life and Man That Drives the Poet On," *New York Times Book Review*. Sept. 14, p. 4.
Eckman, Frederick W.
1948. "Modern Replicas," *Golden Goose*. Autumn, pp. 36–38.
Ellmann, Richard
1950. "From Renishaw to Paterson," *Yale Review*. Spring, pp. 543–45.
Emerson, Richard Wirtz
1952. "The Recent Books of WCW," *Golden Goose*. Oct., pp. 33–40.
Farrelly, John
1950. "To Live and to Write," *New Republic*. May 15, pp. 19–20.
Fiedler, Leslie
1948. "Some Uses and Failures of Feeling," *Partisan Review*. Aug., pp. 924–31.
Fitts, Dudley
1951. "Three Brilliants," *Saturday Review of Literature*. July 21, p. 23.
Fitzgerald, Robert
1948. "Poetry and Perfection," *Sewanee Review*. Autumn, pp. 685–97.

Flint, F. W.
  1950. "I Will Teach You My Townspeople," *Kenyon Review*.
  Summer, pp. 537–43.
Fowler, Albert
  1961. "Shopping for Poetry in Paterson," *Approach*. Winter, pp.
  31–33.
Frankenberg, Lloyd
  1951. "The Year in Poetry," *Harper's*. Oct., pp. 108–12.
Freemantle, Anne
  1946. Review, *Commonweal*. Oct. 4, p. 601.
Gram, William
  1946. "Williams & Williams: Pro & Con," *Voices*. Autumn, pp.
  42–44.
Grigsby, Gordon
  1962. "The Genesis of *Paterson*," *College English*. Jan., pp. 277–81.
Gunn, Thom
  1959. "Poetry as Written," *Yale Review*. Winter, pp. 297–305.
  1962. "New Books in Review: Things, Voices, Minds," *Yale Review*. Autumn, pp. 129–38.
  1965. "William Carlos Williams," *Encounter*. July, pp. 67–74.
Hazel, Robert
  1952. "The Method of Paterson," *Hopkins Review*. Fall, pp. 120–23.
Honig, Edwin
  1947. "The City of Man," *Poetry*. Feb., pp. 277–84.
  1949. "The *Paterson* Impasse," *Poetry*. Apr., pp. 37–41.
  1952. "Three Masters," *Voices*. May–Aug., pp. 34–38.
Jarrell, Randall
  1946. "The Poet and His Public," *Partisan Review*. Sept.–Oct., pp.
  488–500.
  1951. "A View of Three Poets," *Partisan Review*. Nov.–Dec., pp.
  691–700.
Kennedy, Leo
  1950. "Williams' Poems Tinged by His Medical Life," *Chicago Sun-Times*. Mar. 20, p. 5.
Kenner, Hugh
  1952. "With the Bare Hands," *Poetry*. Aug., pp. 276–90.
  1959. "To Measure Is All We Know," *Poetry*. May, pp. 127–32.
Kerr, Walter
  1949. "Regenesis," *Imagi*. pp. 10–11.
Koch, Vivienne
  1950. *William Carlos Williams*. New York: New Directions.
  1952. "William Carlos Williams: The Man and the Poet," *Kenyon Review*. Summer, pp. 502–10.

Lechlitner, Ruth

1946. "A Patersonian Poem Begins," *New York Herald Tribune Book Review.* Sept. 22, p. 3.

1948. "Lyric Satire, Stark Revelation," *New York Herald Tribune Book Review.* June 27, p. 3.

1951. "Geeze, Doc, I Guess It's All Right, but What the Hell Does It Mean?" *New York Herald Tribune Book Review.* July 1, p. 3.

Lowell, Robert

1947. "Thomas, Bishop, and Williams," *Sewanee Review.* Summer, pp. 493–503.

1948. "Paterson II," *Nation.* June 19, pp. 692–94.

McCandless, J. H.

1961. "Christ and the Critic," *Approach.* Fall, pp. 36–41.

Mercier, Vivian

1950. Review, *Commonweal.* Mar. 3, pp. 564–65.

Martz, Louis

1948. "Recent Poetry," *Yale Review.* Autumn, pp. 144–51.

1951. "On the Road to *Paterson,*" *Poetry New York.* Spring, pp. 18–32; reprinted in *The Poem of the Mind.* New York: Oxford Univ. Pr., 1966.

1960. "The Unicorn in *Paterson:* William Carlos Williams," *Thought.* Winter, pp. 537–54; reprinted in *The Poem of the Mind.* New York: Oxford Univ. Pr., 1966.

Mills, Barriss

1961. "The Method of Paterson," *Approach.* Winter, pp. 23, 26.

Morgan, Frederick

1947. "William Carlos Williams: Imagery, Rhythm, Form," *Sewanee Review.* Autumn, pp. 675–90.

Nash, Ralph

1953. "The Use of Prose in *Paterson,*" *Perspective.* Autumn-Winter, pp. 191–99.

O'Connor, William Van

1948. "Sentient America-Gross, Directionless," *Saturday Review of Literature.* Sept. 25, p. 30.

1950. "Search for the Redeeming Tongue," *Saturday Review of Literature.* May 20, p. 41.

Olson, Charles

1959. "Paterson (Book Five)," *Evergreen Review.* Summer, pp. 220–21.

Quinn, Sr. Bernetta

1955. *The Metamorphic Tradition in Modern Poetry.* New Brunswick, N. J.: Rutgers Univ. Pr., 1955, pp. 89–129.

Rodman, Selden

1950. "William Carlos Williams: Serious, Humane, Tireless, New as in 1909," *New York Herald Tribune Book Review.* Mar. 5, p. 5.

Rosenfeld, Isaac

1946. "The Poetry and Wisdom of Paterson," *Nation.* Aug. 24, pp. 216–17.

Rosenthal, M. L.

1951. "In the Roar of the Present," *New Republic.* Aug. 27, pp. 18–19.

1958. "Salvo for William Carlos Williams," *Nation.* May 31, pp. 497, 500.

Snodgrass, W. D.

1959. "Spring Verse Chronicle," *Hudson Review.* Spring, pp. 114–23.

Southworth, James G.

1954. *More Modern American Poets.* New York: Oxford Univ. Pr., pp. 1–17.

Spears, Monroe K.

1950. "The Failure of Language," *Poetry.* Apr., pp. 39–44.

Sutton, Walter

1960. "Dr. Williams' 'Paterson' and the Quest for Form," *Criticism.* Summer, pp. 242–59.

Thirlwall, John

1961. "William Carlos Williams' 'Paterson': The Search for the Redeeming Language—a Personal Epic in Five Parts," *New Directions 17.*

Thompson, Frank

1955. "The Symbolic Structure of Paterson," *Western Review.* Summer, pp. 285–93.

Tyler, Parker

1946. "The Poet of Paterson Book I," *Briarcliff Quarterly.* Oct., pp. 168–75.

Wells, Henry

1959. "Two Poets: Time Unlimited," *Voices.* May–Aug., pp. 49–52.

Zabriskie, George

1953. "The Geography of Paterson," *Perspective.* Autumn-Winter, pp. 201–16.

CHAPTER 4

Floodtime: The Response to Williams, 1946-1963

C all them parallel rivers: the response to *Paterson* forming the major current, the response to Williams's other books creating a wide channel of its own. The latter, published between 1948 and 1962, consisted of eight volumes of poetry, including a selected poems and a collected earlier and later poems; the collected stories; the third leg of the Stecher trilogy; the collected plays; a selected essays; a selected letters; a translation of a Spanish novella; a memoir; and an autobiography—all sent spinning up out of the vortex of Williams's demon-driven final phase.

This astonishing productivity not only staggered some critics and delighted others; it also sent many of them scurrying in search of a way to adequately measure that achievement. Other critics, interested in the work of a whole new generation of younger poets writing in both America and England, saw by the early fifties that the age of Eliot was on the wane. Almost overnight they discovered that many of the younger people were listening to Williams (and Pound) in spite of the academy and the academic poets. Ironically, it was only now that a viable criticism of Williams began to be generated in the American universities; one thinks not only of Vivienne Koch's pioneering study, but also of essays by Randall Jarrell, Roy Harvey Pearce, Sr. Bernetta Quinn, Louis Martz, and Hugh Kenner. Largely because of Williams's own emphasis in his lectures and essays, the issue of his experimental prosody received the most extensive treatment by both the young poets coming into their own in the fifties and by the editors of a whole new line of little magazines. Some, realizing that Williams was now golden, began in Boswellian fashion to collect his "remains"; the collected essays, plays, fiction, and a selected essays and letters all appeared between the late fifties and early

sixties. It was a late but nonetheless bountiful harvest time. In his
last years, the critical channels began running decidedly in Williams's direction.

In the years 1946–50, the years when Williams was creating
Penelope-like the vast tapestry of *Paterson*, the choric response of
the critics remained miniscule. But from Rutherford, Williams was
preparing to innundate New York with the sheer weight of the
work of his last years. "I MUST BEGIN COMPOSING again,"
Williams wrote to Horace Gregory on New Year's Day, 1945, in
a depressed state. He had been experiencing a creative blockage
for some years, and feared that, in his sixty-second year, his own
river was drying up. Objectivism had ended in a stale backwater
for him: "The old approach is outdated, and I shall have to work
like a fiend to make myself new again. But there is no escape.
Either I remake myself or I am done. I can't escape the dilemma
longer. *THAT* is what has stopped me. I must go on or quit once
and for all." That tremendous remaking of a self in old age, that
sense of a new and viable identity, the willingness to slough off an
old skin when most writers were content to settle into theirs and
become parodic images of themselves for the final short haul: it
is this renewal in Williams which astonished the reviewers and
critics and caught many of them off guard. A terminology, a way,
however narrow, had been established for "seeing" Williams:
Williams was antipoetic, a tough sentimentalist, the last and best
of the old Imagists, a figure whose collected poems had already
appeared twice—in 1934 and 1938—before the war. At least one
reviewer had grumbled that Williams was like the person who
sticks around after his own bon voyage party, reemerging pe-
riodically and causing no end of embarrassment, as he had in
1941 in the Poet of the Month series, after the reviewers had
already solemnly celebrated the *Collected Poems*. Now there was
a new generation of poets—Auden chief among them—who were
clamoring to be heard. Williams had had his chance.

But the real breakthrough was still in the future. There was the
flurry of recognition in late 1946 by Norman Macleod, editor of
the *Briarcliff Quarterly*, a little university-sponsored magazine.
Then came a settling back into another period of occasional reviews as Williams produced the parts of *Paterson* (1946–51);
The Clouds and *A Dream of Love* (both 1948); the *Selected
Poems* and *The Pink Church* (both 1949); the *Collected Later
Poems, Make Light of It: Collected Stories*, and *A Beginning on
the Short Story* (all 1950); and then the *Autobiography* and the

Collected Earlier Poems (both 1951). And so the reviews also had to be cranked out, but these soon began to expand geometrically, especially in the early fifties. Furthermore, in early 1950, the first book-length study, Vivienne Koch's *William Carlos Williams*, commissioned by James Laughlin for the Makers of Modern Literature series, appeared. It was a book which raised Williams to an ersatz pantheon with such figures as T. S. Eliot, Forster, Hopkins, Joyce, Lorca, Shaw, and Virginia Woolf. Williams may be said to have "arrived" officially on December 17, 1950, at the age of sixty-seven, when he finally made the front page of the *New York Times Book Review* as "Major Poet and Literary Innovator," with double-barrelled reviews by Eberhart (the poetry) and Robert Gorham Davis (the short stories), angelic presences surrounding the central figure of Williams enjoying a highball.

Shifting Currents, 1945-1950

Williams, of course, saw the importance of having a special issue of a magazine "devoted" to him, even one with the necessarily limited circulation of the *Briarcliff Quarterly*. Its importance lay not so much in giving him recognition, as in presenting a "lucid," "coherent," unified image of what he had been after all his life. "I know," he told Macleod on July 25, 1945, "that whatever my life has been it has been single in purpose, simple in design and constantly directed to the one end of discovery, if possible, of some purpose in being alive, in being a thinking person and in being an active force." But, he added, that "composite" had never yet been made clear by any critic, and he could not stop to do the difficult job of articulating the unity at the heart of all he had written. He had no illusions about belated honors. "It's strange to be sixty-three and to think of the honors that have recently come my way," he wrote Charles Sheeler on October 12, 1946, "this issue of a small magazine devoted to my history along with the rest. It's pleasant but that's about all." The celebration was for others; what he wanted to do was to get on with his work. But the recognition had given him more confidence, made him surer of his words. "For if with what has already been written I have had some success, knowing inside myself how much better it might have been, I can go ahead and improve that." And for Williams, it was that future thrust, and not the settling into the achieved, that mattered.

If the *Briarcliff Quarterly* did not exactly create the unified image of himself that Williams was after—and how could it, drawing tribute as it did from many sources—it did contribute to the rise of Williams's spirits, to his sense of himself, of what he had done and could do. Many of those tributes were short and to the point: Marianne Moore, Hilaire Hiler, Charles Sheeler; a precise comment by Wallace Stevens; a poem addressed to "the first/Great Franciscan poet since/The Middle Ages" by Rexroth; a rerun of Louis Zukofsky's fifteen-year-old note on Williams which had first appeared in the *Symposium* in 1931; Parker Tyler on the poet of *Paterson*; a congratulatory note by James Laughlin of *New Directions* to this "pioneer of a great new American movement," this master of a "new American rhythm"; and essays by Horace Gregory and T. C. Wilson. There were, besides, photographs of Williams and his family, a gathering of Williams's recent poetry, and his essay-letter to an Australian editor.

Stevens's comment was a reassessment of his own influential introduction to the *Collected Poems* of a dozen years before. There the talk had been of Williams's romanticism, of the tension between a sentimental and an antipoetic self. But here he stressed what was uppermost in his own development: the poet daily at his work trying to get down his subject on paper. Williams, he said, was "a writer to whom writing is the grinding of a glass, the polishing of a lens by means of which he hopes to be able to see clearly. His delineations are trials. They are rubbings of reality." The holistic implication here was that all of Williams's work was an attempt at *the* poem, a counterpart to Stevens's own "The Whole of Harmonium" as signature for all his poetry. (Williams himself around 1945 toyed with the idea of entitling his "central" writings till then "The Complete Collected Exercises Toward a Possible Poem.") Stevens maintained that, like Picasso, like the Communists, like the eighteenth-century German pietists, Williams was after a sharpened focus, a realization of the intelligence on which the modern mind had come solely to rely. It was a quiet, sophisticated, significant revaluation, itself a rubbing of reality.

Wilson saw Williams as a poet of the natural world, rendering that world clearly, sharply, with a sense of wonder, demonstrating its reality through the imagination. He was a man who had "sought to recover the sources of . . . contact" with the local, to uncover the freshness of the world he inhabited. But he was also a powerful witness of the "bleak aftermath," of "plentitude plundered beyond recognition," of the perversions arising out of the loss of a living contact, an aftermath in fact crippling to all of us. Horace Gregory, too, lamented that the "common reader" for whom Williams had always written never read the little magazines where he was always published. The suburban housewife of whom he had written would rather read Somerset Maugham's latest novel than see the familiar things of her world: the plums in the icebox, "the rain falling through 'Botticellian' trees." Williams was one of the few real descriptive poets, vehemently set against speculation, against "transcendental thinking and emotion." He was one of the few writers who consistently wrote in his own language, going beneath "literature" to "uncover 'unliterary' sources."

At the same time that the *Briarcliff Quarterly* was published, Horace Gregory and Marya Zaturenska's *A History of American Poetry 1900–1940* also appeared, with a ten-page chapter on Williams called a "A Formal 'Objectivist.' " The chapter constitutes a brief introduction to Williams's poetry, summing up his achievement by quoting in full or in part such pieces as "The Young Housewife," "Nantucket," "Rain," "The Jungle," "The Yachts," and "Burning the Christmas Greens." Taking his cue from Wallace Stevens's comment that Williams's strategy was to add the implied image to his imagism (as in implying the serpent image in describing the "Young Sycamore"), Gregory demonstrated how this grafting had led to a masterpiece like "The Yachts," "one of the finest poems of his generation." Williams's verse was "protestant, yet formal," a presentation of the reality of the object before us, each "notation . . . scrupulously selected," each detail firmly chosen. Gregory's essay has a viability which attends to Williams's completed Objectivist phase (up through the afterthought of *The Wedge*), and Williams himself thought of the book as "a very good textbook on the modern poets"; but even as it was published, Williams had leapt far beyond it, as Gregory suggested later in his own note in the *Briarcliff Quarterly*.

Objectivism itself was a "drugged, curiously nihilistic kind of poetry," William Van O'Connor wrote in *Sense and Sensibility in Modern Poetry* (1948), a poetry "in which people . . . live but have no meaning," where objectivity, "the presentation of uninterpreted facts, reaches its *reductio ad absurdum*." O'Connor had Zukofsky specifically in mind, but Williams was swept into that orbit by explicit association. Williams was mentioned several times in passing, but O'Connor's best comment on the poet is a glossing of "Queen Anne's Lace," which demonstrates how the imagistic symbol—that grafting of which Stevens and Gregory both spoke—works in one of Williams's poems, specifically, the white flower expressing the quality of a woman's love for a man. Still, Williams remained in O'Connor's pantheon one of the attendant figures meant to swell a train.

While *Paterson* I and II were being looked at with growing interest, Williams published, during the summer of 1948 in a special edition of 310 copies, *The Clouds*, "Aigeltinger," *Russia and Other Poems* with the joint cooperation of two small presses, the Wells College Press and the Cummington Press. Then, that September, New Directions brought out *A Dream of Love*, the play Williams had struggled with for years with a serious Broadway audience in mind. There were few reviews of either. In his "Verse Chronicle" (*N*, Dec. 25, 1948), Rolfe Humphries threw out some tired chestnuts about Williams as a poet of the eye who, if he did not write sloppy lines, never tired, either, of "adventurous, delighted, or intricate movements for sound's sake purely." David Daiches, reviewing both *The Clouds* and *A Dream of Love* (*Books*, Jan. 30, 1949), noted Williams's "curiosity about his fellow men." If his poetry was uneven, "slapdash or inadequately pulled together," still, he was never uninteresting. He remained "one of the central modern American poets," a pioneer in poetic methods, still as busy as ever writing for the avant garde little magazines.

A Dream of Love was also uneven, Daiches thought, but it did present an ambiguous tenderness between a man and his wife with force and conviction. And when the "We Present" group put on *A Dream of Love* at the Hudson Guild Playhouse in a little off-Broadway theater during one of the city's worst heat waves, William Saroyan himself gave the play a rave review in the *New York Herald Tribune*. Unfortunately, without air-conditioning, the play was forced to close after only two weeks.

When *The Selected Poems* of Williams was published in March, 1949 (thirty-six hundred copies), the volume was introduced by Randall Jarrell, largely, one suspects, because of his strong praise for *Paterson* I two years before. Jarrell's essay makes a number of astute comments on the kind of poems Williams had written up through *The Wedge*, and, as usual, the prose alone would hold one's interest even if every one of Jarrell's judgments were flawed. But by the time Jarrell wrote the essay, in early 1949, *Paterson* II had appeared, and Williams's stock was beginning to fall again in

Jarrell's estimation. Jarrell heard a voice which he interpreted as being at once original, unique, outspoken, good-hearted, generous, and flawed—flawed as Whitman and Hardy were flawed. Of *Paterson* Jarrell could still feel that one would have "to be determinedly insensitive to modern poetry not to see that it has an extraordinary range and reality, a clear rightness that sometimes approaches perfection." And if the list of Williams's "perfect" poems was small—a list which would have to include "The Yachts," "To Elsie," "By the road to the contagious hospital," and "Burning the Christmas Greens"—still, there was about the imperfect pieces, and even the bad or mediocre poems, that which repaid reading. Williams was one of those poets one took in large doses.

Like Stevens and Marianne Moore, Williams was rooted in Imagism, but also like them, he had gone far beyond its tenets. His was a nature poetry notable for its "muscular and emotional identification with its subject." He had come to fill his landscapes with people seen neither as the illiterate mass nor as the romantic "little man," but as people like himself (and, except for Frost, how few realized people there were in American poetry)—a people seen in the realized context of their northern New Jersey industrial and suburban environment. In terms of Williams's metrics, Jarrell admitted his own proclivities were for an accentual-syllabic verse, but admitted too that Williams had achieved unqualified successes with his free verse which could not be duplicated using traditional modes. (It should be noted that Jarrell wrote his essay before Williams had come to understand his own achievement with the variable foot.) Finally, Jarrell laid stress on the fact that the critics had not done justice to Williams, that most had simply ignored him, and that "one or two of the best [such as Blackmur], when they did write, just twitched as if flies were crawling over them."

Reviewing the *Selected Poems* (*NR*, Apr. 25, 1949), Robert Fitzgerald focused on Williams's free verse techniques, which "meant consigning to the ashcan even such neutral instruments as the iambic line," and working in "the rich tradition of prose." Williams was able to evoke "the details of his notation" and to regulate the speed of his lines "according to how much white space he offers to the eye or breath to the reading voice." Rolfe Humphries (*N*, July 9, 1949) merely reiterated his admiration and personal dislike for Williams's poetry. Like Fitzgerald, he was a translator of the classics, and one suspects he felt that a regular metrical grid would provide a wider base, a greater range of tonal effect than free verse. Richard Wilbur, another formalist, in a long review, "Seven Poets" (*SR*, Jan. 1950), admitted that Williams's poems were often successful but that the underlying metrical form was, finally, insusceptible of analysis; often, in fact, the poem was simply left incomplete in a formal and logical sense. "Many of his poems," Wilbur noted, "seem notes to a text—to the dense and fluid text of reality," something reaching beyond the poem to the reality of the thing itself.

Koch's Formalist Commentary

In early 1950 Williams received a number of kudos, including election to the National Institute of Arts and Letters and a short, crisp interview with Harvey Breit (*Times*, Jan. 15), followed in April by the National Book Award for *Paterson* III and the *Selected Poems*. In the midst of all this, in February, Vivienne Koch's critical study of Williams appeared. The reviews of this first book-length study of Williams (and the only study to appear in Williams's own lifetime) were at best ambivalent. Richard Eberhart, reviewing the book along with *Paterson* III (*Times*, Feb. 12, 1950), recommended it "to those who do not know him or have scattered notions about his intentions." The study was a running commentary, not pretending to "finalities of criticism," refreshing in eschewing "critical jargon." And while it was a subject outside Koch's professed, self-imposed limits, Eberhart would have welcomed a discussion of Williams in relation to the other writers of his generation. Selden Rodman (*Books*, Mar. 5) found Koch "an interpreter whose intellect, perceptiveness and style . . . [were] adequate to the task of establishing [Williams's] position." Working out of a near chaos of material, she had managed to create an order, had written criticism, in fact, not achieved since Edmund Wilson had written *Axel's Castle*, a comment which may have embarrassed Koch herself. F. W. Flint (*KR*, Summer 1950) called it a "sturdy, painstaking book" which yielded a passage through "a mass of contradictory prejudice."

Louis Zukofsky, on the other hand, dismissed Koch (*Poetry*, June 1950), finding the study's only redeeming quality in the string of quotations from Williams flung throughout the book. The study for him was "an unfeeling seminar" in Williams's works to 1950, a writing around the subject without giving us the man. Hayden Carruth (*N*, July 15, 1950) was somewhat kinder but still unimpressed. If the study was "capable and fairly thorough," it remained too much of "a march, often too deliberate, through Williams' writings from beginning to end." He too would have preferred that Koch had attended to "some of the knottier problems, such as his mysterious prosody and the exact nature of his extraordinary gift for language." Her neo-critical proclivities, in fact, reduced the study to little more than "a series of notes" to the *Complete Collected Poems*. And Grover Smith, reviewing Koch's study in a long review essay in the *New Mexico Quarterly* in the fall of 1953, called it "a disappointing study," "chaotic" and "slapdash," although he was willing to concede that this "*philosophe manque*'s tendency towards disorganization" was so "characteristic of his whole poetic output . . . that no very systematic analysis is likely to ensue."

Louis Martz, who was writing his own perceptive overview of Williams's progress up to *Paterson*, noted in the *Yale Review* in September (1950) that Koch's closely-packed interpretation was "a study without development." If her chronological analyses of the poems were good in themselves, seriatim commentary on "the great mass of short poems" was like "a scattering of buckshot that may drop the reader in his tracks." If the book seemed hastily patched together, it contained, "potentially, a sound and penetrating view of Williams's achievement." But Fred B. Millett (*AL*, Jan. 1951) lamented the "obvious weakness" of the book, its "elementary errors in style or form," its deprecation of other poets to raise Williams, its "defective taste" that could find Williams's prose "Jamesian." Koch's real strength, he felt, lay in her glossings on specific works, many of them difficult to come by. And, too, she had shown that Williams was indeed a "far more important figure than most students of modern American literature have realized."

Vivienne Koch undertook her project of a full-scale study in 1945 at James Laughlin's instigation. She interviewed Williams that summer and, although she did not tell Williams what she was up to, he seems to have suspected something of the sort. (He wrote "The Visit" as a commentary on the nature of such interviews after one of her early visits.) If we are to justly appreciate Koch's achievement, we should understand what materials she had to work with. Besides the *Complete Collected Poems* of 1938, she had copies of Williams's other major works: *In the American Grain, First Act* (the first two parts of the Stecher trilogy), the first two parts of *Paterson*, and rare copies of the 1909 *Poems, A Voyage to Pagany, Spring and All, The Descent of Winter, The Great*

American Novel, and the 1929 translation of Soupault's *Last Nights in Paris*. In addition, she had access to the voluminous but uncatalogued files in the Lockwood Memorial Library at the University of Buffalo, a collection assembled through the farsightedness and industry of its librarian, Charles Abbott. Koch herself was clearly at home in the tradition of the New Criticism, and most of the book's 278 pages are given over to a seriatim glossing, some of it good, some usable, of Williams's opus. She divided her book into four unequal chapters under the generic headings: "The Poems" (145 pages), "The Plays" (40 pages), "The Novels and Short Stories" (60 pages), and "Prose Other Than Fiction" (20 pages). Each of her chapters usually begins in a promising manner. So, for example, her discussion of Williams's poetry with its incisive overview of his early influences—Pound, Imagism, American "regionalism"—and his development into an original voice. But her chapter soon breaks down into a fragmentary, poem-by-poem analysis of the contents of the *Complete Collected Poems*, and an acceptance of the central misunderstanding of Kenneth Burke towards the *Improvisations*. *Spring and All* was a consolidation of Williams's achievements to 1923, followed by the stalemate of *The Descent of Winter*. The *Collected Poems* of 1934 were merely a further consolidation. *An Early Martyr* (1935) showed signs of the economic and social realities of the moment out of which it had sprung, while *Adam and Eve and the City* (1936) was more introspective and showed that Williams had finally achieved mastery over the longer poem. She noted that Williams's "long" poems differed from the long poems of many of his contemporaries in eschewing both the narrative scaffold and a direct didactic intent. And the "Recent Verse" of 1938, in oscillatory fashion, had moved out again to encounter the polis, foreshadowing Williams's movement towards *Paterson*. But *The Broken Span* (1941), *The Wedge* (1944), and *The Clouds* (1948) had not noticeably extended Williams's poetic achievement. Rather, they seemed further consolidations of the 1938 collection, spun off from Williams's 1940s central preoccupation: *Paterson*.

Koch's text, however, spends relatively little time with such general overviews of the Williams terrain. Her most characteristic gesture is the close-up of the individual poem, until the sheer weight of gloss on glossing tends to become claustrophobic. With the larger canvasses, such as *A Dream of Love, A Voyage to Pagany, White Mule, In the Money*, and *In the American Grain*, there is a sufficient focusing and many of Williams's works are treated to their first analysis. *A Voyage to Pagany*, in particular, is given a substantial reading. But there is again that admixture of attention to detail together with a shortchanging of the larger thematic interweavings between Williams's various works which do, indeed, all fit together as parts of a single fabric. Vivienne Koch meant her study to stand as an introduction to a major author, much of whose work was, at midcentury, out of print and nearly impossible to come by. This state of affairs helps to explain a major shortcoming of the study, which, interestingly, the reviewers did not even comment on: its almost total neglect of Williams as a major prosodist and poet-critic. Those critical tenets and statements were scattered in a hundred little magazines and a thousand uncollected letters, which Koch simply did not bother to incorporate. But, then, her explicit intentions were much more modest. For her, criticism was "not written as a signature for eternity but as a discipline in extending the limits of that receptivity with which the reader approaches the work criticized." If that was her modest intention, she seems to have succeeded.

Reevaluating Williams's Poetics

In his review of Koch's study in the August, 1952, *Poetry*, R. L. Beum stepped back to take a hard look at Williams's real reputation in America. For all the hoopla, for all the reviews, Beum saw that Williams's belated recognition was really "ninety per-cent publicity and ten per-cent discovery." For Williams was "still the most critically neglected writer, in proportion to his importance, of the first half of the American century." The real test was that the big critics—those who had formed American critical standards, figures like Ransom, Winters, Tate, and Eliot—had refused to alter their original low estimates of the man. It was American poetry rather than Williams which had suffered, because there was still "no generally prevailing understanding of Williams' theory of poetics."

Nor did Vivienne Koch's study help, for she had not undertaken to define or evaluate Williams's poetic revolution. American poetry kept tumbling "along the old iambic trail with its attendant European implications." The trouble was that Koch had been trapped by her own New Critical strategies into gratuitous and laborious analyses of the poems without ever understanding the nature of Williams's revolution. That she could read the details of

"The Red Wheelbarrow" as intrinsically antipoetic was a basic failure to see what Williams was after. Beum suggested, rather, that the critics would do well to attend to the kinetic dynamism, the centrality of the verb as being at the core of Williams's strategical development in poetics.

Beum continued his emphasis on the central importance of the verb in Williams in his review of the *Collected Earlier Poems* and the *Collected Later Poems* two months later in the October, 1952, number of *Golden Goose*, for which he served as an editor. "Williams' personal restlessness and superabundance of energy spill over into the poems by way of strong transitive verbs," Beum noted. And he again attacked the popular misunderstanding of the antipoetic in Williams: "Mushrooms and cinders may be informed [Beum was using the term in its scholastic sense] quite as beautifully as lilies and May clouds," since art made use of the ugly while itself remaining beautiful. For Williams, Beum insisted, there was simply no distinction between "things poetic" and "things anti-poetic."

And in the special Autumn 1953 number of *Perspective*, Beum saw Williams as spearheading a revitalization of poetry as far-ranging in its significance as the revolutions of Chaucer and Wordsworth. Like Wordsworth, Williams was one of the most uneven poets in the language, ascending from sheer bathos to poetry of a very high order. Beum attacked the "wide charm" but essential wrongheadedness of Stevens's "anti-poetic" dictum, especially as lesser critics had distorted that term. What Williams had really achieved was a new "unmetrical" mode, closer to plain speech. What poets as unlike each other as Bridges and Williams had realized, was "that the rhyming iambic metrical line as a means of serious expression is an exhausted tradition." Williams's plain or low material meant to many that it was therefore antipoetic. In fact, however, Williams was "a realist in the classic tradition, . . . temperamentally and aesthetically closer to the poets of the Greek Classic period than any other important poet writing in our language in this century." There was no essentially ugly subject matter, Beum insisted, following Aquinas. Ugliness was a matter of formal imperfection, a manifestation of two extremes: incompleteness and redundancy, but the root, the sand, the rubble were as much a part of the poem as the flower. Aware of and himself printing poets like Creeley, Beum saw that Williams seemed "likely to gain a general critical acceptance only after a profound change in our aesthetic tradition, a change to which his own work must contribute most heavily." Yet, ironically, Williams's poetry was more accessible to more people than the work of poets more widely accepted and acclaimed.

Beum's insistence on Williams's strong verb-consciousness is especially interesting in the light of poet-critic Josephine Miles's statistical findings in her ambitious *The Primary Language of Poetry in the 1940's,* published in 1951 and subsequently as the last part of *The Continuity of Poetic Language: The Primary Language of Poetry, 1540's–1940's.* There she treated Williams briefly as a prime example of the substantival rather than the predicative poet, noun-centered rather than verb-centered. Without naming it specifically as an Imagist bias, Miles saw Williams as "devoted to defining [and preserving] the quality of the instant as it is eternal," a strategy similar to Pound's "setting down of the complex event, however simple, in all its fullness and particularity of meaning." But she noted too that purer verb-centered poets—such as Yeats, Frost, Cummings—were relatively rare in the forties, since they had "learned how to think even of event as at stasis," the action frozen, encapsulated. Williams was essentially a footnote in Miles's study. Her real emphasis was on such poets as Stevens, Eliot, Yeats, and Pound and, among the "younger" poets, Auden and Robert Lowell. While her comments are suggestive (she gleaned from her statistical charts that Williams's "nouns are simply human as in *hand, eye, mind, dream, face,* or natural in *flowers, sea, day, night, water, world*"), Beum's emphasis on Williams's verbs is more correct. It is not the number of verbs that Williams uses, but their force, as in his mimesis of objects and people moving from stasis to process in the very art of a poem's unfolding ("Fine Work with Pitch and Copper" will serve as an example).

Analyzing the various worksheets of a then unfinished Williams poem, "Philomena Andronico," for Charles Abbott's *Poets at Work* (1948), Karl Shapiro focused on Williams's strategy of verbal acceleration and arresting of the object on the page. Like Stevens, Shapiro noted, Williams was affiliated with those painters who freeze the surface of their work into a tense stasis. The poem was typical in centering on the ideographs: those "symbols of the objects thought of" so presented that the objects themselves seemed to leap up before us in the mind's eye. Changes in the various manuscripts of the poem were as much concerned with "the spacing of unchanged words and groups of words" as with the lexis. What Shapiro noted about Williams's methodology was closer to what Miles was to stress in contradistinction to Beum, adding that Williams's poetry was in effect antisymbolic, its force residing in its "surface tension" which was "so great that it seems impossible for submerged material to break through, or for the reader to see down through the exterior." Shapiro's commentary is true, but only of one mode of Williams's poetry: the Imagist poem.

Collected Poems and Short Fiction

On November 30, 1950, two publishing houses brought out two collections of Williams: New Directions issued the *Collected Later Poems* in an edition of forty-seven hundred copies, and Random House published *Make Light of It: Collected Stories* in an edition of five thousand. When David McDowell left New Directions for Random House he convinced Williams to come along with him, and it was Random House which eventually published the *Autobiography* (1951), *The Build-Up* (1952), *The Desert Music* and the *Selected Essays* (both 1954), and *Journey to Love* (1955). And when McDowell started his own press—McDowell, Obolensky—Williams published his *Selected Letters* (1957) and his memoir of his mother, *Yes, Mrs. Williams*, with them. In June, 1965, fifteen months after Williams's death, Random House sold the rights (and remaining plates) of the five books it had published to New Directions. The two McDowell, Obolensky books were simply sold out in time and not reprinted.

Make Light of It, which gathered all of the stories published in *The Knife of the Times* (1932) and *Life Along the Passaic River* (1938), together with twenty-one stories not yet collected—many of which had appeared in magazines in the late thirties and forties—was, for the most part, reviewed as the spin-off product of a major poet. Babette Deutsch (*Books*, Dec. 3, 1950) compared Williams to Chekhov in his fidelity to the facts and his indifference to stylistics, praising his "exuberant vitality," his gusto, his ability to capture the life of the people among whom he worked and the "very accent of the people talking." But the stories were seriously flawed by their inattention to form, by their "irrelevant details" and superfluous commentary. Robert Halsband (*Sat R*, Dec. 9, 1950) remarked that the short stories were really sketches, impressions, anecdotes. Quoting from Williams's own pamphlet, "A Beginning on the Short Story: Notes," which the Alicat Bookshop Press of Yonkers had just published, Halsband pointed to Williams's own definition of the short story as "a medium for nailing down a single conviction," or as "a single flight of the imagination complete: up and down." Still, in spite of its fragmentation, the book held together as a unity, largely because of Williams's voice, with its wide variety and fluid moderation of pitch. The stories themselves, Halsband noted, were Joycean epiphanies; Williams's attitude towards his characters was respectful and involved rather than compassionate.

Robert Gorham Davis, in his page one review of the stories for the December 17, 1950, *New York Times Book Review*, wrote that the sense Williams's fiction gave was "of immediate experience got down as quickly and cleanly as possible in the few minutes before the next patient calls . . . while phrases and gestures and tones of voice are still vividly remembered." If Williams's situations were the kinds which usually enlivened "back-fence and back-parlor conversation in America," still, he treated his subjects "without condescension of sentimentality." The forms for the stories were minimal, fitting the "formal canons of neither slick fiction nor the New Criticism." It was the texture of a living language, a "pure vernacular all spoken," which carried the human facts without the aid of objective correlative or of literary symbol.

The first serious analysis of Williams's craftsmanship in his short fiction appeared in Mona Van Duyn's essay in the Autumn 1953 issue of *Perspective*. Lamenting that Williams's stories were still "nearly as innocent of critical examination as if they were newly published," Van Duyn undertook to demonstrate the nature of Williams's artistic control. Critics had been taken in by his evasion of "the expected sequence," his "illusion of aimless talking and telling." The fifty-one stories of *Make Light of It* formed a unity of "attitude and point of view" suggesting "a socially-sensitive memoir." But many of them were also formally independent stories, perfect in themselves. If Williams seemed merely to be presenting a piece of confused and meaningless reality, he was obliquely "making light of it": on the one hand seeming to shrug off what had happened in an unrehearsed gesture at the same time that he revealed the occurrence's deeper social, economic, and above-all human significance to us. The fact of the depression was everywhere in the grain of these stories, shaping our very moral responses, as in "Jean Beicke." Williams's own attitudes towards his subjects were consistently strong: his love for the human spirit which refused to break, his tenderness, his complete openness to experience, his honesty with himself. His characteristic technique in the story was to casually drop "the crucial insight along the way," the impact hitting the reader even as he continued to read on to an anticlimactic finish. And even the details which the critics had dismissed as extraneous were there to reinforce the story's impact, as Van Duyn demonstrated in her fine, extended analyses of "The Burden of Loveliness" and "Jean Beicke."

The *Collected Later Poems*, which gathered the poems Williams had written while he was preoccupied with *Paterson*, also came in for their share of praise. Eberhart, writing across from Davis on page one of the *New York Times Book Review* in December, 1950, wrote a highly complimentary review which evoked all of the settled clichés about Williams: Williams was interested neither in metaphysical ideas nor in tired forms (the metonymic sonnet). Eberhart's own formulation of Williams's poetics went like this: "It isn't what he says that counts as a work of art, it's what he makes with such intensity of perception that it lives with an intrinsic movement of its own to verify the authenticity."

Babette Deutsch (*Books*, Dec. 17, 1950) stressed Williams's "imagist" techniques, things seen and felt, "presented with veracity of detail, economy of statement," in "the language of our time, unenhanced but enlivened by the poet's individual voice." He had learned to use the American idiom in a way that Pound himself never had. Like his early work, these poems were "genuine," catching the very "indigenousness" of the American suburb.

Hayden Carruth (*N*, Mar. 3, 1951) saw several of the poems as "specimens of great poetic bravery" available to those who wanted them. Rosenthal (*NR*, Aug. 27, 1951), noted how all of the poetry converged, revealing a "sophistication and virtuosity" underlying even "apparent simplicities." He saw in Williams "a compassionate and humorous spirit" with "a dizzying physical awareness of the body's existence as the central fact of truth and art." Williams was a master of the juxtaposition, "taking us from shock directly into meaning," one of the few writers of his generation who had "gone on from the twenties and thirties without rejecting what once was valid for them but always ready to find new meanings and better ways to state them."

David Daiches (*YR*, Autumn 1951), concocting a kind of ad hoc poetics for Williams by quoting from his prose introduction to *The Wedge* and his "Writer's Prologue to a Play in Verse," praised Williams's unique emphasis on form, his concentration on word patterns rather than on "the expression of a state of mind."

Williams, "so scornful of traditional helps, so insistent on the poet's individual responsibility for using language altogether in his own way, so contemptuous of any formal structure that is not uniquely contrived for the individual occasion," was "both the most truly original and the most profoundly American of our poets."

"Between us and our appreciation of American poetry there is often the difficulty that we are unresponsive to the subtlest effects of the American language," wrote the anonymous reviewer in the *Times Literary Supplement* for March 23, 1951. "With diffuse poetry the barriers are lower: with terse, lyric poetry the obstruction which prevents our appreciation is sometimes insuperable." He admitted that, while Williams was not difficult in his own American context, nevertheless, "many English readers will find it hard to reach the centre of the poems." The reviewer was hard put "to say exactly what [Williams's] style is." The forms of his poems were so irregular that they defied measurement; they looked, in fact, like nothing so much as "pruned rose trees."

As a kind of popular measuring rod of Williams's literary reputation and stature at mid-century, we can turn to John Ciardi's piece, "Poets and Prizes," in the December, 1950, issue of *College English*. Reflecting on Williams's tardy recognition by a committee of judges—in this case the National Book Award judges—Ciardi presented a quick overview of the poet's achievement. Williams, he said, had moved from the imagist poem to the sophisticated interplay of prose and poetry in *Paterson,* with its concern for "the idiom of the spoken American language." Williams's prosody, on the other hand, completely baffled Ciardi. It relied neither on the iambic line nor the breath unit and seemed, in fact, arbitrary. Yet Ciardi was willing to concede that Williams had indeed "created a world and entered it meaningfully."

Autobiography

When Charles Henri Ford asked the fifty-four-year-old Williams about the possibility of writing his autobiography in 1938, Williams answered that such a venture would "have to be a monastic, brooding, gay sort of lonely thing that cannot be hurried." But the actual circumstances of its composition were quite different. "You ain't never gonna see none of it until it's presented to you at Randam [sic] House, Thursday, March 1, 1951, at 9 A.M., finished," he wrote David McDowell on January 14, 1951. ". . . I now have it at 1,008 pages longhand with 200 to go outside of the fifty original pages already printed. That ought to hold you. 1,000 pages in 6 weeks, longhand, no dictaphone phonies permitted, is a record anybody can shoot at as wants to. But if they equal it I'll do 2,000 pages next time if I have to give half my time to it."

Williams did not keep that deadline. Sensing that he was finally earning the recognition he had always wished for, he was trying to crash through to the top. On March 13 he sent McDowell another of his progress reports, remarking that there was "more to getting this script ready than meets the eye." And then, twelve days later, he suffered the stroke that nearly killed him and left his right arm dangling and the right side of his face paralyzed. "It was a great surprise to me," he wrote Wallace Stevens late in April, "for although I know I am far from invulnerable, I didn't expect THAT! Quite a surprise. It seems to have resulted from trying to write a book in three months while carrying on a practice of medicine. Just couldn't bring it off." And then he added, "I almost had the book finished at that."

Williams did finish the book in May and the *Autobiography* appeared on his sixty-eighth birthday. "I hope this script will prove worth reading," he wrote Norman Macleod on June 11. "I told it in the only way I could tell it, in a series of incidents as I lived them. . . . It isn't a story of the times during which I lived. It is as though I were a trout living in the water of my own stream, shut away in its waters, only rarely breaking the surface."

Several of the reviews of the *Autobiography* stressed the tone and style of the book, noting its apparent randomness. There was a general sense of disappointment that Williams had not revealed more of himself. Nearly all were flattering, as reviews tend to be when dealing even with the flawed work of an artist who has arrived. Certainly, whatever the final critical consensus of the man was to be, he had finally arrived—by the sheer weight of several collections either published or about to be published. Conrad Aiken, whose own poetry in many ways ran counter to Williams's, could nevertheless write a laudatory if qualified review for the front page of the September 16, 1951, *New York Herald Tribune Book Review*. Williams was a unique phenomenon, the writer who had "gone his own way, and played his own game, in his lifelong battle against the 'poetic' " as well as against a dead tradition. Yet the *Autobiography* only imperfectly demonstrated how Williams had come to his "late flowering and eminence," or how he had come to influence two generations of poets. For the book itself was "immensely crowded," "rambling," "disproportioned," revealing Williams's power "slowly and confusedly" by an osmosis of "discontinuous notes and recollections and observations." Aiken suspected Williams's intellectual framework, questioned whether indeed Williams had a unified, considered aesthetic, and attacked Williams's conception of a new line, which he thought Williams had pushed enthusiastically but without clarity or intellectual conviction. Nor had Williams sufficiently attended to the mnemonic quality necessary to all true poetry (and here Aiken's own preference for the traditional music was unmistakable). He had never learned properly how to select, had insisted on dumping "insoluble, indigestible lumps" among the lyrics of *Paterson* as well as his *Autobiography*. What saved the *Autobiography*, Aiken suggested, in spite of its absence of formal excellence, was the man himself with his "comprehensive, warm, animal, perhaps all-too-inclusive love."

Selden Rodman's review (*Times*, Sept. 16, 1951) was a mixture of flattery and lightweightedness. Williams was generous, singleminded, selfless, a man who had caught his own life breathlessly, seen it in terms of "a ceaseless curiosity and wonder." Organization had "never been Williams' forte and parts of the book read like pages from a notebook." But there were fragments here "as 'pure' as anything in 'Life on the Mississippi' or 'Democratic Vistas.'" What "made" the book, however, was Williams's "naïveté"—what Aiken had called his "all-too-inclusive love." Williams was "an unspoiled primitive, without inhibitions, affectations or compulsions to make his generosity a self-conscious gift." Rodman was closer to the truth when he commented that it was the conflict between the two Williamses—the smalltown country doctor, the exponent of the local, and "the apostle of Objectivism or Projective Verse" whose sights were always grudgingly turned towards Europe—that formed the central fascination of the book.

In a condescending piece for the October 8, 1951, issue of *Time* magazine called "Part-Time Poet," the anonymous reviewer praised Williams's kindness and humanity, and admitted that Williams was a figure to reckon with. But the *Autobiography*, like *Paterson*, was "oddly erratic, even pointless at times, with commonplace anecdotes and trailing reminiscences . . . random recollections never meant for a critical eye." Matthew Josephson (*Sat R*, Oct. 20, 1951), who had reviewed Williams's *The Great American Novel* nearly thirty years before, gave the *Autobiogra-*

phy a lukewarm review, calling it an embodiment in literature of "what we used to call the 'amateur spirit.' " Williams was too impatient to present "balanced judgments of complex personalities such as Pound and Gertrude Stein," nor could he deal with "the intellectual content of artistic movements." And yet this enigma to the New Critics had written a great deal of first-rate literature in his own unorthodox fashion, employing an *ars poetica* already fully formed by the time he came to write his Dadaist *Improvisations* in the late teens. For Harvey Breit (*AM*, Oct.) the *Autobiography* was "immensely honest," reminding him of Stendhal's *Memoirs of Egotism*, "in which that autobiographer promises the reader he will only put down honest lines." The book was "refreshing," "absorbing," "informative," particularly in its vignettes of other writers like Pound, Joyce, and H. D.

Vivienne Koch reviewed the *Autobiography* twice: once for *Poetry* in May, 1952, and again that summer in the *Kenyon Review*. She was disenchanted with the book. There was about it a "kind of destructive pursuit of honesty." Nor was it really an image of "the American as a man of letters." Instead, it was Williams's "singularity" which was the real interest in the book. The "Emersonian ethic of honesty and self reliance" was there, as was "the Whitmanian celebration of the sexual," but Williams was a far more complex figure than this. If the book was American, it was American in its voice: "colloquial, slangy in the durable sense, invigorating, in the concrete pitch that the movement takes." Its artlessness was a part of Williams's social mask. And if Williams had himself maintained in his introduction that "the hidden core of my life will not be easily deciphered" from the outer circumstances of that life, still, these "peripheral illuminations" did, by their cumulative weight, "suggest a way to the centre of his being." It gave insights too into the social and literary history of the first half of this century, "seen through the special and . . . highly selective experience of one gifted American." But Williams's real autobiography was in his poetry and fiction. She reiterated most of these ideas in the *Kenyon Review*, stressing that a poet's autobiographical self-image (and she included Yeats as well) was "always at variance with the self-image dramatized more intensely by the objective work of art."

Back to back with Koch's essay in the *Kenyon Review* was Richard Ellmann's cool reception of the *Autobiography*. What particularly troubled Ellmann was Williams's continual pursuit of the naked, the unadorned, the unembellished, which even went so far as to eschew the explicit sentence. "Cleansing the gates of perception," while valuable, could also strip the object of everything. And the amassing of particulars, as Pound had done in the *Cantos* and Williams in his *Autobiography*, often resulted merely in a heap of unfocused fragments.

Byron Vazakas, reviewing in the *New Mexico Quarterly* (Spring, 1952) the books of three modern old masters—Williams, Stevens, and Marianne Moore—insisted on a political bias in his commentary on the *Autobiography*. Williams, Vazakas wrote, was a liberal after science and humanity rather than a conservative after tradition and myth. His lives as a doctor and as a poet were really one life dominated by a single moral criterion: "the alleviation of pain, mental as well as physical." As his poetry itself showed, Williams believed "that the law should fit the needs of the individual rather than that of abstractions or institutions." Williams, Vazakas insisted, was "a *genuine* liberal," an "unacknowledged legislator" (in Shelley's famous phrase) who should be listened to.

Irving Stone, himself a biographer of some reputation, commented in his pastel-light review of the *Autobiography* (*YR*, Winter 1952) that, even though the book was loosely constructed, he liked it for its portrayal of a selfless, dedicated doctor-artist and for its portrait of Pound, a story told "in terms of pity and terror, pity for Pound . . . and terror lest Pound, in some of his criticisms of our country, may be partially right." Finally, Frederick Eckman (*GG*, Oct. 1952) counterattacked that army of reviewers who kept treating Williams's prose either superficially or as the "embarrassing but necessary waste product of poem-making." Rather, he insisted, Williams was "all of a piece." In both the poetry and the prose he had fought "against dead language, dead syntax."

In October, 1952, the long-delayed third part of the Stecher trilogy was finally published by Random House as *The Build-up*, but it attracted little attention. Winfield Scott (*Books*, Nov. 2, 1952) noted its biographical nature, based as it was on Williams's in-laws and his wife. Scott must have been ironical when he called the novel an "American success story" based on an immigrant family's memories of itself. Structurally, the book had failed. It was not only plotless; it was "planless." Events were summoned, characters created, and then allowed to disappear. And the book did not end; it simply stopped. (What Scott failed to see was that the ending is really a brilliant epiphany about the human cost of achieving "success" in America.)

Eberhart (*NR*, Nov. 10, 1952) was unintentionally comic in his attempt to speak about the novel. He kept trying to say something about the book's relative greatness or at least goodness, admitted that he was somehow deeply moved by it. He marvelled at Williams's ability to capture on paper the very life of his people, observing them with objectivity and love, without the consolations of either religion or myth. Williams's style, he commented, had "little subtlety of phrasing" in the way that Henry James was conscious of phrasing. But there was an "adroit management of the paragraph, the revealing of character through the timing of events, the build-up of chapters." It was, somehow, powerful writing.

Collected Earlier Poems

In fact, the critical response crested with the publication of the *Autobiography*. The National Book Award was history and the *Collected Earlier Poems* were by their nature anticlimactic. There were, accordingly, fewer reviews of that volume. I. L. Salomon's review (*Sat R*, Mar. 15, 1952) was typical. Noting that the collection had been published to increase Williams's prestige, he insisted that Williams would have been an important poet even if he had stopped writing after 1939. Even so, he had continued to grow since that time.

The most significant review was Jarrell's essay, "The Situation of a Poet" collected in *Poetry and the Age* (1953). In spite of writing in free (accentual) verse, he wrote, Williams was "one of the most tensile, dynamic and kinesthetically engaging of poets," a voice which had the urgency of "a delicately graduated riveting machine," a signature for his exclamatory, galvanic nature. He courted "arbitrariness, chanciness, mere contingency" in the language of his poems. But this was precisely how Williams saw his world. The collected poems documented Williams's concern with his America with his own situation in his own place from the beginning. America was "his own family, so that he says awful things about it but cannot bear for anyone else to." He had a way of looking at other poets along Paterson's streets with a greater distrust than he looked at the people. Jarrell took the opportunity to chide him for his insistence that American poets create a new language in which to write. The truth was, Jarrell maintained, that Williams was already writing in it, and so were they. Williams had been too parochial, too much "the chiropractor impatient of anything but his own fragment of the truth."

But it was the British reviewers, really, who acknowledged the collection as a "new" voice to contend with. G. S. Fraser (*NS*, Apr. 12, 1952) dismissed the poems as "charmingly impudent," democratic, not especially memorable. Williams, he noted, had almost no standing in England, but he could recommend him as the one poet to study for the visitor going to America (read province). On the other hand, the February 1, 1952, *Times Literary Supplement* carried a long, thoughtful review of Williams's recent work which attempted to evaluate his "contributions to American letters." Here was a poet who had embraced his world, championing "the cause of Blake's Minutely Particular." He had written a poetry so stripped that some had accused him of simply being unable to write a complex, resonant poem. He noted that his own countrymen, brought up on the resonances of Marlowe, Milton, and Dylan Thomas, would be disappointed with this thinner music. On the other hand, he recognized that the English tradition, which included medieval order and Augustan elegance, was not felt as immediately by the American poet with his "legacy of Twain and Whitman." Furthermore, the American poet, having no privileged legacy, was in greater danger of being swallowed up by a democratic and cultural barbarism; Williams had had to rub up against a more chaotic, less settled world. He gave every indication of being a major figure: he had a recognizable philosophy, a developed style. But he was not memorable. One could not quote passages from his work. His language was so alien, so different from the accepted tradition, that he would probably not gain a very wide audience of English readers. Williams, of course, had anticipated as much back in the early thirties.

Reassessing the Early Prose

In the summer of 1953 the *Western Review* published a symposium on the value of impressionistic writing (in a New Critical age), using Williams's *In the American Grain* and D. H. Lawrence's 1923 *Studies in Classic American Literature* as examples and models. Russell Roth (*WR*, Summer 1953) wrote a ten-page essay championing the return to an impressionistic criticism

in the wake of the failure of Marxist criticism, which had had its
day in the thirties, and the New Criticism of the forties. *In the
American Grain* is an infectious book; there is always the tempta-
tion to want to style one's own critical prose after its taut, nervous
illuminations. Roth's essay is a case in point of what happens when
an enthusiastic amateur attempts what is, in fact, a treacherously
deceptive style. Roth interpreted Williams as pointing towards an
America that would become "immediate (Eric), Latin (Cortez),
Catholic (Rasles), passionate (Boone), aristocratic (Burr)." That
figure had perhaps been most fully realized in the person of William Faulkner. Exponents of the New Criticism like Tate and
Ransom could not have revealed this manifestation to us, he insisted, because that mode tended towards obscurity and the cere-
bral, carefully avoiding the local. It was concerned with the lofty,
the universal.

When one reads the devastating rejoinders (*WR*, Summer
1953) of Elizabeth Hardwick, William Van O'Connor, and especially of Robert B. Heilman, one wonders what could have
prompted Roth to set himself up as such an easy mark. *In the
American Grain*, Elizabeth Hardwick confessed, was a beautiful
book, but Williams was certainly a weak contender in the field of
literary criticism. It was "almost a subtle disparagement of Williams to use *him* as an attack on the criticism of Tate and Ransom,"
for Williams was unhappily barren in this regard. (Except for
Hugh Kenner's lone championing, it was not until the early seventies that Williams began to be taken seriously as a critic.) Critical writing, of whatever school, Hardwick insisted, was first of
all *writing*, and so what Roth was really attacking was second-rate
criticism by second-rate writers. America was big enough to include Williams *and* Tate. Besides, even Faulkner's frontier characters owed as much to Joyce and Conrad as to Twain.

O'Connor was not interested, really, in going after Roth; he
dismissed him in a long footnote and then went in pursuit of the
real problem: the widespread American concern for the recovery
of a radical innocence, the quest for "a single tradition with a root
. . . center." Such a quest had given us an "official" American
prose in *Huckleberry Finn* and an "official" American poetry in
Leaves of Grass. Their acceptance had crippled good writers like
Sherwood Anderson and Hart Crane. O'Connor dismissed *In the
American Grain* as being of the same stuff as Jay Gatsby's chim-
erical dream: "there is somewhere in the valleys or on the plains
or in the clouds over the United States the elusive spirit of inno-

cence, which once was here in its untrammeled freedom, and if we look hard enough, why one day . . . ."

Behind Heilman's razor-sharp attack on Roth was the combined weight of a convincing knowledge of the New Critical, Humanist, and Marxist schools of critical thought together with an ability to marshall facts against Roth's flawed "impressions" of how things must have been. Heilman too was for a critical pluralism, not to replace one school with another, but "as a means of guaranteeing a number of approaches adequate to the complexity of literary objects, so that no possibility may be neglected in the evolving of a sufficiently inclusive method." To pursue an "American style" consciously was dangerous, since the American artist would be "infallibly . . . American without trying." Even such an impressionistic writer as Williams could best be interpreted by the New Criticism. Did not *In the American Grain* use "a diversity of methods ranging from direct exposition and quotation to internal monologues and hypothetic dialogues"? And didn't it use such recurrent themes as "fertility and death, each rendered by numerous images and concepts (touch, procreation, seed, flowering; carefulness, fearfulness, protectiveness, disease)"?

Four years later Jean Garrigue, reviewing the first paperback edition (ten thousand copies) of *In the American Grain* for *Poetry* (Aug. 1957), also exhibited the book's infectiousness. The book was, Garrigue wrote, "all style—was, is, and will be—an American tension of style if you will—imitative form and no fallacy!—an American Original, too." What made this book—Williams's elusive quest "to disentangle the obscurities that oppress me"—was in part the materials of our past which Williams had uncovered and in part his "alert, passionate interpretation of it," the juxtapositioning of scenes and styles to "let significance shock out." Garrigue presented sharp, incisive pictures of several of Williams's chapters, particularly "The Destruction of Tenochtitlan," where "the more indirect, unconscious will" stepped "back before the dry, rational aggression of the West, armed with the cross." She saw the Puritans as running counter to Williams's belief "in the powers of the immediate, the local, and the validity it gives to those who remain directly, closely connected with it." The whole book was "a mine of suggestibility on how to take on these not yet humanized public personages of the war-making, history-shaping world and make something of them imaginatively." Its very "angers and criticisms," she noted, were "more dreadfully pertinent than ever," particularly as they were addressed to a people who then as now thought little of their own history, whose "compulsion is always towards the future," and whose present, thus ignored, had become "ambiguously frenzied in the cities, monotonous and dull in the suburbs."

Reflecting on "The Legacy of Fenimore Cooper" (*EC*, 1959) Donald Davie examined the "bastard" genre of impressionistic history. Both Pound's strategy of pastiche to document historical sources in the *Cantos* and Lawrence's vocabulary and use of myth in *Studies in Classic American Literature* had decisively shaped the texture and tone of *In the American Grain*. Williams had been one of the first Americans to incorporate Lawrence's understanding that the myths of America could be profitably extracted from its literature because those myths had been shaped after the invention and dissemination of print. Williams was probably the only writer who had absorbed a "Lawrencian vocabulary, along with a centrally Lawrencian idea" with "other than calamitous effect." He had, in fact, surpassed even Lawrence in "approximating" the "rhythms and contours of excited speech" in the central "Rasles" section. Given the context of that chapter as the emotional climax of the book, Davie found the manner not only justified; it was, indeed, "a remarkable if eccentric achievement."

Hugh Kenner's brilliant "A Note on *The Great American Novel*" in the Fall 1953 *Perspective* showed what could be done in terms of analyzing Williams's experimental prose of the twenties. He demonstrated convincingly and briefly how the style of that seventy-page prose piece was the content, how it maintained "a remarkable poise, midway between spoof and earnestness." The book itself was about the difficulty of grubbing for both a subject and a fit language in order to write the impossible "great American novel." For our language itself is "distinguished by a sort of amnesia," which makes lyrical flight at best difficult. Williams, Kenner showed, had caught the inelegant cadence of Jersey speech rhythms with their flat insistencies which, if they meant less than Latinate rhythms, "mean it with greater finality." Interlocked with this cleansing of words from their European connotations was Williams's eschewal of the techniques of traditional fiction as well: plot, epithet, fine cadence. Williams insisted, rather, on "a wide range of textures," held together only by "a suitably balanced sensibility" which could digest and parody all styles, including the symbolic gestures at the close of the "novel." Williams had insinuated his own fictional strategies into the success story of the merchant who had met the American demand for cheap, attractive shoddy.

Debate over the Variable Foot

In March, 1954, Random House brought out Williams's first volume of new poems since *Paterson* IV: *The Desert Music*. The volume included a number of poems employing the variable foot, a form Williams had stumbled upon in "The Descent," which first appeared in *Paterson* II. The book was widely and, for the most part, favorably reviewed. Rexroth, who had insisted for years that Williams was a classic—in fact the great Franciscan poet of our time—saw in Williams (*Times*, Mar. 28, 1954) America's "only writer who stands any chance of being assimilated into our culture permanently at his face value." Williams's line was welded to the American idiom, as "the choruses of Euripedes were welded to the speech of the Athenians in the market place." The book itself was a summing up, in tone "unpretentious and unworried," filled with a mature wisdom concerned with "simple, indisputable" ideas.

Winfield Scott also noted (*Books*, Mar. 28, 1954) Williams's new ease. And if there was heard now "a thinner speech" than that heard in the "nervous, intense complexity" of the earlier poetry, there was also a new purity and clarity in these new poems, especially those employing the variable foot. Richard Wirtz Emerson (*GG*, Apr. 1) was sure that the lyric achievement of this book would make more people aware of Williams's greatness.

Ciardi (*N*, Apr. 24, 1954) praised Williams for his zest and for his ability to evoke the richness of things. But the variable foot, he insisted, was "haunted by the richest memory of meter," its triadic structure often resolving itself into iambic pentameter. Imagism had insisted on the constant destruction of old forms and the creation of a new one every time a poem was made. This was too high a price to pay, Ciardi insisted, and pointed to *Paterson*, which had been crippled because it lacked "an assured line." But the variable foot, with its echo of the older metrical tradition to support it, gave Williams the kind of relative form he needed.

Nearly five years later Ciardi came back to the question of just how free free verse was (*Sat R*, Oct. 11, 1958). Explaining that he did not "wholly understand" the metric theory behind Williams's three-line stanza, he saw (1) that the three steps were roughly equal to each other, and (2) that there was a caesural pause after each step-down. But in practice what he heard in such poems as "The Artist" was "a series of variations on an iambic-pentameter line divided into three equal units by the careful control of caesuras," a rhythm similar to jazz improvisations on a basic theme.

"In no small part due to the theory and practice of William Carlos Williams, much American poetry of the last thirty years has had about it a calculated flatness, an anti-poetic flavor that has come to be peculiarly American," John McCormick wrote in the Autumn 1954 number of the *Western Review*. There was a new serenity in Williams coupled with the old freshness in communicating a series of mental objects immediately and sensuously. The tone was "elegiac and gay, retrospective and tragic." There was also a religious sense in these poems new to Williams, unobtrusive and natural. If Williams's triadic structures restricted the fluency of the line, there was a concomitant increase in emphasis and immediacy. What struck McCormick most was that the old man was "still developing, still making constant and new connections."

Unconvinced by Williams's theory of a "relatively stable" poetic foot, particularly as this was heralded in the *Selected Essays*, Thomas Fitzsimmons (*NR*, Feb. 7, 1955) insisted that what he heard in the variable foot was "a flexible, careful prose using many of the devices of poetry and broken up on the page for dramatic effect." Fitzsimmons was unconvinced by this technique and pointed to the key lesson which the French Symbolistes and Yeats (he might have added Stevens and Eliot) had learned from the past: the necessity of retaining a developed music in poetry which could "pierce through and beyond the categories of the intellect, into the imagination, *while still retaining their intellectual content*." Fitzsimmons came down hard on Williams because he felt that the poet's forty-year revolution against the old forms (as plotted in the *Selected Essays*, also under review) had itself become a fashionable institution, accepted too easily by other poets and critics. He felt that Williams himself had begun to swing towards some kind of measure. But that new measure was insufficient—was, finally, prose.

Babette Deutsch (*Poetry*, Mar. 1955) heard a speech-like quality in these new poems, but in a cadence narrower than prose and carrying the emotional charge of music. There was a new clarity here, a gay seriousness in the face of encroaching death, "the eloquent simplicity" of the Chinese masters of the lyric. J. E. Palmer (*SR*, Spring 1955) admitted that he had been converted late to Williams's poetry, which had often seemed tedious and arbitrary. But *Paterson*, for all its crankiness, had altered his opinion of the man, and *The Desert Music* had fully converted him. Louis Martz (*YR*, Winter 1955) was less fully won over, but admired the spacing of the poems in the new form, which gave "just the right pace and emphasis when the poem is read aloud." Only "The Desert Music" itself refused to shape itself into a dance.

Thomas Cole (*Voices*, Jan.-Apr. 1956) read the variable foot as based "not on a set foot as a ground for the poem," but rather on the "conversational foot which varies continually as speech progresses," that is, on an accentual line. The three-line stanza was "the perfect form for a swift, uncumbered reading." The late poems were poems of statement, handled like the *things* they were. The old man, he noted, was "writing circles around the younger poets" and even "most of the fashionable older" ones.

Thomas Carter (*Shenandoah*, Spring 1955) wavered in his review of the poems. Williams was no doubt "one of our finest minor poets," whose "methods work *for him* again and again, miraculously." Against all the odds, Williams had extended his range from the tense, "short-winded movement" and "strained syntax" of *Spring and All* to a subtle, sure, relaxed control—surely a formal advance—in *The Desert Music*. And if a poem like "The Host" should have failed by all the "rules" of the game, somehow it had worked and worked well.

Robert Creeley (*BMR*, Summer 1954) focused instead on Williams's treatment of women in the book, giving that theme a force all the more insistent by its distillation, in the space of four pages, of quotations from the whole range of Williams's work. Creeley noted in Laurentian terms the masculine force, clarity, and directness of Williams's strategy in addressing the woman; it was a force all the more stunning coming as it did from a man in his seventies. "I have never come down as hard on that as I would like to or, better put, as I have dared to," Williams wrote Creeley in August, 1954, in a letter partially printed in J. Hillis Miller's 1966 collection of critical essays on Williams. "Yet what you have seen and assembled under one head is for that all the more forceful."

Creeley, of course, was already one of the sons of Williams, as the spareness of his imagery and line in poems then appearing in the little magazines show at a glance. Reviewing the *Selected Essays* (Random House, Nov. 1954) for *Black Mountain Review*

(Winter 1954), Creeley noted that some of Williams's best essays, like the "Letter to an Australian Editor" (1946) or "With Forced Fingers Rude" (1948) had not been reprinted; that, in fact, the book was only half as long as Williams had originally intended. Creeley was surprised to find Williams championing poets like Pound whose poetry seemed to confute his own. In other essays, it was not so much what Williams said of the poets whom he was reviewing that mattered, but what, rather, was struck off in chance remarks about the nature of the craft. But most of Creeley's essay was devoted to a wrestling with the implications of Williams's new measure, which was, of course, central to Creeley's own concerns. Creeley pointed to what he saw as a confusion in Williams between a metrical construction and a typographical construction, both of which he seemed to endorse in practice, but both of which he rejected in theory. For Creeley, what Williams's twenty-year concern with measure came down to was this: "that the words in a poem must cohere in terms of their rhythms and sound weights," and that we must rethink the possible extensions of quantitative verse in terms of the practice of the "poets in our own immediate tradition," (who, like the reviewer in the *Times Literary Supplement*, kept harping back to diminished orthodoxies).

Eberhart (*Sat R*, Nov. 20, 1954) noted that Williams's critical ideas were "coherent, alive, and brisk." His essay style was too hurried, only a cut above journalese, but it was still direct, informative, and eminently readable. Williams had also limited himself as a thinker in being unconcerned with the tragic sense, with suffering, or with religion—marks of the contemplative and, as such, alien to Williams. (Interestingly, Williams's next book, *Journey to Love*, would deal directly with at least the last two of those themes.)

Sidney Alexander's review of the *Selected Essays* for the January, 1955, *Commentary* swung from distant amusement to impatience. There was "no connective tissue in Williams's thought," Alexander wrote. "Indeed, 'thought' is hardly the word for this mishmash of dazzling epigram and arrant nonsense, these sparkling insights embedded in a marshmallow-minded heap of hunch." In particular, he disliked Williams's treatment of the Jew, and considered "an unattached intelligence" superior to any "intense localism." The trouble with Williams was that he "really hates ideas," that he was "simply incapable of coherent thought." The book showed signs of being rushed through the presses by a "master of hot flashes" who did not have the time to proofread his own essays. He attacked, too, Williams's pronouncements on usury, which were just "baloney by the Pound," and the *ignis fatuus* of trying to come at an unconceptualized thing. If Williams had done literature a service in helping "to rid us of accumulated rhetoric," his "spontaneous disorder," supposedly "more 'true' than reflected-upon order," was merely "a loafer's conviction."

Thomas Carter (*Shenandoah*, Spring 1955) called Williams's essays "strategems," "campaign bulletins" by a modern who had been in the front lines since the beginning. They were interesting, even rich, but several of them were self-indulgent, more in the nature of "an affected prose stutter." There was a strong human attractiveness about the essays which tended "to disguise his weakest points," namely, a "genuine incoherence" and an "inability to deal in logical relations." There were, threading their way through these essays, two major concerns. The first was a conception of America as the "combined sum of gains and regressions of an alien people trying to erect a new life and a new language in a strange, hostile land" (a concern which too easily became a Laurentian mystique of America). The second was a concern with the search for a new language for a new world. But, Carter insisted, there already existed an American language whose minimum essentials could be shaped by artists as dissimilar as Faulkner and Hemingway.

Hugh Kenner's essay, "Dr. Williams Shaping His Axe" (*Gnomon*, 1958), presents the most cogent argument (in an area where it is difficult to scare up debaters) for accepting Williams as a literary critic of major proportions. If Williams was not "known as a major critic" (which, incredibly, remains true fifteen years after Kenner's essay), it was partly because of Williams himself, who had always been too busy concentrating "on the *nature* of writing, especially the writing that somebody ought to be doing right now," to put "into hierarchies an array of poems closed off forty years ago." Nor had Williams bothered to collect the literally hundreds of prose statements and polemical arguments and introductions to little-known and well-known poets until he was seventy. The *Selected Essays*, Kenner wrote, should have been in circulation before the war, to ferment along with Eliot's book of the same title. As it was, its advent was "nicely timed to disturb the afternoon peace of a bureaucracy that has lately been supposing all the major criticism of the present time to be well known and sifted, the orthodoxies established." Another reason why Williams was not recognized as major was because of his trick of coining "aphorisms as little suitable for ruminative mastication as so many bricks," as opposed, by implication, to T. S. Eliot's "dozen or so formulations, some of them dangerously succinct and memorable" which made up nine-tenths of his criticism. If Williams was less "urbane" than Eliot, he was no less catholic; and if he seemed impatient with much of the great tradition, Eliot was as impatient with much of the present. It was not a question of the one "superseding the other," but rather of two valuable critics "each so perfectly the other's complement."

Williams had concerned himself with "writing so good it hasn't been done yet," had read the new writers tenaciously to find glimpses of this unwritten writing. He was impatient with the idea that the poem could be resolved into "a few of its detachable parts," image-gems stuck together by a neutral prose paste. It was, rather, in Williams's words, "in the minute organization of the words and their relationships in a composition that the seriousness and value of a work of writing exist—*not* in the sentiments, ideas, schemes portrayed." And, in discussing Williams on Marianne Moore, Kenner gleaned "a poetic of great interest": that poetry is not a mystical but a secular art, "deriving its illuminations directly from the quality of the mind that has done the work," using images without conscripting them as gestures pointing away from the poem to "the lower borders of the supernatural." Words were not copies of nature, but real . . . as real as paint.

Coming as it did only eighteen months after *The Desert Music*, *Journey to Love* (which Williams thought would be his last volume of poetry) attracted less attention. The reviews were favorable, commending especially Williams's long "Of Asphodel, that Greeny Flower" and "The Sparrow." Much of the commentary again focused on Williams's measure. Eberhart (*Sat R*, Feb. 18, 1956) singled out the line of "Asphodel," which appeared deceptively light and easy, but which had in fact "a very tough and tensile strength which cannot be broken down." The three-line, step-down stanza was, as Paul Goodman saw (*Poetry*, Mar. 1956), "an achieved norm for Williams." Goodman's analysis of the measure is particularly thoughtful. Each line, he wrote, "is a beat of meaning [a word or word cluster that can momentarily, relative to its place in the given sentence, be attended to in itself] that may contain from one to about ten ametric syllables, one to six or seven words. . . . The versification is such as to keep you running on." This pattern "is laid across a serious nervous common speech [arising out of a prose matrix] given just as it might actually be spoken, without inversion, compression or other alteration by which poets tailor speech." Goodman noted what Ciardi had also seen: that each of Williams's three-line stanzas *approximated* the three beats of meaning of a line of English blank verse, with occasional variations of from two to four beats per line. But Goodman also noted that "each beat of meaning is to be if possible taken also in isolation, as an image," which demonstrated Williams's imagist and ideogrammic genealogy as well. Cummings had taken the painter's technique of isolating the word to one extreme, but Williams had achieved a balance between the stasis of the isolated word or word cluster on the one hand, and the rhythmic forward thrust of a language approximating the actuality of speech on the other.

There were, however, two impediments to the widespread reception of such a measure: (1) the difficulty in breathing, in reading the lines with the kind of halting, nervous voice demanded by the exigencies of the frequent caesuras themselves and (2) the resistance of ametric line units to flow together into larger wholes, gathering strength and power as blank verse can. But Williams had found the perfect vehicle for the voice he wished to portray in a poem like "Asphodel": gasping, filled with interruptions and parenthetical comments, yet moving haltingly forward towards its intense, tentative resolutions.

"Having tried many types of line," Edwin Honig wrote (*PR*, Winter 1956), "Williams has settled down to a cascading triplet of short, successively indented phrases." If there were here the "falterings, the asides, the almost too casual loosenesses of phrase" so characteristic of Williams, there was now also "a strength, a serious, unabated, almost effortless clarity" in the new work since *The Desert Music*. While not his best work, the late poems were "his purest, his simplest in design." Norman Holmes Pearson (*Lit R*, Autumn 1957), in a discussion of Williams's "semi-philosophical nativism," saw in the lines of *Journey to Love* (he pointed to pieces like "A Negro Woman" and "The Sparrow") "the stamp of more firmly controlled metrics and subsequently gained powers of rumination and absorption."

What Pearson called "rumination," Eberhart called a "mature wisdom" about love. But Goodman went further. He saw a dark wisdom in *Journey to Love*, which he called "a disturbing book." He "saw through" Williams, whose strategy was to look hard

without letting on to what he had really seen, throwing out in-
genuous questions which were really smokescreens as he ventured
out into "lonely and unsafe" territory in his halting steps towards
love.

Williams's Boswells

In his reminiscence, "William Carlos Williams and John C.
Thirlwall: Record of a Ten-Year Relationship," published in the
July, 1970, *Yale University Library Gazette*, the late John Thirlwall of the City College of New York recalled his difficult friendship with Williams, for whom he served as a surrogate Boswell and
editor of the *Selected Letters of William Carlos Williams*, which
McDowell, Obolensky brought out in August, 1957. Thirlwall
met Williams in May, 1953, and "came to Rutherford weekly
(with occasional lapses) for ten years," to gather Williams's ideas
and memories for a projected critical biography which he never
finished. In early 1954 Norman Holmes Pearson of Yale instigated
the suggestion, seconded by Williams, that Thirlwall collect Williams's letters. That collection grew by fits and starts into the
1957 selection of 218 letters from the thousands available, the
whole effort prefaced by a modest introduction. When Thirlwall
sent Williams a rough draft of the *Selected Letters* in 1955, which
knotted the letters together with biographical material, Williams
did his own editing, rejecting the biography as redundant. Thirlwall scrapped it, replacing it with very short introductory notes
on the various correspondents. Even so, something of a behavioristic commentary leaked into Thirlwall's "introduction" to the *Selected Letters*—commentary such as, "His mother and father had
inculcated an ideal of absolute purity and perfection which proved
impossible, the nonattainment of which, however, left . . . Williams uncomfortable for life."

Morton Dauwen Zabel (*Times*, Sept. 1, 1957) called the *Selected Letters* "a major document on modern American writing,"
giving "one of the liveliest and most energetic accounts of the life
in literature to appear in the last quarter-century." Where Williams's *Autobiography* failed—lacked "proportion, judgment, self-
revelation joined with self-distancing"—the letters succeeded in
their consistency of purpose and personality. They were not
works of art, written for posterity, and they showed "clearly the
marks of that enthusiasm, intimacy, carelessness, rudeness of zest

and energy that originally sped them from the pen or typewriter."
There was in them "a continuous sense of the confusions that
have beset the artist during the last fifty years"; at the same time
they showed "with what persistence, honesty and spirit one writer
untangled his language . . . and made it unmistakably . . . his
own."

Winfield Scott (*Sat R*, Sept. 7, 1957) also stressed the sense of
urgency in the letters, the "spirited, hasty, offhand, high-tempered
letters of a busy man." Comparing the divorce Wallace Stevens
had effected between his role as insurance company executive and
as poet with Williams's alignment of his roles as pediatrician and
as poet, Scott saw Stevens as having retreated into an insulated
esthetics, where, he felt, all but a handful of his poems would in
time fade. Williams, on the other hand, was the whole man, "one
of God's spies" on his rounds as a doctor, his locale thoroughly informing his poetics. (This kind of invidious "populist" comparison
says little about the relative merits of each, but even Williams was
convinced that Stevens's poems were doomed to slide shortly into
oblivion, as he wrote in his "eulogy" to Stevens in 1956 in the
pages of *Poetry*.)

Phoebe Adams (*AM*, Sept. 1957) noted that the letters, while
lacking that "intimate and unexpected quality which is one of the
traditional charms of the genre," mapped the growth of "a forceful, simple style." The real value òf the letters lay in their "record
of a working poet" whose poetics showed "little basic change"
from 1913 to the mid-fifties. Katherine Hoskins (*N*, Oct. 5, 1957)
called the letters "a spiritual autobiography of such high stature
and integrated structure" as to make the *Autobiography* irrelevant.
The recurrence of Pound throughout the letters acted as a kind of
"fictional device to point up the intense Americanism of the Williams story." For Williams's was an American success story of
sorts, with Williams succeeding in giving "the local an airy habitation and a name," having arrived, finally, at a metric satisfactory
to himself. Reed Whittemore's comments on the letters (*YR*,
Winter 1958) were general, even confused. The letters, he said,
were good, energetic, benevolent, but "conventional, . . . the
letters of a conventional rebel recommending war." And yet the
letters showed Williams to be "one of the healthiest, least eccentric
literary figures of our time," even if he did preach "much the same
gospel of eccentricity for verse as did Stevens."

Hugh Kenner (*Poetry*, June 1958) focused on Williams's "continuous, directed, unfaltering intention" toward discovering, in

Williams's own words, "some purpose . . . in being an active force," which Williams had realized in his search for a language, a measure. "For two-thirds of a lifetime," Kenner wrote, "we see Williams doing the right thing (in his writing) by instinct, or doing the wrong thing and by instinct discarding it." Kenner's remark that it was only as Williams approached fifty that he could articulate seriously prosodic theory to Pound is misleading, however, for he was discussing Yeats's metrics in an original manner as early as 1912. But Kenner's central drift that Williams came to satisfactorily articulate only in his sixties what he had been doing often enough successfully by instinct is clearly demonstrated. "What Williams has been laboring to achieve since 1912, it turns out, is simply [the] separation of the strict musical form from the free pulse of the words." This parallel progression of the words and the measure was the principle Williams had groped for so long, a principle for which the terminology had still not been developed, a principle understood (darkly) by Wyatt and Chaucer, developed by Shakespeare (he might have added Milton and Hopkins), but lost again and again by the poets and prosodists. It was this principle, unenunciated, which had governed such poems as "By the road to the contagious hospital," mistakenly called "free verse" by everyone, including Williams. To understand Williams's measure was in fact to understand the poetic activity of Kenner's own moment: late Pound, Creeley, Olson, Zukofsky, Charles Tomlinson, the Layton-Dudek-Souster group in Canada, Alan Neame. It was unequal but honest work, and Kenner warned that, unless we listened to the poets who were at work, we might some day find ourselves in a position analogous to "those who carried on disputations concerning quantitative and accentual verse, not knowing that they were contemporaries of Shakespeare."

While McDowell, Obolensky was bringing out Thirlwall's edition of the letters, *New Directions 16* published "The Lost Poems of William Carlos Williams." In going through Williams's collection of little magazines as well as the papers at Buffalo and Yale, Thirlwall uncovered sixty-three uncollected or unpublished poems dating from 1909 to 1950. These take up most of Thirlwall's forty-odd page essay; the rest is commentary, "a study," as he called it, "of [Williams's] techniques of poetry." Thirlwall marked in general terms Williams's movement from conventional forms like the sonnet, to a free verse pursued under Pound's and Whitman's magistry, and, finally, to a "variable regularity" which "leads to the rhythm of daily speech without distortion." He pointed to the influence on Williams's sense of measure of Einstein's theory of relativity; the *versos sueltos* ("loose verses") of Spanish poets like Martinez and Lorca, whom Williams was translating; and, from 1952 on, the Greek lyric poets.

Edith Heal's *I Wanted to Write a Poem* is a running commentary folded into a slim bibliography (one hundred large-print pages), the commentary prompted by Florence Williams's passing all those books—in the order of their publication—under his nose to stir Williams into reminiscing. "As bibliography, the book is undistinguished," Winfield Scott wrote (*Times*, Apr. 13, 1958). There were typographical errors; books had been omitted or chronologically misplaced. Its chief value was autobiographical; it had managed to catch the charm of the man's "directness and truth." Babette Deutsch (*Books*, July 6, 1958) also noted that it was the commentary that made the book.

"They don't set up as a knowing pair, these two," Kenner wrote (*Poetry*, May 1959). "There is ample excuse for the reviewer who concluded from this volume that Dr. Williams was an agreeable man without talent. . . . We nearly conclude that Miss Heal simply wasn't talking to the man who wrote *The Descent*, or 'The pure products of America/go crazy. . . .' She was encouraging a retired New Jersey doctor to leaf through his albums." Yet even in this form, Williams's strengths as a writer were clear. For Williams's strategy in uniting his energy with the ready word, intimate in "the casual social gusto" of the book, was a strategy of idiom Williams had perfected over thirty-five years, a rare "balance of literacy and impulse . . . only possible to naiveté of a certain order."

Late Prose and Prose Collections

The reviews of *Yes, Mrs. Williams: A Personal Record of My Mother*, which McDowell, Obolensky published in June, 1959, were tepid, deferential, pale salutations to a grand old man. Williams had contemplated at least since the late thirties doing a biography of sorts about his Spanish-French-Jewish mother, had worked on it sporadically, publishing sections in two little magazines: *Twice a Year* in 1940 and the *Literary Review* in 1957. In 1954 he cut off another section of his reminiscences, pasted it to a translation he had done with his mother of *El Perro y la Calentura* by the seventeenth-century Spanish satirist, Quevedo, and

published it with the Shoe String Press as *The Dog and the Fever*.
Yes, Mrs. Williams is a fragment of a portrait of his mother, a likeness assembled from notes he took, surreptitiously, while translating Quevedo with her. At the time, she was confined to her bed
with a broken hip which never healed; she was in her eighties
when she fell, and lived on under Williams's care until 1949, when
she died at 102.

For Babette Deutsch (*Books*, June 21, 1959), the memoir was
"a mixed bag, set forth without regard to eliminating repetitions
or reconciling contradictory statements of fact," where trivia
rested side by side with epiphany. Still, the old woman, "locked
in the prison of her infirmities," had been summoned candidly and
with piety in her "pitiful, outrageous, admirable" complexity.
Ciardi (*Sat R*, July 11, 1959) called the book "secondary," dull,
although valuable for throwing off clues about a fascinating poet.
Williams should have known better, he felt, than to simply throw
down impressions which could never capture "that experienceable
illusion of personality which is the essence of achieved writing."
The radical attempt to eschew form had resulted this time in
failure. The book fell short, too, for Phoebe Adams (*AM*, July
1959) because the old woman might have been any "patient" or
even "a talkative dining-car acquaintance." There was no book
here, Reed Whittemore complained (*VQR*, Autumn), "merely
the raw material for an as yet unwritten biography."

Williams's aesthetic practice from *In the American Grain* up
through *Paterson*, Janet Fiscalini argued (*C*, Sept. 18, 1959), had
been "to present, to pile up particulars . . . in such rhythmed arrangements that the development and reflection of motives are
possible, though explicit connections, narrative or 'logical,' are
abandoned." But the risk in using such a strategy was that "the
particulars, the untrimmed and trailing 'facts', are apt to show an
ungainly 'bulk'; the thematic, 'musical' structures are apt to be lost
in eccentric reverie." It was precisely these excesses which had
ruined, first, the fourth book of *Paterson*, and then *Yes, Mrs. Williams*, which formed a kind of parody of Williams's fictive strategies gone to seed.

On September 22, 1961, New Directions brought out two
Williams collections. One was *The Farmers' Daughters*, his collected stories, printed from the Random House plates of *Make Light
of It* (1950), together with the addition of the long title story which
Williams had tinkered with from 1940 until its magazine publication
in 1956, and an informal, biographical introduction by Van Wyck

Brooks. The other volume was *Many Loves and Other Plays*, which collected Williams's five mature plays: *The First President* (1936), *Many Loves* (1942), *A Dream of Love* (1948). *Tituba's Children* (1950), and *The Cure* (1960). Neither volume, however, received much notice. Williams was a poet, it was tacitly understood, who dabbled in the other genres.

Irving Howe (*NR*, Nov. 13, 1961) said as much. Williams was, indeed, an overrated poet who had written at moments some very fine fiction, for example, "The Use of Force" and "Jean Beicke." Essentially, however, the man was a miniaturist, out of his league when he attempted "more complex structures" as in *Paterson*, where the results were often either "sentimental incoherence," romantic simplification, or contrived simplicity. Philip Rahv, Howe recalled, had observed years before that for Williams "formal means of expression would not only be superfluous but might nullify the incentive to creation," that the stories were, in fact, formless. But Howe disagreed: "If ever I have been persuaded of the validity of 'organic form' as a critical notion—the form that is said to proceed not from executive techniques but from an inner harmony or consistency of feeling—it is in reading these stories. What holds them together is the presence of Williams himself, not always a likeable man but usually vibrant with energy and purpose." It was Williams's persona which held these stories together, an image of the "man who has found pleasure and fulfillment in useful work." (Along with Howe, one might consider Mona Van Duyn's 1953 study of the short fiction, and her location of Williams's formal preoccupation in the oblique, anticlimactic strategies of his best short fiction.)

Kenneth Rexroth praised both collections highly (*NL*, Dec. 11, 1961). Not only was Williams "the finest poet writing in America," he was also "a consummate master of prose," writing in "the tradition of Stendhal and Flaubert as it branches off into Chekhov." He was a master of the naturalistic detail, whose narrative unfolded with "a continuous surgical interference" to the "nervous system." Norman Holmes Pearson (*YR*, Winter 1962) placed Williams among the American local colorists; he had "established a locale and filled it with natives," had taken the commonplace of the area around Paterson and created out of this locale "classics" like "Old Doc Rivers" and "The Girl with a Pimply Face." And if certain of the "sketches" were unfelt, unrealized, Williams had still succeeded in creating a new style by easing the cliché—the unforced idiom—into the very fabric of his fiction. "If we do not have here a supreme fiction," Arthur M. Kay wrote (*AQ*, Winter 1962), "we have something very good and very distinctive." True, these stories employed many forms: monologue, vignette, autobiography, essay, sketch. But the stories were also without density of design. Their real value lay in their "stark authenticity" and "utter verisimilitude" which exposed to view "nearly every sort of neurosis and abnormality."

John Thirlwall's "Notes on William Carlos Williams as Playwright" (1961), appended to *Many Loves*, is a good, short biographical survey of Williams's lifelong, amateur interest in the drama from 1903, when "he played Polonius in a Mask and Wig production of *Mr. Hamlet of Denmark* at the University of Pennsylvania," until 1960, when he finished *The Cure*, a therapeutic exercise he had worked on intermittently since his stroke in August, 1952. One found, Pearson noted, that, at their best, Williams's dramatic figures and fictional figures spoke "the same fresh language," had "the same capacities for feeling." *Many Loves* still remains Williams's most successfully performed play: it had excellent notices; ran for nearly a year after its opening on January 13, 1959, at Julian Beck's Living Theatre in New York; and was highly recommended by Donald Malcolm of the *New Yorker* and Henry Hewes of the *Saturday Review of Literature*. However, Pearson insisted Williams's *best* play was *A Dream of Love*.

Williams, Rexroth wrote (*NL*, Dec. 11, 1961), was "the only major poet . . . who has written effective, more or less realistic, plays about contemporary people." Eliot's drama by comparison was pale. What baffled Rexroth, therefore, was that, while Williams's plays were made for (uncorrupted) Broadway audiences, they had been consistently ignored. Benjamin T. Spencer (*MD*, May 1963) praised Williams's experimental impulse in his impressionistic opera, *The First President*, for using music to reveal Washington's real character. He considered the authentic simplicity and the mastery of colloquial idiom in *Many Loves*, but he too found *A Dream of Love* "the most durable of all the plays." It was Williams rather than Eliot, he also insisted, who could supply a "viable and cogent American drama and poetry."

Massachusetts Review Garland, 1962

The *Massachusetts Review* (Winter 1962) included a sixty-four-page supplement, "A Gathering for William Carlos Williams," edited by Stanley Koehler, who was to interview Williams later that year for the *Paris Review*. The garland was rich and included prose, letters, and recent poems by Williams; photographs; essays by John Thirlwall, Gael Turnbull, Mary Ellen Solt, Cid Corman, and Hugh Kenner; an old note of Louis Zukofsky's; and a section on Williams and the theatre, with contributions by Clinton Atkinson, Raymond Kennedy, and H. E. F. Donohue. Thirlwall's essay, "Two Cities: Paris and Paterson," outlined Williams's lifelong interest in French literature, despite his own disclaimer that the French writers had had any influence on him. There was Rimbaud's influence on *Kora in Hell*, as René Taupin had demonstrated in 1929; the influence of surrealism and Phillippe Soupault's *Les Derniers Nuits* which Williams translated in 1929; and Valery Larbaud, who figured so centrally in *In the American Grain*. And there were René Char, Yvan Goll, and Nicholas Calas (the last a Greek writing French poetry)—all of whom Williams had translated. Here was a tradition of Williams's own: fantastic and romantic.

Mary Ellen Solt's essay on Williams's idiom and structure reviewed his search for the new mode and the American idiom in much the same terms that earlier critics had already done, but more philosophically, more attuned to linguistic and rhythmic subtleties. Much of Solt's lexis owes a great deal to Objectivist verse theory, as in her statement that "it is the spaces between phrases, the sense-breaks we make in the flow of speech, rather than the spaces between words on the printed page, that are significant." But Williams's search for the idiom also carried a sociological weight, for "the conflict between Williams' recognition of the present, tragic state of decay of the American idiom and his conviction that its true potential is still to be realized has produced what is probably the major tension in his art."

The publication of Williams's collected plays in 1961 prompted the three essays on Williams as dramatist in the *Massachusetts Review*. Clinton Atkinson reiterated much of Thirlwall's afterword to the collected plays and then treated each of the major plays chronologically. *The First President* employed avant-garde techniques years before Broadway invented them. *Tituba's Children* was "a frank and violent attack on . . . McCarthyism," written at least three years before *The Crucible*. *Many Loves* was Williams's "theatrical manifesto," the "avant-garde in its traditional theatrical appearance." Furthermore, *A Dream of Love* was "certainly a major American work, whose greatness lies in its theme and Williams' handling of it." In performance, he said, the play was "unbearably vivid," its "seemingly flat lines rise into three-dimensional shock, the characters excite the actors into spontaneous creativity of a depth" unmatched by any other contemporary American playwright.

Raymond Kennedy qualified his praise of *Many Loves*. He was "annoyed with Williams' attempt to bewilder." After all, *Many Loves* was simply three short one-acters yoked together by the "contrived and tedious" vehicle of Hubert and Peter, who more than anything fragmented the play and confused the issues. H. E. F. Donohue's remarks on Williams as playwright were humorously balanced between spotting Williams's occasional lapses into the banal and his strange power to move us. Williams was a pro in his "exploration of [the] process by which a person, a people, a country, a time, or merely a vulnerable notion determines what is genuinely needed for itself." Yet his plays were "neither absurd enough to enhance our peripheral perceptions, nor 'realistic' enough for the 'suspension of disbelief,' for effective identification." How might he reconcile Williams's clumsy faults with his masterful creations? For this he turned to Williams's own portrait of Washington (a psychological portrait, really, of the artist himself) as a man richly endowed and deserving who "had been all his life used to defeat—so that it never surprised him and out of it he built his genius."

Pictures from Brueghel

Pictures from Brueghel, containing *The Desert Music* and *Journey to Love*, together with a note by Thirlwall on Williams's new measure, came out in late June, 1962. The last book Williams saw through publication, it was to receive the Pulitzer Prize in poetry the following May, only two months after his death. Thirlwall's note served to remind the reader that critics had found "some of his best poems written in the last ten years." Phoebe Adams (*AM*, Aug. 1962) sensed "a crackling energy" in Williams's line. Stanley Kunitz, writing his annual critique for *Harper's* (Oct. 1962), called "Asphodel" one of the best love poems in the language and thought the latest poems danced "as smartly as anything he ever wrote." In his poems Williams presented himself as "the man of our time, fallible, vulnerable, full of marvels." Kunitz singled out

"The Stone Crock" for its balance of prose flatness and a taut discipline, with its "sensitive manipulation of the short fourth line of each stanza" reinforcing the "isolated power of the very last word of the poem after we have been led to expect it to be thrown away." Williams, almost eighty, was still experimenting with the line.

Creeley (N, Oct. 13, 1962) adopted the stance that it was difficult to talk about the book because it was too much a part of Williams himself, of the things and feelings of his world. The poem's technique derived from the man's deepest needs. He focused on the dance in Williams as a metaphor of this life felt along the pulse, "a music of survival," the acts of life moving two and two with the music, the life-force itself.

Alan Stephens (Poetry, Feb. 1963) compared Williams to Hardy in that the poems of both men had remained essentially stable over a long career. Williams's earlier techniques had not radically altered; they had simply been "more efficiently established." At his best, Williams could "be matched by only a very few of his contemporaries." But Williams's talk of a "variable foot" was misleading, since the options for choosing a unit of measurement were strictly limited. In fact, "to speak of the variable foot," he wrote in a quip which was to become widespread, ". . . is like speaking of an elastic inch." For the norm of poetry was not finally an audible rhythm, Stephens insisted, but "the formal architecture of the sentence" itself.

A. Frederic Franklyn (Trace, Spring 1963), dismissed the variable foot as a minor device not worth the fuss it had stirred up. What did interest him about the device, however, was the resemblance he saw (but did not clearly communicate) between it and John Cage's "silence stresses" employed rhythmically in music. As for the Brueghel pieces themselves, they were finger exercises which failed "either as appreciations or interpretations." If Williams was not evading "the customary honesty of perspective" in his copies (how little Franklyn understood Williams's use of tradition), then he was simply ignoring Brueghel's themes. Alonzo Gibbs (Voices, Jan.-Apr. 1963) questioned "the validity of writing poems about pictures," where an "emotional impact pre-exists." Williams's eschewal of standard punctuation both confused and startled him. Samuel French Morse (CL, Autumn 1963) spoke of Williams's "modest" poems, many of them "one-finger exercises . . . perfectly realized" and carrying the signature of the poet in their unquenchable vitality. In this review of the year's work in poetry Morse evoked other ghosts: Oppen and Reznikoff from the old Objectivist days, and a son, Robert Creeley.

"I take 'American Prosody' to be that approach to metric initiated by WCW and carried on by Chas Olson . . . [as] the salient markers," Gilbert Sorrentino wrote in his stimulating "Some Notes Toward a Paper on Prosody" (*Yugen*, 1961). Sorrentino was sure Williams had found the variable measure he had been searching for for so long, but he was also aware that Williams had made "a hundred charlatans possible." Williams had forerunners of a flexible measure as far back as Chaucer, who had used the iambic pentameter, but always with a great range of freedom, the line contracting and expanding aurally, according to natural speech patterns. American Negro blues, with their variations played against a constant line, suggested an analogue for what Williams and Olson were after. Amidst all of the critical talk, one thing stood clear: even as he was leaving the stage, the old man was bequeathing a new music for others to use as they could.

Charting the Pound/Williams Line

By early 1964 some of the necessary spadework on the literary relationships between Williams and Pound had been done. Glauco Cambon (*CE*, March 1961) wrote of the two as practitioners of an open poetry, both viable, and both claimed by younger poets like Olson, Levertov, Creeley, and Duncan. There was a literary affinity between the poetry of the two men, both receptive to change and to an open-ended, processive form. In his essay, "Poetic Form Today," Paul West (*CE*, Spring 1960) also discussed Williams's formal experiments, using *Paterson* as an example. Williams's typographical experiments allowed for the charting of emotional effects which the traditional line could not hope to duplicate. "The gaps in grammar and spatial continuousness," together with the partial repetition of motifs, could suggest on the page the "mental incoherence and spiritual torsion" characteristic of the poet's tentative, groping frame of mind in much of *Paterson*.

Edgar F. Racey (*BR*, Mar. 1963) emphasized that what Williams had taken from Pound was not his erudition, but the discovery of a new metric, which, of course, Williams had acknowledged in several essays on Pound: "It is in terms of the variable foot that Williams measures Pound's contribution to the language of American poetry, and he maintains that this variable foot is most often found in the middle Cantos." Williams's "without invention nothing is well spaced" section in *Paterson* II was in fact a direct echo of Pound's "Usura Canto" (45). Since Williams had pointed to Shakespeare's practice in the late plays of incorporating prose rhythms into his blank verse lines, this suggested to Racey that Williams's lines were counterpointed against the felt rhythm of the decasyllabic line. Finally, Racey reaffirmed Roy Harvey Pearce's distinction (in his 1952 essay, "The Poet as Person") that if Pound was a poet of culture, Williams was a poet of personality. Racey expressed that difference this way: Williams was "the ultimate sanction, as perceiver, for the myriad subject matter of *Paterson*." Where the *Cantos* were, finally, but "one more document in the cultural tradition which they commemorate," culture had its significance for Williams only as it was filtered and became part of his experience.

But the best six pages available on the Pound-Williams cross-fertilization are in Donald Davie's 1954 study, *Ezra Pound: Poet as Sculptor*. Davie showed the direct borrowing of Williams's three-ply line from Pound's reproduction of Guido Cavalcanti's "Donna mi pregha" in *Make It New*. He compared the relationship between the sharpness of the image and the radical dismemberment of the line in Pound and Williams alike. He suggested that Williams had learned from Pound the technique of "cutting" (in its cinematic sense) to achieve the clear juxtaposition of hard images. Pound's wholesale incorporation of chunks of historical materials into a new framework, as in the Malatesta Cantos (published in 1923), was followed in 1925 by Williams's borrowings from Cotton Mather, Ben Franklin, and John Paul Jones in *In the American Grain*. Williams had learned how to present "history" from Pound.

General Assessment, 1950-1963

When we look at Eliot or even Stevens, Williams's own contemporaries, the critical response to Williams in the textbooks in the last decade or so of his life is hardly visible. Most of the critics simply refused to acknowledge him or made comments about him which were hopelessly outdated even as they appeared. Lloyd Frankenberg gave Williams eleven pages in his *Pleasure Dome:*

On Reading Modern Poetry (1949) which appeared a year before
Vivienne Koch's study. But Eliot received eighty pages, Stevens
seventy-five, Cummings nearly forty, and Pound thirteen. Of
those eleven pages, more than half were given over to a selection
of the poems. Williams, Frankenberg noted, was a "happy champion of the vernacular," an advocate of contemporary speech and
subject matter, a practitioner of free verse, antipoetic, a novelist,
the writer of a "geographical biography" [sic] called *Paterson*.

Williams makes an appearance too in R. P. Blackmur's "Lord
Tennyson's Scissors: 1912–1950" (*KR*, Winter 1952), where he
figures as "the imagism of 1912 self-transcended." Williams felt
almost harassed by Blackmur and one can see why in the professor's "cute" summary of Williams's achievement at seventy: "He
is contact without tact; he is objectivism without objective;
l'anima semplicetta run wild, with all the gain in the zest of immediate wonder, with all the loss that strikes when memory and ex-
pectation, the double burden of the true music, are both gone.
The neo-classicist and the neo-barbarian are alike in this: their vitality is without choice or purpose."

Babette Deutsch's thirteen-page section on Williams in *Poetry
in Our Time* (1952, rev. 1962) still makes interesting reading and,
with the necessary caveats, serves as a good general introduction
up through *Paterson*. Years of reviewing and corresponding with
the poet had helped her see his achievement clearly and succinctly.
She stressed Williams's naked, antipoetic style, his eschewal of
rhyme, meter, metaphor, his fine ear. She saw the presence of
both Wordsworth and Joyce behind *Paterson* (the growth of the
poet's mind, the man-city identity). She marked the themes of
divorce, language, the river, noted in general the borrowings from
Pound. She quarrelled with *Paterson*'s large chunks of unassimi-
lated prose, had hoped that more of the city would find its way
into the poem. On the other hand, if *Paterson* was a lesser
achievement than the *Cantos*, it was "far more alive." It was a
better poem than "The Bridge" in that it had escaped "inflated diction and sentiment." Williams was better than his disciples, more
vigorous, more immediate. Compared with Eliot, he was a poet
who "declares the sacredness of the secular," one who grasped
reality *in* and not *beyond* phenomena.

In his influential essay, "The Poet as Person," for the March,
1952, *Yale Review*, Roy Harvey Pearce borrowed from Edward
Sapir the idea of dividing poets into poets of culture and poets
of personality. And while the distinction between the two is too

pat and therefore suspect, it can serve as a useful working model. Pound, Eliot, and Frost were poets of culture, who shaped their own sensibilities in accordance with models or sources outside of these sensibilities. Williams, Cummings, and Stevens were poets of personality, who started with their "own radically individuated sensibility," aggrandizing and rejecting models as they could use them, in fact infusing those models with meaning. Williams was a poet of perception whose immediate contact with the object gave it its meaning. *Paterson,* therefore, was a city only in the sense that Williams had made it a city. There was no city, only the city perceived by "a community of infinitely different, infinitely varied selves." In fact, the only order possible in Williams's world was an order of process, an order of "living, discovering, and dying." And, one might add, the constant unfolding, the constant becoming . . . of the self.

Williams's "ideal poetic manner depends resolutely upon factual integrity," Frederick J. Hoffman wrote in a section published first in *Poetry* (Apr. 1954), and subsequently in *The Twenties: American Writing in the Postwar Decade* (1955, 1962). Hoffman stressed Williams's primary concern from the beginning for the integrity of things. Williams had always insisted that ideas develop out of the careful presentation of those things, and not the other way around. The problem of presenting his world, the world of northeastern New Jersey, had been for Williams both a formal and a moral problem. It meant discovering a language which could yield his world, and this necessarily meant considering the various barriers others had "unwittingly or maliciously" set up to block him. Pearce and Hoffman were among the more responsible academic critics who were seriously attempting to revaluate Williams by the mid-fifties. (By marked contrast, however, the English could hardly be said to have been attending to this American. In *The Literature of the United States,* a Penguin paperback published in 1954 and revised in 1964, for example, Marcus Cunliffe could still "introduce" Williams to an English audience by serving them a half-dozen pages of rehashed clichés. Williams, he said, was a poet of the antipoetic, the writer of "The Red Wheelbarrow" with its "childlike immediacy," the proponent of "No ideas but in things," and the writer of *Paterson,* a poem which had not sustained its early promise.)

In his 1957 general estimate of Williams, William Bittner (*Sat R,* Sept. 7, 1957) saluted the poet's almost legendary generosity to little magazines and to fledgling poets over four decades. If Williams had published too much, he had created a significant number of established masterpieces. *In the American Grain,* "a search for origins," with its troubled love of America, was unquestionably great. His short stories, too, were "among the best in the language," had expanded "the horizons of the form in a way not even Joyce attempted." If *Paterson* had not succeeded "in generating a new technique for poetry in our prosaic age," it had brought us a long way towards that poetry. And if there were more successes among the earlier poems (up through the late thirties) than since, Williams was still developing. What Bittner was suggesting, then, was that Williams was, finally, a *prose* master writing "to bring poetry through its most difficult period since the time of the Puritans."

Charles Hartung (*UKCR,* Autumn 1958) defined Williams's poetry as "a record of individual moments of perception with a minimum of literary allusion," with "a carefully thought-out aesthetic" behind it. If he had been associated with several theories of art, he had always remained independent. If Hartung was wrong in calling him an impressionist, he was right in seeing a movement in Williams's poems from the clear image to a poetry informed with a larger, implied social significance. He pointed to "Nantucket" and "By the road to the contagious hospital" as examples of Williams's treatment of "still" lifes and nature, and to "The Orchestra" as an example of the poet's observation of human behavior. But the essay was essentially a rehashing of earlier critics.

Denis Donoghue's "For a Redeeming Language" (*TCL,* June 1958) may be the best short overview and appreciation of Williams we have. Donoghue considered Williams's poetry under Cicero's three headings: teaching, delighting, moving. *Teaching:* "Williams has had plenty to say, mostly about language, and things, and women, and formal invention, and divorce, and the American rôle in culture, and 'poem as a field action.' " Williams had made enemies, and he had published too much—Donoghue offered a plan for a *Selected Writings* which would include all of *In the American Grain* and *Paterson* and examples from all the rest, including the letters. He stressed Williams's "piety toward *things,*" his sense of tradition, and his concern with "a new measure consonant with our day." He convincingly demonstrated Williams's ability to handle ideas, dismissing the notion of "the great big lumpkin who . . . wouldn't be caught dead in the company of an idea." There was the poetry to prove it, as well as the man's "vigorous idea of culture." What Williams had given us, in fact, was "a grammar of

American culture; American because that is what he has at hand and knows best and cares most about, not because he thinks it the richest culture ever achieved." *Delighting:* Williams's best poems caught modes of consciousness which would otherwise have remained neglected. Donoghue understood Williams's three-ply measure in terms of bars in music, where "each bar may contain any number of syllables." The measure, difficult as it was to define, was "sufficiently *there* to enforce discipline." *Moving:* Williams, Donoghue saw, was closer in temperament to Henry James than to Whitman. To compensate for this he had swung to "the Redskin, the frontiersman, creating a pantheon of heroes of exceptional achievement: Franklin, Columbus, Boone, Washington, Lincoln, Madame Curie, his mother, Herbert Clark fighting yellow fever. Finally, what Donoghue appreciated were the man's traditional priorities: that life and people were important, that a person's dignity depended on his power of moral choice. And it was moving to see a man like Williams opting for "clarity, self-knowledge, understanding."

Karl Shapiro's "William Carlos Williams: The True Contemporary" (reprinted in his *In Defense of Ignorance*) is a mixed bag. Written forcefully and with no apologies for its iconoclastic bad manners, it is a cross between a twenty-one-gun salute for Williams, this "godfather . . . of nearly all the existent *avant-garde* poetry, all the free poetry that exists in the English world today," and a using of the old man as a handy bat with which to smash Eliot and Pound and the "orthodox" critics over the head. Anyone raised on a new critical diet comes to Shapiro with a sense of giddy elation as the restraints are finally removed, but Shapiro's antiintellectualism, his unsupported statements, his impressionistic lunges and, finally, his bad manners, wear on one. Still, as his heavy two-handed engine clangs off the rocks he throws off enough brilliant flecks to see by, at least by fits and starts. *Paterson* was bad, he maintained, because it had been written to impress the culture critics. Still, there were hundreds of other lyrics which, taken together, made up an American poetry written in "a foreign language, my language." Williams was not much of a critic because he couldn't get said well what he wanted to say, although one sensed that *what* he was saying was usually on the right track. There was so much talk about prosody in Williams that it had assumed the stature of a mystique. The New Critics on Williams (he singled out Koch and Tyler without naming them) were worse than comic—they were useless. Shapiro reviewed the vari-

ous influences on Williams's poetry, saw him early reject Pound
and move towards a poetry without metaphor, "a pure spoken
idiom," in a direct, sensuous relationship with daily experience.
Shapiro saw him fighting alone "against the growing orthodoxy of
Eliotic criticism" after "the great catastrophe" of *The Waste
Land*. Williams's concern with prosody, really, was a concern
with language, with getting down on the page the cadences of his
own idiom without falsification. In fact, what he was doing was
"approximately what Hopkins did in sprung rhythm, creating a
total form rather than a unit form." His "step-down kind of ty-
pography" (the three-ply line) was simply another form, to be
used and discarded when it no longer served. In fact, what really
saved Williams and made his poetry "the chief development of
the American poem since *Leaves of Grass*," was his final indifference to form. Shapiro was willing to fly in the face of Williams
himself to mold him in his own divine Laurentian likeness. And
damn the sissy critics.

M. L. Rosenthal, one of the critics Shapiro had singled out for
scorn, gave over ten pages of his 1960 *The Modern Poets: A
Critical Introduction*, to Williams, many of the remarks culled
from his earlier reviews. Williams was an "aesthetic of existence,"
grounded "in the local and immediate without loss of larger perspectives." What Rosenthal stressed, in fact overstressed, was Williams's social consciousness, his struggle, together with Pound,
against the economic and cultural drift of America. But, unlike
Pound and like Lawrence, Williams's emphasis was on what he
had himself called "the secret gardens of the self," our basic kin-
ship with all of life. What Williams was after, finally, was the
"poetic repossession of the intractable." *In the American Grain*
was "one of the truly germinative American prose works of this
century"; *Paterson* I-IV "a devastating comment on every phase
of our life, though one relieved by momentary oases of perceived
or imagined beauty"; *Paterson* V "a mellowing without loss of
energy," a sharper refocusing on the "archetypal oppositions and
symbols" of the earlier books.

Reviewing Williams's long quest to find a viable measure, Roy
Harvey Pearce, in "Williams and the 'New Mode'" (a section of
his *The Continuity of American Poetry*, 1961), called Williams's
new measure "nothing less than the poet's means of taking absolute
control over his world and of baptizing it in his own name."
Williams had realized that new mode most fully in *Paterson*, towards which the earlier poetry, with its ability to make Williams

(and us) see the vital sense of the thing's existence, had been tending. The earlier poems had concerned themselves with seeing the
world and with talking about that world, usually to oneself. In
Paterson, Williams's "new mode," as Pearce saw it, was "to control and modulate revelation according to the nature and needs of
poet and reader." Williams was the poet of preconceptual awareness, presenting the object as it first impressed itself upon the
mind, before things were categorized by the intellect.

But in the poetry after the four parts of *Paterson*, Williams had
tried to move beyond this act of mediation *between* subject and
object to a poetry where subject and object fused, where Williams's world became, in essence, *the* world. For Pearce this was
expecting too much from the poem; he saw Williams's search for
a new mode as a "mystique," an eschewal of the old orthodoxies
replaced by the light of the imagination. The world of *Paterson*
had been filled with many things, but the later poetry only with
Williams. In short, a poem like *Paterson* V lacked that "fecundating sense of the place and its inhabitants" present in Williams's
earlier books. All of the late poems verged toward the incantatory,
"the Adamic poet's unmediated vision." They were not discoveries but a celebration of the imagination's power to invent, where
discrete objects merely became grist in a world inhabited by one
man alone. J. Hillis Miller's essay on Williams in *Poets of Reality*
(1966) is a forceful reply to many of Pearce's arguments, especially in their respective valuations of Williams's last phase.
Where Pearce saw a falling-off, with Williams retreating into the
self and the new space of memory, Miller was to see the reconciliation of the poet and his world, with time and space successfully
"annihilated" by the imagination. Looking at the two, Pearce
reads more like the classicist, Miller like the romantic.

Another view of Williams's new mode was Bernard F. Engel's
two position papers delivered before the Michigan Academy of
Science, Arts, and Letters in 1960 and 1961, summing up Williams's achievement with a new poetics, and tying it in with his
search for America. In "The Verse Line of Dr. Williams: A Fact
of the Thing Itself," Engel stressed the uses and effects of Williams's line, a line which attains its "distinction not by rhetoric or
overt melody but by care in statement." It was a line grounded
firmly on the prose rhythms of the American idiom, where each
line has "one moment of climactic stress," and where "line divisions are intended to force a momentary examination of each
important segment of the presentation." Reading Williams's three-

ply lines as loose iambic pentameters was "disastrous." These lines
had one stress each with only the "barest suggestion of convention . . . present." Williams's line was "craggy, abrupt, muscular," a strategy of presentation rather than of commentary, "suited
to the desperate analyst who would urge a new beginning."

In his second paper, "Dr. Williams as Exhorter: The Meaning
of Americanism," Engel focused on Williams's long battle to get
Americans to first know the ground from which they had sprung.
That meant a paring to the ground, a return to the beginnings of
things and a rejection of those (Eliot in particular) who would
turn to outmoded, sterile philosophies. Turning to *In the American Grain*, Engel stressed Williams's rejection of the self-repress-
ing Puritan heritage and the contrasting image of the Catholic
fathers who attempted a psychological communion with the Indian and who refrained from judging them in terms of themselves. *Paterson* was a continuation of the diagnosis first worked
out in *In the American Grain*, with "rapacious individualism" our
primeval sin, and divorce from our roots giving rise to the mon-
strous, the cancerous. Hand-in-hand with our need to truly per-
ceive our world was the need for a new line which would present
that world, which meant inventing a language adequate to the task.
It meant a poetic strategy relying "heavily upon juxtapositions and
subtle repetitions" which would order facts with a minimum of
editorializing and present things as they are.

In an essay called "Doctor Williams' American Grain" (*TSL*,
1963), Benjamin T. Spencer considered Williams's Americanism
from another angle. Williams, he said, had "probed the nature of
an indigenous American literature more zealously than any other
major writer since Whitman." His poetry and criticism, for all its
muddle, revealed "a tonic diagnosis . . . which [has] made him
one of the inescapable forces in Twentieth-century American
writing." Spencer's essay is a careful, heavily-documented paper
on Williams's concept of the local and of his reliance on the
examples of Poe and Whitman in particular. Williams found in
Poe, Spencer showed, "a literary virtue in [his] failure to mirror
explicitly and sensuously his milieu," and found that Poe was
the first American writer in terms of style and temper to spring
from his agonizing encounter with his place. Williams "measured
the real character of the New World by Poe's psychic response
to it, not Poe's picture of it." In Whitman, however, Williams
found his real mentor, even as he tried to hide it or only grudgingly acknowledge it. For, if Williams liked to think of himself as

a hard-headed classicist for whom the poem was, finally, "a small (or large) machine made of words" with nothing redundant about it (the legacy of Poe), his deepest impulse was to view the poem as organic, charged, spontaneous feeling.

Spencer also demonstrated that America for Williams was three-ply: "a kind of Platonic idea of America historically expressed in the American dream; a covert America intuited by poets like Poe and Whitman; and finally an existential America, vulgar and re-calcitrant in its temporal pursuits." Williams's search for America, then, included a return to the ground, to those who had been in contact with the New World—the Indian, the black, his early heroes—as well as a return to the essential American idiom, stripped of its imported connotations and rhythms, a search for the non-English word, for the new mode. American poetry had to be grounded in the phenomenological world out of which the poet had sprung, *all* of that world lifted up by the imagination.

Written after repeated conversations with Williams in the late fifties, Mary Ellen Solt's "William Carlos Williams: Poems in the American Idiom" (*Folio*, 1960) reveals a perceptive understand-ing of the nature and viability of Williams's prosodic theories as a means of reviewing American poetry and establishing it on a sound theoretical basis. Williams, she explained, "begins with na-tive linguistic materials, seeks to establish language and experience, and hopes to achieve a dance of words." The poem "creates its own form as the words combine rhythmically and work toward it," so that the form is "not specifically definable although it ex-hibits certain characteristics." She recognized modes of rhetoric which Williams characteristically used and others which he es-chewed, always with the end in view of affecting, in his own words, "a transference—for psychic relief—from the actual to the formal," carrying the energy which originally compelled the poem into the sharp perception of the poem itself.

She described the quantitative, melodic basis of Williams's measure as "far closer in structure to the Greek lyric than to the ballad." Her long discussion of "The Red Wheelbarrow," despite that poor poem's having been done to death, is a model of clarity in its explanation of the kinds of patterned variety possible with a relatively stable foot. (That Williams was not to use the term variable foot until nearly three decades after "The Red Wheel-barrow" is not critical to her discussion, since Williams was late in articulating what he did in part by instinct.) Summing up, Mary Ellen Solt wrote that Williams seemed "to be advocating

. . . a new American classicism founded upon the objectification of language as it relates to the perception of experience that has as its goal a distinctive American poetry" in the native language. This was, she insisted, a necessarily moral concern and not, as some would claim, a chauvinistic parochialism.

William Pratt's fine "Introduction" to *The Imagist Poem* (1963) treats, among others, Williams's poetry as basically Imagistic. However far Williams went beyond the original movement, his poetics were nevertheless grounded in a "complex quantitative music" and a "further accuracy of the image," phrases which Williams himself used to describe his own poetics. *Paterson*, like the *Cantos* and *Four Quartets*, employed the central "effect of instantaneous perception, or simultaneity," present in "the shortest Imagist poem." Quoting Herbert Read, Pratt read "one clear line of progress" in the development of modern poetry in England and America: "the isolation and clarification of the image, and the perfecting of a diction that would leave the image unclouded by rhetoric or sentiment." Those two thrusts define in shorthand Williams's concerns over half a century.

A footnote here: in *Metaphor and Reality* (1962), Philip Wheelwright tried to demonstrate that "simplicity cannot for the most part be conveyed simply" by using "The Red Wheelbarrow" as an example of Williams's failure to present the image adequately. That poem failed because "the associations that connect the statement with the experience of one person are unlikely to be available, except by miracle, to another." Only by building up the associations of "simple" components in a poem could a reader "succeed in feeling about it as the poet does." (Perhaps, though, Williams's little poem derives its power through its surface tension. It was not meant, after all, as an example of the deep image.)

Two years before Williams died, Donald Hall's "Introduction" to the Penguin *Contemporary American Poetry* commented succinctly on the passing of the thirty-year orthodoxy led by T. S. Eliot and the academic New Critics. "The only contrary direction which endured throughout the orthodoxy was the direction . . . [of] the colloquial, or the line of William Carlos Williams." And while the orthodoxy was admiring him for his descriptive powers, Williams had really been preoccupied with the American idiom. His line was concerned more with experience than with ideas, and so grounded more solidly in his world. What helped this line to surface, as Hall saw it, was the presence of good editors willing to publish poets like Creeley and Levertov and Duncan and Olson, who "erected a critical standard" for a new poetics. Lowell, the central figure in American poetry in the early sixties, had attempted a synthesis between the orthodoxy and the colloquial in *Life Studies*. (When he added a preface to the second edition of his anthology in 1969, Hall saw Williams's line as "more salient than any other line" in that decade. But he saw, too, that a new orthodoxy of fantasy or neo-surrealism was nudging out Williams's line, and a whole world of black poetry was thriving, largely unnoticed by white America.)

Stephen Whicher and Lars Ahnebrink, in their paperback anthology, *Twelve American Poets* (1961), originally compiled for a Swedish audience, ended a short introduction to a selection of Williams's poems with the comment that, "if American poetry has a future, the road to it is likely to lead through Williams." In the same year Kenneth Rexroth affirmed in his long essay, "The Influence of French Poetry on American" (collected in *Assays*) that Williams was the greatest of "the classic American modernists" and "America's greatest living poet," whose "localism has become international and timeless." Williams was completely at home among the French and the one American poet besides Whitman whom the French could learn most from. His idiom was "identical with that which is the end product of centuries of polish, refinement, tradition and revolution."

By contrast, A. Alvarez's influential "The New Poetry, *or* Beyond the Gentility Principle," his "Introduction" to the 1962 Penguin paperback, *The New Poetry*, did not even mention Williams. Instead, Alvarez focused on Lowell's new nakedness in *Life Studies*. Here was a poetry of "skill and intelligence," coping "openly with the quick of [his] experience, experience sometimes on the edge of disintegration and breakdown." But Alvarez did not mark how it was that Lowell was no longer an adherent "of the cult of rigid impersonality."

With *Life Studies* behind him, Lowell paid tribute to the old man, acknowledging the nature of Williams's influence on him (*HR*, Winter 1961–62). That influence can be at least partially substantiated by comparing *Life Studies* (1959) with *Lord Weary's Castle* (1946) or *The Mills of the Kavanaughs* (1951). There is a marked shift from the academic formalism of Tate and Ransom, which dominated academic poetry during the forties and which was concerned with "making the old metrical forms usable again to express the depths of one's experience," to the freedom and "common style" characteristic of Williams. But even as

Lowell acknowledged his debt to Williams, he also showed why he and Jarrell and the other young American poets of the second generation who grew up in the years just before World War II (except for "our only strong and avant-garde man" at Harvard, James Laughlin) would not then have learned much from Williams. English professors in the late thirties and early forties were "worthy, but outworn and backward-looking scholars, whose tastes in the moderns were most often superficial, random and vulgar." Williams himself was a byline revolutionary whose work was "fresh, secondary and minor," who had done the best work "that free verse could do." By the fifties, formalism had stiffened and the times demanded an experimental art. Lowell had gone to school to Williams again. (Recall, incidentally, that Lowell was one of the first to appreciate *Paterson*, years before his own verse was radically affected by Williams.) When it did come, that change went deep, and Lowell had an understandably difficult time in articulating the precise nature of that debt. But he did come to see the power of Williams's descriptive passages and the "wide clarity and dashing rightness with words, his dignity and almost Alexandrian modulations of voice." He touched something remarkably accurate about the nature of Williams's influence: "Williams enters me, but I cannot enter him. . . . He sees and hears what we all see and hear and what is most obvious, but no one else has found this a help or an inspiration. . . . When I say that I cannot enter him, I am almost saying that I cannot enter America."

When Jarrell delivered his lecture, "50 Years of American Poetry," to the National Poetry Festival in Washington, D. C. on October 22, 1962, he simply presented what he had rifled from his earlier reviews and essays when he came to talk of Williams's place in the American pantheon, which came *after* Frost, Stevens, and Eliot. In the nearly ten years since he had given his verdict on *Paterson*, Jarrell's opinion of Williams had completely frozen. To some of the younger writers hearing his eloquent, rhetorically finished commentary in the fall of 1962, Jarrell's judgment must certainly have sounded a little distant and even unreal, a voice already washed by time.

Speaking for a group of younger writers, LeRoi Jones's introduction to *The Moderns: An Anthology of New Writing in America* (1963) acknowledged that figures like Creeley, Kerouac, Edward Dorn, and himself owed their prose styles "much more to the poems of . . . Williams . . . than to Hemingway's short stories." The restoration of "American poetry to the mainstream of modern poetry after it had been cut off from that tradition by the Anglo-Eliotic domination of the academies" (how closely Jones echoes Williams here) had led, consequently, to a new and fresher American prose. Jones's stress on the local as "what one can see from where one is standing" obviously owes something to Charles Olson's topical divisions, but ultimately it too stems from Williams's preoccupations.

In 1963 John Malcolm Brinnin's *William Carlos Williams*, number 24 in the Pamphlets on American Writers series, also appeared. It was a good, brief overview of its kind, a summary of the preoccupations and biases of critics like Burke and Jarrell, and borrowing heavily from Williams's own critical statements, especially the *Autobiography*. Brinnin commented in turn on the influence on Williams of Keats, Whitman, Pound, the Imagists, the 1913 Armory Show, the Ashcan school, Cubism, and, interestingly, Williams's affinities with Edward Hopper. He gave short, pointed readings of a number of Williams's early poems, including a particularly good one of that cubist experiment, "St. Francis Einstein of the Daffodils," and, of course, "The Red Wheelbarrow." He ignored, curiously, Williams's entire late phase, except for a comment on *Paterson* V. He pointed out Williams's methods of contrast and dispersion in *Paterson*. The method of contrast Brinnin read as a concession to an "academically certifiable poetry" like *The Waste Land*, where the "present is compared with the past in terms of spiritual grace and spiritual vulgarity." But the method of dispersion was uniquely Williams's, shared with action painters like Jackson Pollock: "the release of energy rather than the reassembling of familiar counters," a process poem continually striving to answer the question which its own structures constantly posed. In a poem like *Paterson*, "energy and force take precedence over organization and the graceful disposition of subject matter." Still, Brinnin agreed with Jarrell that *Paterson* was a flawed creation. If it possessed an intellectual integration and a master strategy, Brinnin asserted confusedly, "on an emotive level the poem is vastly uneven and at times hopelessly fragmented." (*If* the poem has an intellectual integrity, the mind, seeing that, assents to the emotional "rightness" of the poem in the same act: integrity is integrity. If Brinnin meant the poem had long flat passages devoid of lyric uplift, that is part of the necessary emotive strategy of every long poem ever written.) Two more commonplaces: as for Williams's prosodic theories,

Brinnin found that to follow them led always to disaster, but that Williams's example "has had tonic effect on a generation of poets not remotely like him." In fact, Williams's theories were so lax as to defy analysis. And yet, in practice, the poems worked. It is, unfortunately, widespread commentary like this—as much as anything—which has led to the acceptance of Williams's concept of the variable foot as a *mystique*, a term which, in the empirical mind, soon collapses to the handier term, "nonsense." Mystique is a critical accretion foreign to Williams's whole sensibility.

Marking the Passing of Williams

When the eulogies came to be written for Williams in the spring and summer of 1963, it was clear the old man had made it. "More than anyone else, he made available to us the whole range of the language," Denise Levertov summed up (*N*, Mar. 16). He had continued to grow until his death, writing his greatest poems in his seventies. For John Ciardi (*Sat R*, Mar. 23) Williams's passing had brought the end of an age, an age when "American poetry threw off its last colonial dependence on England and came securely to rest in the American language." Williams's poetry had returned poetry to the world, Hayden Carruth argued (*NR*, Apr. 13). The man had gone counter to the whole intellectual movement which had tried to constitute itself as "a new reality with its own self-revealing authority." Williams was, instead, "committed to our life, our reality, our enigma." Kenner (*Nat R*, Mar. 26) made one of the boldest claims for Williams, and yet a claim which time will very likely sustain, when he wrote that the man had done his job as a poet "with such passion and tenacity that American poetry groups itself around twin peaks, Williams and Whitman." If *Paterson* was "his most solid achievement," it was his last poems, typed out letter by letter with one finger, which were his "most poignant, simplest and loveliest."

One of the most touching tributes to Williams came from Kenneth Burke (*NYRB*, May 10). This was the man who had known Williams since the early days, who could still harbor a special affection for *Al Que Quiere!*, and who could still wish some publisher might reissue the book "just as it was in the original 1917 edition" for its verse "written into the very constitution of our country." He knew Williams in a way that few others could—as friend, advisor, champion, and he summed up the man's poetics in this way: "whatever may be our uncertainties about the accidents of his doctrine, its essence resides in the kind of physicality imposed upon his poetry by the nature of his work as a physician." Burke had come to see just how deeply "contact" had gone into this man, whose very impatience at not being among things in his retirement was signalled by a rapid gesture of the hands as if he were delivering a baby.

In less than a year three other American poets also passed from the scene as well: Jeffers, Cummings, Frost. Williams, Josephine Jacobsen wrote (*C*, May 10), was "the least inky" of them all. He was a moral poet and a great singer of love. "Asphodel" was "as fine as any poem written in English in the last fifty years." Stephen Stephanchev (*Books*, June 16) commented that Williams had "produced enough work of fine formal control to justify his eminent position." But Kenneth Lamott (*Contact*, July) had his doubts about the notice of Williams which the popular press had given him. "One is moved to despair," he wrote, ". . . by the ease with which the popular press can reduce a first-rate poet into the more palatable picture of a lovable, crotchety small town doctor." Charles Angoff's eulogy (*Lit R*, Summer) was the most embarrassingly romantic of them all. Williams, he said, "was the Great Democrat, searching for more and more rivers and mountains and for lowly men and women to love and to sing about." He was also "Walt Whitman and Abraham Lincoln and Brann the Iconoclast" and many more, "all rolled into one."

Jack Hirschman (*S*, Summer) praised highly Williams's American idiom, which seemed "true to the time and space" in which the poet had lived. Here was a man who could write in the mode of Joyce, could make his "multilevel, multilingual excursions." Still, "he was not at home in that world," but in the world of his own locale. His followers already included Levertov, Creeley, Olson, Gorman. Williams had shown American poets how to care and attend to words within their own language, a language not available to traditional poetry. But even now there were dissonances. "I am tired of all agonists, missionaries, and philosophers engaged in the cause of finding A REAL TRUE HONEST TO GOD AMERICAN-TYPE POETRY," Lewis Turco slammed into Hirschman in the next issue (*S*, Autumn). Turco wished that Hirschman and Shapiro and all the others who wanted poets to "go out and memorize . . . Williams and say . . . 'Song of Myself' every evening before bedtime" might be rounded up and sent to Sheboygan to howl as they would.

In a quieter vein, the *Beloit Poetry Journal*, under David Ignatow's editorship, published a "Memorial Chapbook" that same fall,
with poems in Williams's honor by, among others, Blackburn,
Merwin, LeRoi Jones, Babette Deutsch, Levertov, Snyder, Am-
mons, Creeley, and Bly. "At this high moment of his fame, it is
almost superfluous to enumerate the man's qualities as poet, they
are so well known, loved and appreciated." Ignatow singled out
Paterson in particular for praise. That poem, like *Leaves of Grass*,
was "a work unprecedented in scope and intent in American literature." *Paterson* too was the product of a "harsh reality in colli-
sion with an exuberant and loving man."

The eulogies were in, the initial summaries registered. Williams
had finally entered the sea. His work was finished, had, in fact, to
enter now a new dimension. In a radically new sense, Williams
became his words.

References

Adams, Phoebe
   1957. "Poetry, an Unrewarded Art," *Atlantic Monthly*. Sept., pp.
   84–85.
   1959. "Lines for a Portrait," *Atlantic Monthly*. July, pp. 80–81.
   1962. "Potpourri," *Atlantic Monthly*. Aug., p. 145.
Aiken, Conrad
   1951. "William Carlos Williams' Rich, Sprawling Memories,"
   New York Herald Tribune Book Review. Sept. 16, p. 1.
Alexander, Sidney
   1955. "Apostle of Impulse," *Commentary*. Jan., pp. 96–98.
Alvarez, Anthony
   1962. "Introduction" to *The New Poetry*. London: Penguin. pp.
   21–32.
   1967. "Introduction" to *Miroslaw Holub: Selected Poems*. Baltimore: Penguin, pp. 9–17.
Angoff, Charles
   1963. "Three Towering Figures," *Literary Review*. Summer, pp.
   423–29.
Anonymous
   1951a. "An American Poet," *Times Literary Supplement*. Mar. 23,
   p. 178.
   1951b. "Part-Time Poet," *Time*. Oct. 8, pp. 118–20.
   1952. "Poet of an Industrial Society," *Times Literary Supplement*.
   Feb. 1, p. 95.

Beum, R. L.
1952a. "The Neglect of Williams," *Poetry*. Aug., pp. 291–93.
1952b. "The Recent Books of W. C. Williams," *Golden Goose*. Oct., pp. 33–35.
1953. "The Baby Glove of a Pharaoh," *Perspective*. Autumn, pp. 217–23.

Bittner, William
1957. "William Carlos Williams: Muse or Patron Saint: His Works," *Saturday Review of Literature*. Sept. 7, pp. 13–14.

Blackmur, R. P.
1952. "Lord Tennyson's Scissors: 1912–1950," *Kenyon Review*. Winter; reprinted in *Form and Value in Modern Poetry*, pp. 369–88. Garden City, N.Y.: Doubleday.

Bompard, Paola
1955. "Profilo di William Carlos Williams," *Studi Americani*. pp. 235–55.

Breit, Harvey
1950. "Talk with W. C. Williams," *New York Times Book Review*. Jan. 15, p. 18.
1951. "First Person Singular," *Atlantic Monthly*. Oct., pp. 82–83.

Brinnin, John Malcolm
1963. *William Carlos Williams*. Pamphlets on American Writers Series, no. 24. Minneapolis: Univ. of Minnesota Pr.

Brooks, Van Wyck
1961. "Introduction" to *The Farmers' Daughters*. New York: New Directions, pp. vii–xii.

Caldwell, James
1949. "A Burly Fact of Nature," *Saturday Review of Literature*. Aug. 20, p. 27.

Cambon, Glauco
1961. "William Carlos Williams and Ezra Pound: Two Examples of Open Poetry," *College English*. Mar. pp. 387–89.

Carruth, Hayden
1950. "The Work of W. C. Williams," *Nation*. July 15, pp. 64–65.
1951. "More Poems by Dr. Williams," *Nation*. Mar. 3, pp. 209–10.
1963. "William Carlos Williams as One of Us," *New Republic*. Apr. 13, pp. 30–32.

Carter, Thomas
1955. Review, *Shenandoah*. Spring, pp. 72–80.

Ciardi, John
1950. "Poets and Prizes," *College English*. Dec., pp. 127–34.
1954. "Thing Is the Form," *Nation*. Apr. 24, pp. 368–69.
1958. "How Free Is Free Verse?" *Saturday Review of Literature*. Oct. 11, p. 38.

1959. "A Flame to Her Son," *Saturday Review of Literature.* July 11, pp. 32–33.

1963. "Manner of Speaking," *Saturday Review of Literature.* Mar. 23, p. 20.

Cole, Thomas

1956. "Give, Sympathize, Control," *Voices.* Jan.–Apr., pp. 35–39.

Cook, Albert

˙ 1959. "Modern Verse: Diffusion as a Principle of Composition," *Kenyon Review.* Spring, pp. 199–220; revised and reprinted in *Prisms: Studies in Modern Literature,* by Albert S. Cook, pp. 3–24. Bloomington: Indiana Univ. Pr., 1967.

Creeley, Robert

1954a. "A Character for Love," *Black Mountain Review.* Summer, pp. 45–48; reprinted in *William Carlos Williams: A Collection of Critical Essays,* ed. J. Hillis Miller. Englewood Cliffs, N.J.: Prentice-Hall, 1966.

1954b. Review of *Selected Essays, Black Mountain Review.* Winter, pp. 53–58.

1962. "The Fact of His Life," *Nation.* Oct. 13, p. 224.

Cunliffe, Marcus

1961. *The Literature of the United States.* Baltimore: Penguin.

Daiches, David

1949. "Four Modern Poets," *New York Herald Tribune Book Review.* Jan. 30, p. 17.

1951. "Some Recent Poetry," *Yale Review.* Autumn, pp. 153–57.

Davie, Donald

1959. "The Legacy of Fenimore Cooper," *Essays in Criticism.* 9, no. 3: 222–34.

Davis, Robert Gorham

1950. "Stories, to Mr. Williams, Are Swift Experiences," *New York Times Book Review.* Dec. 17, p. 1.

Deutsch, Babette

1950a. "Gusty Tales from Over Passaic Way," *New York Herald Tribune Book Review.* Dec. 3, p. 5.

1950b. "His Arcadia Lies in the American Suburbs," *New York Herald Tribune Book Review.* Dec. 17, p. 4.

1952. "The Earthly and the Definite" in *Poetry in Our Time,* pp. 84–128. New York: Doubleday. Revised 1963.

1955. "The Morality of the Poet," *Poetry.* Mar., pp. 351–55.

1958. "Good Poetry and Good Talk," *New York Herald Tribune Book Review.* July 6, p. 9.

1959. "Picture of a Poet's Mother," *New York Herald Tribune Book Review.* June 21, p. 4.

Donoghue, Denis

1958. "For a Redeeming Language," *Twentieth Century Liter-*

ature. June, pp. 532–42; reprinted in *William Carlos Williams: A Collection of Critical Essays*, ed. J. Hillis Miller, pp. 121–31. Englewood Cliffs, N.J.: Prentice-Hall, 1966.

1965. *Connoisseurs of Chaos: Ideas of Order in Modern American Poetry*. New York: Macmillan.

Dudek, Louis

1958. "A Note on Metrics," *Delta* (Cambridge). Oct., pp. 15–17.

Eberhart, Richard

1950a. "The Image of Ourselves," *New York Times Book Review*. Feb. 12, p. 5.

1950b. "Poetry, for Mr. Williams, Is as Natural as Breathing," *New York Times Book Review*. Dec. 17, p. 1.

1952. "Things as They Are," *New Republic*. Nov. 10, pp. 20–21.

1954. "Prose, Poetry, and the Love of Life," *Saturday Review of Literature*. Nov. 20, pp. 37–38.

1956. "American Passion," *Saturday Review of Literature*. Feb. 18, p. 49.

Eckman, Frederick

1952. "The Recent Books of W. C. Williams," *Golden Goose*. Oct., pp. 35–38.

Edelstein, Sanford

1953. "William Carlos Williams: Essential Speech," *Perspective*. Autumn, pp. 224–28.

Ellman, Richard

1952. "The Doctor in Search of Himself," *Kenyon Review*. Summer, pp. 510–12.

Emerson, Richard Wirtz

1952. "The Recent Books of W. C. Williams," *Golden Goose*. Oct., pp. 38–40.

1954. "Books and Opinion," *Golden Goose*. Apr., pp. 133–35.

Engel, Bernard

1961. "The Verse Line of Dr. Williams: A Fact of the Thing Itself," *Papers of the Michigan Academy of Science, Arts, and Letters*, pp. 665–70.

1962. "Dr. Williams as Exhorter: The Meaning of Americanism," *Papers of the Michigan Academy of Science, Arts, and Letters*, pp. 579–86.

Fiscalini, Janet

1959. "Poet Americanus," *Commonweal*. Sept. 18, pp. 519–21.

Fitzgerald, Robert

1949. "Bejewelled, the Great Sun," *New Republic*. Apr. 25, pp. 22–23.

Fitzsimmons, Thomas

1955. "A Box of Old Forms," *New Republic*. Feb. 7, pp. 18–20.

Flint, F. W.
  1950. "I Will Teach You My Townspeople," *Kenyon Review*.
  Summer, pp. 537–43.
Frankenberg, Lloyd
  1949. *Pleasure Dome: On Reading Modern Poetry*. New York:
  Houghton Mifflin, pp. 286–96. Reprinted. Staten Island, N.Y.:
  Gordian Pr., 1968.
Franklyn, A. Frederick
  1963. "The Truth and the Poem," *Trace*. Spring, pp. 32, 79–83.
Frazer, G. S.
  1952. "Old Tricks and Young Dogs," *New Statesman*. Apr. 12,
  p. 440.
Garrigue, Jean
  1957. "America Revisited," *Poetry*. Aug., pp. 315–20.
Gibbs, Alonzo
  1963. "Naer Het Leven," *Voices*. Jan.–Apr., pp. 46–49.
Goodman, Paul
  1956. "Between the Flash and the Thunderstroke," *Poetry*. Mar.,
  pp. 366–70.
Gregory, Horace
  1946a. "William Carlos Williams and the 'Common Reader,'"
  Briarcliff Quarterly. Oct., pp. 186–88.
  1946b. (and Marya Zaturenska) "A Formal 'Objectivist': William Carlos Williams" in *A History of American Poetry, 1900–
  1940*, pp. 207–16. New York: Harcourt. Reprinted. Staten Island,
  N.Y.: Gordian Pr., 1969.
Hall, Donald
  1962. "Introduction" to *Contemporary American Poetry*. Baltimore: Penguin, pp. 21–22.
Halsband, Robert
  1950. "I Lived among These People," *Saturday Review of Literature*. Dec. 9, pp. 14–15.
Hardwick, Elizabeth
  1953. "A Large and Difficult Place," *Western Review*. Summer,
  pp. 286–88.
Hartung, Charles
  1958. "A Poetry of Experience," *University of Kansas City Review*. Autumn, pp. 65–69.
Heal, Edith
  1958. "Introduction" to *I Wanted to Write a Poem*. Boston:
  Beacon Pr., pp. v–ix.
Heilman, Robert
  1953. "Some Notes on Impressionistic Literary Criticism," *Western Review*. Summer, pp. 288–92.
Henderson, Archibald
  1963. "The Gypsy and the Monk: Lorca and W. C. Williams,"

Voices. Sept.–Dec., pp. 51–53.

Hewes, Henry

1959. "Head-Shaking and Shakespeare," *Saturday Review of Literature.* Jan. 31, p. 24.

Hiler, Hilaire

1946. "A Rare Phenomenon," *Briarcliff Quarterly.* Oct., p. 188.

Hirschman, Jack

1963. "William Carlos Williams," *Shenandoah.* Summer, pp. 3–10.

Hoffman, Frederick

1954. "Williams and His Muse," *Poetry.* Apr., pp. 23–27; revised and reprinted in his *The Twenties: American Writing in the Postwar Decade.* New York: Viking, 1955.

Honig, Edwin

1956. "Poetry Chronicle," *Partisan Review.* Winter, pp. 115–20.

Hoskins, Katherine

1957. "Sweating Out a Brithright," *Nation.* Oct. 5, pp. 225–27.

Howe, Irving

1961. "Stories: New, Old, and Sometimes Good," *New Republic.* Nov. 13, pp. 18–19, 22–23.

Humphries, Rolfe

1948. "Verse Chronicle," *Nation.* Dec. 25, pp. 730–31.

1949. "Verse Chronicle," *Nation.* July 9, p. 44.

Ignatow, David

1963. "Introduction to William Carlos Williams: A Memorial Chapbook," *Beloit Poetry Journal.* Fall, pp. 1–2.

Jacobs, Willis

1967. "The Attic which is Desire," *Explicator.* Mar., p. 61.

1970a. "Williams' 'Great Mullen,' " *Explicator.* Mar., p. 63.

1970b. "Williams 'Between Walls,' " *Explicator.* Apr., p. 68.

1970c. "Williams' 'The Young Housewife,' " *Explicator.* May, p. 81.

1970d. "Williams' 'To Waken an Old Lady,' " *Explicator.* Sept., p. 6.

1971. "Williams' 'The Hunter,' " *Explicator.* Mar., p. 71.

Jacobsen, Josephine

1963. "Legacy of Three Poets," *Commonweal.* May 10, pp. 189–92.

Jarrell, Randall

1949. "Introduction" to *Selected Poems of William Carlos Williams.* New York: New Directions, pp. ix–xiii.

1963. "50 Years of American Poetry," *Prairie Schooner.* Spring, pp. 1–27; reprinted in *The Third Book of Criticism,* pp. 295–334. New York: Farrar, Straus and Giroux.

Jones, LeRoi

1963. (editor) "Introduction" to *The Moderns: An Anthology of New Writing in America.* New York: Corinth, pp. ix–xvi.

Josephson, Matthew
   1951. "Memoirs of a Doctor-Poet," *Saturday Review of Literature.* Oct. 20, pp. 10–11.
Kay, Arthur M.
   1962. Review, *Arizona Quarterly.* Winter, pp. 368–70.
Kenner, Hugh
   1953. "A Note on *The Great American Novel,*" *Perspective.* Autumn, pp. 177–82; reprinted in *Gnomon* and in *William Carlos Williams: A Collection of Critical Essays,* ed. J. Hillis Miller. Englewood Cliffs, N.J.: Prentice-Hall, 1966.
   1958a. "Dr. Williams Shaping His Axe," *Gnomon.* New York: New Directions, pp. 55–66.
   1958b. "Columbus's Log-Book," *Poetry.* June, pp. 174–78.
   1959. "To Measure Is All We Know," *Poetry.* May, pp. 127–32.
Koch, Vivienne
   1950. *William Carlos Williams.* New York: New Directions. Rev. ed. New York: Kraus, 1973.
   1952a. "Williams: The Social Mask," *Poetry.* May, pp. 89–95.
   1952b. "The Man and the Poet," *Kenyon Review.* Summer, pp. 502–10.
Kunitz, Stanley
   1962. "Frost, Williams, & Company," *Harper's.* Oct., pp. 100–3, 108.
Lamott, Kenneth
   1963. "A Pilgrimage to Rutherford," *Contact.* July, pp. 41–43.
Laughlin, James
   1946. "A Publisher's Report," *Briarcliff Quarterly.* Oct., pp. 189–92.
Levertov, Denise
   1963. "William Carlos Williams," *Nation.* Mar. 16, p. 230.
Lowell, Robert
   1961. "William Carlos Williams," *Hudson Review.* Winter, pp. 530–36.
McCormick, John
   1954. "Poet and Anti-Poet," *Western Review.* Autumn, pp. 65–72.
Malcolm, Donald
   1959. "Off Broadway," *New Yorker.* Jan. 24, pp. 74, 76.
Martz, Louis
   1950. "Poets of Our Climate," *Yale Review.* Sept., pp. 152–54.
   1955. "New Poetry: In the Pastoral Mode," *Yale Review.* Winter, pp. 301–9.
Miles, Josephine
   1951. "The Primary Language of Poetry in the 1940's," in *The Continuity of Poetic Language.* Rev. ed. New York: Octagon.
Miller, J. Hillis
   1966a. *Poets of Reality: Six Twentieth Century Writers.* Rev. ed. New York: Atheneum.

1966b. (editor) *William Carlos Williams: A Collection of Critical Essays*. Englewood Cliffs, N.J.: Prentice-Hall.

Millett, Fred B.
1951. Review, *American Literature*. Jan., pp. 533–34.

Mitchell, Rogers
1963. "Wallace Stevens's 'Spaniard of the Rose': William Carlos Williams," *Notes and Queries*. Oct., pp. 381–82.

Moore, Marianne
1946. "With Regard to William Carlos Williams," *Briarcliff Quarterly*. Oct., p. 192.

Morse, Samuel French
1963. "Poetry 1962: A Partial View," *Contemporary Literature*. Autumn, pp. 367–80.

O'Connor, William Van
1953. "The Hero with the Guileless Face," *Western Review*. Summer, pp. 293–99.

Palmer, J. E.
1955. "Seven Voices, Seven Styles," *Sewanee Review*. Spring, pp. 287–96.

Pearce, Roy Harvey
1952. "The Poet as Person," *Yale Review*. Mar., pp. 421–40; reprinted in *Interpretations of American Literature*, eds. Charles Feidelson, Jr. and Paul Brodtkorb, Jr. New York: Oxford Univ. Pr.
1961. "Williams and the 'New Mode'" in *The Continuity of American Poetry*, pp. 335–48. Princeton, N.J.: Princeton Univ. Pr.

Pearson, Norman Holmes
1957. "Williams, New Jersey," *Literary Review*. Autumn, pp. 29–36.
1962. "Williams Collected," *Yale Review*. Winter, pp. 329–32.

Pratt, William
1963. (editor) "Introduction" to *The Imagist Poem: Modern Poetry in Miniature*. New York: Dutton, pp. 11–39.

Racey, Edgar F.
1963. "Pound and Williams: The Poet as Renewer," *Bucknell Review*. Mar., pp. 21–30.

Rexroth, Kenneth
1946. "A Letter to William Carlos Williams," *Briarcliff Quarterly*. Oct., pp. 193–95.
1954. "A Poet Sums Up," *New York Times Book Review*. Mar. 28, p. 5.
1961a. "Master of Those Who Know," *New Leader*. Dec. 11, pp. 29–30.
1961b. "The Influence of French Poetry on American," in *Assays*, pp. 143–74. New York: New Directions.

1961c. "A Public Letter for William Carlos Williams' Seventy-fifth Birthday," in *Assays,* pp. 202–5. New York: New Directions.

Rodman, Selden

1950. "William Carlos Williams: Serious, Humane, Tireless, New as in 1909," *New York Herald Tribune Book Review.* Mar. 5, p. 5.

1951. "A Primitive Unspoiled," *New York Times Book Review.* Sept. 16, p. 6.

Rosenthal, M. L.

1951. "In the Roar of the Present," *New Republic.* Aug. 27, pp. 18–19.

1958. "Salvo for William Carlos Williams," *Nation.* May 31, pp. 497, 500.

1960. *The Modern Poets: A Critical Introduction.* New York: Oxford Univ. Pr., pp. 113–22.

1962. "William Carlos Williams and Some Young Germans," *Massachusetts Review.* Winter, pp. 337–41.

Roth, Russell

1953. "In the American Grain," *Western Review.* Summer, pp. 277–86.

Salomon, I. L.

1952. "Candor and Science," *Saturday Review of Literature.* Mar. 15, p. 14.

Schneps, Maurice

1961. "William Carlos Williams; A Dialogue," *Orient/West.* pp. 77–82.

Scott, Winfield T.

1952. "Odd, Wonderful Love Letter," *New York Herald Tribune Book Review.* Nov. 2, p. 6.

1954. "William Carlos Williams, Poet, at 71: Thoughtful, Grave and Lively," *New York Herald Tribune Book Review.* Mar. 28, p. 5.

1957. "William Carlos Williams: Muse or Patron Saint: His Letters," *Saturday Review of Literature.* Sept. 7, pp. 14, 37.

1958. "Some Talk About Verse," *New York Times Book Review.* Apr. 13, p. 26.

Shapiro, Karl

1948. "Study of 'Philomena Andronico'," in *Poets at Work,* ed. Charles D. Abbott, pp. 105–11. New York: Harcourt.

1960. "William Carlos Williams: The True Contemporary," in *Start with the Sun: Studies in Cosmic Poetry,* pp. 206–25. Lincoln: Univ. of Nebraska Pr. Revised and reprinted in *In Defense of Ignorance,* pp. 143–69. New York: Random House, 1960.

Sheeler, Charles

1946. "In a Handful of Pebbles," *Briarcliff Quarterly.* Oct., p. 204.

Smith, A. J. M.
1954. "Refining Fire: The Meaning and Use of Poetry," *Queen's Quarterly*. Autumn, pp. 355–56.

Smith, Grover
1953. "On Poets and Poetry," *New Mexico Quarterly*. Autumn, pp. 317–29.

Solt, Mary Ellen
1960. "William Carlos Williams: Poems in the American Idiom," *Folio*, pp. 3–28.
1962. "William Carlos Williams: Idiom and Structure," *Massachusetts Review*. Winter, pp. 304–18.

Sorrentino, Gilbert
1961. "Some Notes toward a Paper on Prosody," *Yugen* 7: 34–37.

Spencer, Benjamin T.
1963a. Review, *Modern Drama*. May, pp. 97–98.
1963b. "Doctor Williams' American Grain," *Tennessee Studies in Literature*. pp. 1–16.

Stepanchev, Stephen
1963. "A Medley of Verse," *New York Herald Tribune Book Review*. June 16, p. 10.

Stephens, Alan
1963. "Dr. Williams and Tradition," *Poetry*. Feb., pp. 360–62.

Stone, Irving
1952. "Two Autobiographies," *Yale Review*. Winter, pp. 316–18.

Tate, Allen
1954. (and Frances Cheney) *Sixty American Poets, 1896–1944*. Washington: Library of Congress. Reprinted. Detroit: Gale, pp. 143–46.

Thirlwall, John
1954. "The Letters of William Carlos Williams," *Golden Goose*. Apr., pp. 124–32.
1957a. "William Carlos Williams as Correspondent," *Literary Review*. Autumn, pp. 13–28.
1957b. "Introduction" to *Selected Letters of William Carlos Williams*. New York: McDowell, Obolensky, pp. xiii–xix.
1957c. "The Lost Poems of William Carlos Williams or The Past Recaptured," *New Directions 16*, pp. 3–45.
1961. "Notes on William Carlos Williams as Playwright," in *Many Loves*, pp. 429–37. New York: New Directions.
1962a. "Two Cities: Paris and Paterson," *Massachusetts Review*. Winter, pp. 284–91.
1962b. "Ten Years of a New Rhythm," in *Pictures from Brueghel*, pp. 183–84. New York: New Directions.
1963. "An Editorial Note," in *The Collected Later Poems*, pp. 249–51. Rev. ed. New York: New Directions.

1965. Review, *American Literature*. Jan., pp. 539–40.

1970. "William Carlos Williams and John C. Thirlwall: Record of a Ten-Year Relationship," *Yale University Library Gazette*. July, pp. 15–21.

Turco, Lewis

1963. "For Poets in Search of Poetry Prose-Wise," *Shenandoah*. Autumn, pp. 67–69.

Turnbull, Gael

1958. "A Visit to William Carlos Williams: Sept., 1958," *Mica*. June, pp. 16–22.

Van Duyn, Mona

1953. "To 'Make Light of It' as Fictional Technique," *Perspective*. Autumn, pp. 230–38.

Vazakas, Byron

1952. "Three Modern Old Masters: Moore-Stevens-Williams," *New Mexico Quarterly*. Spring, pp. 431–44.

Wasserstrom, William

1963. *The Time of the Dial*. Syracuse, N.Y.: Syracuse Univ. Pr., pp. 92–93, 136, 144–45, passim.

West, Paul

1960. "Poetic Form Today," *College English*. Spring.

West, Ray B.

1954. "The Modern Writer," *College English*. Jan., pp. 207–15.

Wheelwright, Philip

1962. *Metaphor and Reality*. Bloomington: Indiana Univ. Pr., pp. 158–63.

Whicher, Stephen

1961. (and Lars Ahnebrink) *Twelve American Poets*. New York: Oxford Univ. Pr.

Whittemore, Reed

1958. "Five Old Masters and Their Sensibilities," *Yale Review*. Winter, pp. 281–88.

1959. "What Is the Secret," *Virginia Quarterly Review*. Autumn, pp. 637–39.

Wilbur, Richard

1950. "Seven Poets," *Sewanee Review*. Jan., pp. 130–43.

Wilson, T. C.

1946. "The Animate Touch," *Briarcliff Quarterly*. Oct., pp. 195–98.

Zabel, Morton Dauwen

1957. "Poet, Doctor and, by Choice, a Member of the Crowd," *New York Times Book Review*. Sept. 1, p. 3.

Zukofsky, Louis

1950. "Poetry in a Modern Age," *Poetry*. June, pp. 177–80.

1958. "The Best Human Value," *Nation*. May 31, pp. 500–2.

1962. "An Old Note on William Carlos Williams," *Massachusetts Review*. Winter, pp. 301–2.

CHAPTER 5

The Critical Current:
Towards Canonization, 1963-1973

In the decade since his death there has been a critical explosion focusing on Williams's central importance for modern American poetry. This chapter will review first Williams's posthumous and quizzical reception in England as a result of his finally being published in that country. Charles Tomlinson's succinct and intelligent review of Williams's British reception in his 1972 *Penguin Critical Anthology* holds that by the mid-sixties Williams was being taken seriously by the British. This seems questionable, for, except in significant but isolated instances (the most important being Tomlinson's own poetic example), Williams does not seem to have made any serious impact on the shape of modern British poetry. And English critics still get their backs up whenever they think Williams is being thrust upon them. (Schmidt and Lindop's *British Poetry since 1960*, published at the same time that Tomlinson's anthology came out, is only one of the more recent cries to resist a "prescriptive" assault on the English literary terrain by Williams's followers.)

This chapter goes on to review the early, quiet, posthumous response to Williams by Americans, and then charts the massive critical reappraisal of him which followed J. Hillis Miller's evaluation of Williams in *Poets of Reality* in 1966. Following the parallel lines established in the two previous chapters, this chapter reviews, first, the essays on *Paterson* (the single work which continues to receive the most critical attention), and then the essays treating Williams's other writings. Finally, the longer commentaries are considered in the following order: (1) the overviews of Williams —Wagner, Ostrom, Whitaker, Guimond, Breslin; (2) the *Paterson* commentaries—Peterson, Conarroe, Sankey; (3) the commentaries on other aspects of Williams—Paul, Dijkstra, the Siegels, and Mazzaro.

Posthumous British Reception

Two days after Williams died, his work found a British publishing house prepared to give him its imprint. MacGibbon and
Kee, sensing "a climate of opinion" favorable to Williams, contracted with New Directions to bind and distribute copies of selected books of Williams's in England. *Pictures from Brueghel*
(containing *The Desert Music* and *Journey to Love*) was the first
to be published, in late October, 1963. It was followed by the
complete *Paterson* (August 1964); *Collected Later Poems* (May
1965); the first two parts of the Stecher trilogy in July, 1965 and
February, 1966, respectively; *Collected Earlier Poems*, *In the
American Grain*, and Rosenthal's *Reader*, all in March, 1967; and
then subsequent volumes until the early seventies.

Williams had "made it" in England, largely through his followers and the Beats, who had made a strong impact on England in
the fifties. That country witnessed a flurry of critical activity over
Williams from late 1963 until late 1967, a period almost exactly
corresponding to MacGibbon and Kee's publication of Williams.
This activity was, on the one side, a mixture of apology for having turned deaf ears for so long on a major American voice and
a determination to rectify that parochialism. Such was the stance
taken by such avant-garde magazines as *Agenda, Chelsea, Review,*
and *Encounter.* On the other side were the polite listeners, sympathetic but uncomprehending, who puzzled over what, really, this
fuss was all about. There were even a few older voices, like Symonds, out of an earlier age, who could still wax apoplectic over
Williams and his influence on young British and American writers.

Few of the English critics or even the Americans writing for
English publications added anything essentially new to an understanding of Williams. Their primary function was, really, to pre-
pare an audience to listen attentively to this most American of
poets. But there were almost insuperable difficulties in understanding what Williams was up to. First of all, until MacGibbon and
Kee had given Williams an imprint, he had been virtually *un-
heard* of in England; Koch's study of the man was almost unobtainable there. And experimental volumes like *Kora in Hell,
Spring and All,* and *The Great American Novel* were almost impossible to come by in America, let alone England. Since a critical
vocabulary grounded in Williams's own theory of poetry did not
exist in print, Williams's English advocates were thrown back on
the formulations of his disciples: Creeley, Duncan, and especially

Olson in his 1950 Projectivist manifesto. J. Hillis Miller's 1966 collection of essays on and by Williams also helped shed more light on Williams and even offered a preliminary critical vocabulary. But it is interesting that Williams's *Selected Essays* was not one of the volumes chosen by MacGibbon and Kee for a British audience, so deep did the feeling persist that Williams was not a theoretician of any real importance.

The October-November, 1963, issue of *Agenda* was the first English publication ever to be given over to Williams. To introduce him to the English, it printed all of "Of Asphodel, that Greeny Flower," one of Williams's most traditionally oriented pieces, with its grave quasi-iambic music, its wide range of flower symbols, its familiarity with a long tradition of painters and writers. Peter Whigham's strategy in his essay introducing Williams to his countrymen was to compare Williams with his widely known counterpart, Ezra Pound. They were both Americans, but Williams was more deeply in the primitive American grain, "like the wagon master of those prairie caravans, [moving] daily through totally new territory." Like most of the English critics, Whigham saw Williams's best work in the later poems. Whigham had special reason for paying his respects to Williams, for it was the old man who had read and admired the Englishman's translations of Catullus in the early sixties when they were still circulating in manuscript, hunting for a publisher. Williams singled out Whigham in his 1960 interview with Walter Sutton as one of the few younger English writers who had dared to go against his entrenched elders. He encouraged Whigham, called him "the most delightful translator of Catullus" and his translations "bawdy," "undisciplined," among the best. Whigham had clearly been listening to Williams's measures, even to rendering Catullus into the variable foot. And when he came to publish his *The Poems of Catullus* in the Penguin Classics in 1966, he dedicated the book to the memory of the master who had in his last great years made Theocritus and Sappho his own contemporaries.

David Ignatow (*Chelsea*, Jan. 1964) stressed Williams's centrality in establishing a voice counter to Eliot and the New Criticism, a voice which had, perhaps, Allen Ginsberg as its chief spokesman. Williams could claim as disciples poet-scholars like Zukofsky and the Olson of the *Maximus* poems. And there were other American poets who had been influenced by Williams's "esthetic of personal confrontation" with one's subject: poets like Levertov, Lowell, Duncan, Roethke, Jarrell, Rexroth, Vazakas. But Ignatow also warned that there was a current which ran counter to Williams and which helped to undermine his most important value as a poet. For writers like Ginsberg, even as they paid homage to Williams, had rejected his "ethos of the integrated individual." In "The New American Decadence" (*Delta*, Spring 1966), Richard Bruce-Wilson also called attention to Williams's difference from younger disciples like Denise Levertov, whose work, he said, did not, "for the unconverted, possess either the same degree, or even the same kind, of merit."

In the same month that Ignatow's essay appeared, Charles Tomlinson interviewed Robert Creeley (*R*, Jan. 1964), focusing on the Black Mountain school and on Williams's influence on that movement. Tomlinson was trying to get the writers in this American camp a hearing in England, and he knew how difficult this would be. "The English reader," Tomlinson noted, "grows lazy once he gets to the American-sounding W. C. Williams—indeed, it is possible for Kenneth Allott in his *Penguin Book of Contemporary Verse* to boast of his indifference to Williams as though it were a matter for self-congratulation." Creeley's own comments on the differences between himself and Williams, and the differences between Olson and Williams and Pound, on the nature of the poetic line stemming out of Whitman were perceptive, discriminating, important. One senses here a man concerned with the living fabric of an ongoing, dynamic tradition rather than with merely summing up a historical event, as one senses in the *Times Literary Supplement* reviews.

"I find it a puzzle what to say about William Carlos Williams," commented P. N. Furbank (*L*, April 1964). And Geoffrey Grigson could still, as he had thirty years before, dismiss Williams as a simple simon, except for his late "Asphodel," with its "European myth and experience" (*NS*, May 1964). Williams's poetry was "full of isolated descriptive acts that are simply neat and inconsequential and in the end it is surprising how narrowly suburban his range of interest seems," the *Times Literary Supplement* reported in May, 1964. Williams's lifelong concern with prosody was really more a concern to free himself "from the English metrical vice than to maintain any really serious endeavour for a distinctively American speech-movement." It was all "trickery and at worst quite arbitrary." "Asphodel," on the other hand, was a fine poem. Tomlinson tried to educate this reviewer's ear in an exchange of correspondence, but the reviewer, typically, opted firmly for his own ear. In September, another anonymous *Times* reviewer, this time looking at *Paterson*, found it lacking as "a unified poem" and as such had to "be judged a failure, probably an irresponsible one," spilling as it progressed with "accelerating abandon."

Williams was uneven, Ian Hamilton wrote (*LM*, July 1964); he was a poet who wrote a thinly documentary poetry which frequently demonstrated "those gifts of observation which one expects from a rather average novelist." At his best he could shape into metaphor "his concrete materials" by the strength of his "difficult compassion." But Williams's "private measure," he complained, "not only assaults the traditional metric but also the conventions of ordinary speech," doing so "in a spirit of gratuitous rebellion." There was too much of "a convention of the halt" in Williams; one tired of it, sought out, rather, those moments which were most alert to "the habits of ordinary speech."

"I agree with G. S. Fraser that British readers cannot *hear* Williams' rhythms," Donald Davie wrote in the December 1964 *Review*. "I often doubt if Americans can hear them either." Davie accused Williams of "a poetics of ad-libbing" in "Asphodel", starting far from his subject and then talking "his way nervously nearer and nearer to it." Still, Williams could at times break through to "a valuably childlike naiveté of perception," to "the tone of the true naif, piercing and unforgettable." And as late as June 1967 Julian Symonds (*NS*) could dismiss Williams's line of development as a new "heresy," and Williams as an "anti-intellectual fake, a purveyor of half a dozen kinds of false simplicity."

There were a few good reviews which sought to educate as much as they judged. Among these was Thomas Clark's review of the *Collected Later Poems* (*NS*, July 23, 1965). Clark pointed out that Williams's work differed from the other Imagists "by his ability to write from within the act of perception, making his poem a mark of the complex interaction between the manifested field and the mind's gesture to apprehend it." His was a syntax which sought to reproduce "the living procedure of perception, a linear, disjunctive, groping movement" in which anything like a total view could "be gained only as hindsight." It was the articulation of a nervous dynamism in Williams's images which particularly impressed him.

There were also a number of intelligent essays on Williams. "American Poetry in the Thirties: Some Revisions and Bearings (*Review*, Fall 1964), by Eric Mottram was one. Mottram's argument was that the line of development springing out of *Spring and All* (1923) and moving through Zukofsky's Objectivist platform (1931) had in fact "produced most of what is good in American poetry" since 1945. Covering some of the ground which Hugh Kenner had covered nearly a decade before, but extending and documenting it more thoroughly, Mottram showed how long had been Williams's concern with poetics and the nature of measure, a concern which had produced a poetics based on "Cubist dislocation and reassemblage." Williams, he warned his British readers, was not a poet who could "be approached with the instruments of culture-criticism." He would have to be listened to on his own terms.

"The Making of Paterson," which Mottram published in *Stand* in 1965 (and reprinted in Mazzaro's collection), makes an excellent introduction to the genesis of *Paterson* and catalogues in workmanlike fashion its various themes. While there was little that was new here, Mottram used his sources judiciously and presented them clearly and vigorously. In particular, he suggested how deeply and how early the *Cantos* became the paradigmatic structure for the long poem. Speaking of Williams's 1931 essay on the *XXX Cantos*, "Excerpts from a Critical Sketch," Mottram wrote that *Paterson*'s solution, like the *Cantos*, would be " 'analytical,' not simply 'mass fusion' or even 'synthesis' at any profound level." *Paterson*'s strategy would imitate the *Cantos:* "a shot through all material—a true and somewhat old-fashioned analysis" of both men's worlds. What Mottram did not take sufficient cognizance of, however, was the unifying nature of that "shot" which magnetized the disparate particles to itself.

David Ferry's "The Diction of American Poetry" in *American Poetry*, edited by Irvin Ehrenpreis (London, 1965), contained a helpful commentary on Williams's poems as *acts*. Ferry saw that Williams's insistence that we write from our own ground was no mere American chauvinism but rather a way of realizing on paper "the qualities of a place in relation to the life which occupies it." Denis Donoghue, comparing Stevens and Williams in his *Connoisseurs of Chaos* (1965) concluded that, while "Stevens was teasing out the problems of epistemology, Williams was hacking through the undergrowth of American history, trying to discover what had happened." He saw Williams as the one committed "to the terms of action, contact, time, history, motive, purpose, direction, end."

Thom Gunn's essay (*Encounter*, July 1965) presented, in effect, an overview of Williams's whole career and his tremendous influence on the younger poets. First Gunn attended to the charge of Williams's anti-intellectual, chauvinist concern for an American language. As Gunn saw it, Williams's concern "embodied a desire that the unknown and unexpressed should not be treated in terms of the already known and expressed." Gunn chartered Williams's development from his early "exclamatory romanticism," through his Imagist phase, to his settling on "a perfect accuracy of description" in *Spring and All*, by means of which the world is both mastered and lived in. There was little further development in Williams from 1923 until *Paterson*. The *Collected Later Poems*, for example, was "surprisingly long, . . . surprisingly dull." Unlike his early masterpiece, *In the American Grain*, *Paterson* contained a great deal of waste, its strongest section being the second part of Book III, dealing with the "Beautiful thing." If Williams was uneven, still, he did offer "a valid alternative of style and attitude to the others available." What he could teach Gunn's countrymen was to be found not only in the expression of a distinctive voice, but in "the clarity of evocation, the sensitivity of movement, and the purity of language," all linked to the man's fine humanity.

Another serious review was Norman Talbot's from down under in the December, 1965, *Poetry Australia*. Here was a poet, Talbot wrote, who was a master "of grammatical positioning and spoken cadences," the poet of the "hard definite word" in search of a local subject and a natural language which would evoke that subject with the least possible distortion. Like the others, however, Talbot considered *Paterson* extremely uneven. It was, finally, only "a series of local sense-experiences, a complex conglomeration of social documents and sheer impressionism, a cubist-and-collagiste portrait of a heterogeneous human context." But Williams, almost alone among his modernist contemporaries, had taken the tremendous risk of embracing a world of humble ugliness rather than recoil or invent substitutes.

In the Summer 1966 *Agenda*, Michael Alexander took a hard look at Williams and Creeley. He puzzled over why Faber had not admitted to its ranks a poet "who is beginning to look like the Whitman of this century for American poetry." Eliot had introduced a new period of dreariness into Britain which had lasted from 1922 until his death. Now many of "the young barbarians" were looking for other voices. Alexander was convinced that English poets would do well to listen to Williams. While Williams was no theoretician, he had learned to construct a fine poetry on two principles: "No ideas but in things!" and "Only the imagination is real." *Paterson* was a wonderful poem, a heroic effort, he

felt, but, finally, "no more than the sum of its parts," for Williams
was not finally able to subsume "the particular in the traditional
universal." Like most of the other English critics, Alexander felt
that *Pictures from Brueghel,* his first volume published in England,
was Williams's best. He saw in these poems "a deliberation, a
weighing, a . . . contrived richness which yet appears natural."
Williams could teach the English poets an eye for detail, vigor,
love, and openness to the universe, as well as delicacy, humility,
and, of course, discipline.

In the November, 1967, issue of *Encounter,* Charles Tomlinson,
reviewing the *Penguin Modern Poets 9* (which included Levertov, Rexroth, and Williams), Rosenthal's *Reader,* and Miller's
collection of critical essays, discussed Williams's cubist techniques
and sketched in the poet's development. Williams, he said, belonged to the line of Emerson, Whitman, and Thoreau in his insistence on contact and an indigenous idiom. In time, having
grounded his technique thoroughly in the local, Williams had
"*earned* the right to address Breughel, Bosch, Dürer, Toulouse-
Lautrec, and the artist of the Unicorn Tapestries—they whose localism was also now a universal affair." In Levertov, Tomlinson
found one of the few disciples of Williams who had refined the
aural as well as the imagistic quality of her poetry successfully.
Rexroth, on the other hand, had not developed his ear sufficiently;
his transitions were labored, the poem at its best too often an
impeded trajectory. In looking hard at some of Williams's disciples, Tomlinson was acknowledging the master's ear.

Looking over the British "reassessment" of Williams from the
vantage of the early seventies, however, the whole flurry takes
on the aspect of an old comatose lion twitching its tail in the general direction of some irritating flies, and then settling back into
its old, comfortable position. But in the decade following Williams's death, there was one English critic who steeped himself in
Williams's literary life to give us the best scholarly treatment of
Williams now available: Mike Weaver's *William Carlos Williams:
The American Background* (1971). "Challenged by Williams to
hear his poems in the American language," Weaver wrote in his
preface, "I realized that as an Englishman there was much in his
idiom which, for lack of his viewpoint, I could not 'hear', and so
I came to understand that the question of idiom is more profound
than a matter of adjusting the ear to a new music; the difference
between the British and American idioms rests on important diver-

gences in attitudes of mind." Weaver's careful style, the implicit judgments in what he chose to tell in presenting Williams's "American viewpoint," reveal that he was by no means fully successful in comprehending Williams's American attitudes. There is throughout Weaver's study a kind of alien buffer, the figure of the outsider peering into a strange landscape and trying to map it for the first time. But the amount of sheer research and detective work that went into his study over a six-year period has yielded an extremely important source book on the poet.

Weaver modestly calls his study a "prolegomena to a study of Williams," but he has given us what no other critic yet has: a wealth of hard information on Williams and his literary world. Weaver bothered to diligently research the extensive holdings of Williams's papers at Yale, Buffalo, Rutherford, and the smaller collections scattered throughout the country. He also corresponded extensively with many of those who knew and worked with Williams, unearthing splendid veins of what are still relatively unexplored but important literary connections. Weaver's book is, essentially, a quilt of separate chapters, a kind of cubist assemblage, stressing some of the various facets of Williams's extraordinarily complex literary biography, which is far more extensive than even his own *Autobiography* suggests. It is Weaver's kind of quiet, prolonged attention paid to the artist which is launching Williams criticism to a new, more serious level. Weaver's "Notes to 'Paterson'," an appendix at the end of his study, for example, identifies many of the letters in *Paterson*. There are the long, distraught letters of "Cress" (Marcia Nardi), for whom Williams once wrote an introduction to *New Directions* readers; letters from Alva Turner; from Fred Miller, with whom Williams once collaborated on his improvisational black novel, *Man Orchid;* from Dolly, a black servant girl from Paterson who wrote the 'Tut' letter; from Gilbert Sorrentino (G. S.); and from Professor Arnold Post (A. P.).

Weaver is good in filling in many of the blank spaces in Williams's literary biography, areas which Williams had either forgotten or for a variety of reasons chose not to recall. Williams's strong interest in the sexual philosophy of Otto Weininger (*Sex and Character,* 1906)—that man is genial, woman material—is carefully mapped out in excerpts from unpublished letters to his brother and to Viola Baxter Jordan; and Weaver demonstrates convincingly that Williams's identity of the virgin with the whore grew out of the poet's correspondence, carried on in the pages of the *Egoist*, with the feminist Dora Marsden.

He has shown some of the relations between Charles Sheeler, the Shakers, and Williams's "precisionist" poetry. He supplements Dijkstra in his section on photographic imagism; he devotes a section to the influence of Louis Zukofsky on Williams; he suggests the importance to Williams of the music of George Antheil and, in the mid-forties, of Bunk Johnson's jazz. He defines Williams's associations during the thirties with the leftist magazine, *Blast*, and with the American Social Credit Movement (an influence or emphasis due largely to Ezra Pound's economic concerns). And he reveals the vicious and unfounded attacks on Williams at the height of the McCarthy period, especially by Mrs. Cummins of the *Lyric*, who made him out to be a Communist. It was an attack which cost Williams his post as Consultant in Poetry at the Library of Congress. (But Williams was always a fighter: he joined a German-American club in New Jersey at the height of anti-German feeling during World War I, largely because he admired his German-American father-in-law.)

Weaver also examines the influence of David Lyle, whom Stieglitz called "The Man from Paterson," upon the structure of Paterson. Lyle, an old radio man, spent a good deal of his life searching for the relationships between mathematics (design) and the complex river of particulars. He sought "a common language which would illustrate the common basis of all organization and so open the way to a sense of common purpose in the world" by taking written communications from all levels of discourse and analyzing the common elements inherent within them (a description which also makes a handy definition of *Paterson*). Lyle is one aspect of the complex central consciousness of Noah Faitoute Paterson, for Lyle came to address his voluminous montages of correspondence to "Dear Noah" and signed himself "Faitoute." Weaver also examines Parker Tyler's work on Pavel Tchelitchew, an artist who affected Williams's tapestry design in *Paterson* as much as Gris and Sheeler had influenced his earlier still lifes. There is also the influence of Tyler's own magazine, *View*, especially those issues which dealt with America in a surrealistic mode. In 164 pages of text, apart from the appendices, Weaver manages to suggest incisively whole areas of influence and background which shaped the literary biography of one of our greatest and most important poets.

Posthumous American Reception, 1963-1966

In America, the critical response in the little magazines and the established scholarly journals, as well as sections of book-length studies, all dealing with Williams, has continued to increase in the ten years since the poet's death. Unlike T. S. Eliot, whom the scholarly industry is now cautiously revaluing, the first genuine wave of critical response to Williams has not yet crested. Much of the criticism in the years immediately following Williams's death, from 1963 to 1966, is for the most part spotty and faulty, either polemical, insufficiently informed, or both. The period looks now like a holding action. Karl Shapiro's "Is Poetry an American Art?" (*CE*, Mar. 1964) resigned itself to the fact that poetry is simply alien to our country and invoked Williams's spirit to bear witness to his despair. Richard Noland's thoughtful essay (*EUQ*, Winter 1964), while praising Williams's criticism of American life, argued that he did not provide "a comprehensive social and political statement about modern America," did not, in short, provide us with anything more sophisticated than a romantic utopianism. There was some further discussion of Williams's idiom and his measure in Gerald Butler's "The Measure of American," printed in *Things (Hanging Loose)* in late 1964. Vittorio Sereni discussed the problems and rewards of translating Williams's *The Desert Music* into Italian in the Winter 1965 issue of *Prairie Schooner*. There were also a few readings of individual poems in undergraduate anthologies as well as a few light reminiscences, such as Charles Angoff's "A Williams Memoir" (*PS*, Winter 1964).

In a long essay for the *New Jersey Historical Series* published the year after Williams's death, A. Walton Litz could still summarize Williams's entire career "as an elaborate working-out of the implications of Imagist theory." For Litz, the controlling force in Williams's art was the dynamic tension between such categories as "the exotic and the familiar, . . . the cosmopolitan and the regional." In collapsing "the distinction between life and the poem," he maintained, Williams had placed himself "at the mercy of every sensation or impulse," thus denying himself "the right to select and control." He had also cut himself off "from the resources of myth," although he had learned to control, develop, and exfoliate the image. His measure was quantitative, isochronous, although the best of his late verse was better described as a loose

pattern of stresses which allowed the unstressed syllables to run
with relative freedom (a description which sounds very much
like Hopkins's sprung rhythm). Litz's essay is interesting, even
helpful, but his categories are conservative and retrospective. The
essay seems years away from critics like Miller, Riddel, or Sr.
Quinn.

In a lighter vein, Cleanth Brooks's 1965 "A Retrospective Introduction" to his *Modern Poetry and the Tradition*, a textbook
which has influenced two generations of American academics
since its original publication in 1939, finally acknowledged Williams's impact (his existence had been duly recorded in the original text by the inclusion of "Spring and All" and "The Red
Wheelbarrow"). But Brooks's tone was defensive, his stance that
of an Horatio at the bridge. "The Red Wheelbarrow"—as if that
poor overworked little poem which Williams had once dashed off
"in a minute" were to be equated with the man's opus—managed
to remain for Brooks "quite inert." It was clear that Brooks was
still Eliot's man.

Recent Collections

Part of the reason for this standstill in the critical response to
Williams was a logistical one; Williams's texts were simply not
available to the reader *or* to many of the critics. New Directions
was working to rectify this situation, not only by supplying sheets
to MacGibbon and Kee, but by publishing new or expanded editions of Williams at home. In late May, 1963, they published a
revised and expanded *Collected Later Poems* and, in October, the
paperback edition of *Paterson* I-V, together with the fragments of
the projected sixth book. In 1966 they published *The William
Carlos Williams Reader*, edited and with an introduction by M. L.
Rosenthal. In 1970 *A Voyage to Pagany*, out of print since its
original publication forty-two years before, was published in a
new edition, with an excellent introduction on the theme of the
innocent abroad by Harry Levin. The publication of Williams's
seminal, theoretical texts written during the twenties, most of
which were extremely difficult to get hold of, were also published
in 1970. Webster Schott, who edited and introduced the texts,
called the volume, with onomastic brilliance, *Imaginations*. Here,
available in paperback, were assembled *Kora in Hell: Improvisations* (1920), together with the 1918 Prologue; *Spring and All*

(1923); *The Great American Novel* (1923); *The Descent of Winter* (1928); and *A Novelette and Other Prose* (1932).

Various other essays, previously unpublished and several left in rough, unfinished form by Williams, have also appeared in journals. The most ambitious of these magazine publications to date has been "A Williams Garland: Petals from the Falls, 1945–1950," which appeared in the Winter 1973 number of the *Massachusetts Review*. This eighty-four page supplement, edited by myself, includes Williams's unfinished collaborative novel using a black protagonist, written in late 1945 and 1946 and called *Man Orchid*; an essay on the novel's genesis; two essays on Ezra Pound, "A Study of Ezra Pound's Present Position" (1947) and "The Later Pound" (1950), both edited from drafts; and a 1950 interview with Williams conducted by John W. Gerber, edited from acetate discs by Emily M. Wallace.

There have also appeared four collections of critical essays on Williams, three of them commercial and one a special issue of the *Journal of Modern Literature*. The first to appear, and also the one maintaining the highest consistent quality, was J. Hillis Miller's collection for *Twentieth Century Views* in 1966. This included an introduction by Miller followed by most of the prose passages from *Spring and All*, then out of print, and then the verdicts of five of Williams's contemporaries and friends: Pound's classic 1928 essay, "Dr. Williams' Position"; three essays on Williams by Marianne Moore written between 1921 and 1934; two judgments by Kenneth Burke written forty years apart; Stevens's two notes on Williams, including the troublesome and influential "antipoetic" essay; and finally, Yvor Winters's negative criticism, written in 1939, followed by his crotchety 1965 postscript. Miller followed this with essays written mostly in the decade from the mid-fifties to the mid-sixties: Martz's essay on *Paterson* V, Kenner on *The Great American Novel*, Sr. Quinn on *Paterson* I, Roy Harvey Pearce, Richard W. Macksey, and the judgments of six younger poets and poet-critics—Robert Lowell, Karl Shapiro, Robert Creeley, Cid Corman, Thom Gunn, and Denis Donoghue.

The other three collections all appeared in 1971, two of them by the Charles E. Merrill Company: Jerome Mazzaro's *Profile of William Carlos Williams*, and John Engel's *Studies in Paterson*. Mazzaro's compilation includes, besides a Williams chronology, late essays written for the most part between 1965 and 1971: Philip L. Gerber on the early Williams (1971); William Heyen's essay-review of *Imaginations* (1970); a memoir by Charles Angoff (1965); Eric Mottram's "The Making of *Paterson*" (1965); three reviews of *Paterson* by Jarrell, Lowell, and Olson; an essay on Williams's poetics by Powell Woods (1970); another essay on the poetics, concentrating on *Pictures from Brueghel*, by Peter Meinke (1967); Kenner's eulogy; and Mazzaro's own "Dimensionality in Dr. Williams' *Paterson*," incorporated into his 1973 study on the later Williams (Cornell).

Engel's compilation, *Studies in Paterson*, is divided into two sections: "Contemporary Reviews" and "Essays." The reviews, by Edwin Honig, Robert Lowell, Hayden Carruth, and Richard Eberhart, cover an eleven-year period. The six essays cover a fourteen-year period: Ralph Nash's influential "The Use of Prose in 'Paterson' "; Linda Wagner's "A Bunch of Marigolds," incorporated into her study of Williams's prose; and essays by Walter Sutton, Bernard Duffey, Roger Seamon, and Sr. Macaria Neussendorfer. Engel's choice of texts was hampered by two considerations: his difficulty in obtaining permissions to reprint such pieces as Kenner's 1952 "With the Bare Hands," and his decision not to include material already reprinted elsewhere. The result is an uneven, perhaps spavined collection.

Finally, there is the special number of the *Journal of Modern Literature* devoted to Williams (May 1971). This contains nine essays and the fullest checklist of writings about Williams till then published, a monumental task ably performed by Jack Hardie. Edited by Maurice Beebe, this 190-page journal includes essays by Joseph Evans Slate on *Kora in Hell;* Louis L. Martz, Sr. Bernetta Quinn, James Cowan, and Cary Nelson, all on aspects of *Paterson;* Neil Myers on "Two Pendants: for the Ears"; Joel Conarroe on "Pictures from Brueghel"; James K. Guimond on Williams's sense of tradition; and Paul Ramsey on Williams's prosody.

Towards a Radical Reevaluation

However we view his approach and strategy, J. Hillis Miller's is one of the most important and seminal encounters in the sixty-year history of Williams criticism. Miller can be argued with and perhaps substantially qualified; he cannot be dismissed. His chapter on Williams in *Poets of Reality: Six Twentieth-Century Writers* (1966) is the first of his encounters. This long essay is a phenomenological graphing of Williams's poetics, an ontological reading of the epistemology. Virtually eradicating the fits and starts and detours of any "direction" through life, Miller's strategy is to create a fictional interior landscape which will reveal the poet's most characteristic mental gestures: his preoccupations, assumptions, the drama of movement *towards* a satisfactory end. In the late Williams, the poetics of immanence, of imaginative incarnation, is achieved, where time becomes a function of space, and where space is coextensive with the mind. "This space, a domain of plenitude and enlargement," Miller writes, "coincides with a time which continually reaches out toward a goal of perennial freshness." From this point of view, Miller is willing to assert that the vision and promise of "Asphodel" is not only "the climax of Williams' writing," it is "the climax too of the development so far of twentieth-century poetry." It is an assertion with such profound implications that it is no wonder that subsequent critical comment, which always feels more comfortable with its time-tested armory of qualifiers, has felt uneasy about Miller. Even if commentators have reservations about Miller's handling of this radically different kind of criticism grafted from the Geneva school and Georges Poulet, the luminous fiction which is his result does open "new places/inhabited by hordes/heretofore unrealized,/of new kinds." Briefly, Miller describes Williams's early sense of loss, of moving beyond the subject/object dichotomy which has plagued Western man since Descartes, towards an outright acceptance of the basic and profound identity and interpenetration between the two worlds. It is for him "a revolution in human sensibility," in which "words, things, people, and God vanish as separate entities and everything becomes a unit." Williams, Miller holds, does not ascribe meaning to things; rather, everything "has its meaning as part of its substance" so that a thing's meaning can be realized in the language itself. It is a language chastened and seen denotatively, the word *not* as symbol but as a thing itself, containing two aspects: verb—process, shimmer, resonance—and noun, so that all words, even the most humble, are *things* in their own right.

Miller's discussion of space and dimension (following leads by Bachelard into the poetics of space) as applied to Williams's poetics is also valuable. In Williams, words become "explosions of linguistic energy, each with its own precise radiance," the words in their dancing moving towards a complex simultaneity. This simultaneity includes a body knowledge, a consciousness which includes all of the senses, often together, including the sense of breathing and a "tactile" seeing. But most pronounced is Williams's pervasive "sexual space" which charges all objects with an erotic value. In Williams's immanent world, there are always three elements in constant tension, one or the other disappearing as the others take precedence. These are "the formless ground, origin of all things; the formed thing, defined and limited; [and] a nameless presence, the 'beautiful thing,' . . . there in every form but hidden by it." Williams's poetic preoccupation is to find an equilibrium between the potential, fecund ground of things and the thing coming over into realized form, an equilibrium achieved by freezing the moment in a shimmering yet static tension, or even by finding ways of extending the moment when shy beauty reveals itself by verbally imitating the *life* of the thing. It was only with the variable foot, where "rising and sinking are not sequential but simultaneous" so that there is an effect of constant renewal, that Williams was able to sustain the effect of a continual flowering, a perpetual dance. Miller's graph raises as many questions about Williams's poetics as it resolves. It is audaciously procrustean, but it is also a provocative and brilliant performance.

But Miller himself seems not to have been satisfied with this first articulation of Williams's radical reconciliation of dualities. And in "Williams' *Spring and All* and the Progress of Poetry," published in the Spring 1970 number of *Daedalus*, he handles the same central issues with greater assurance and hence with greater clarity. *Spring and All* has undoubtedly had a profound impact on Miller; he refers to it constantly in his chapter on Williams in *Poets of Reality* and in his "Introduction" to his collection of essays. He also reprints a large part of its prose passages in that same collection, because it was almost unobtainable until its publication in *Imaginations* in 1970. In his new essay, Miller discusses the idea of progress in the humanities and in the arts themselves, focusing particularly on the theories of Matthew Arnold, W. J. Bate, Harold Bloom, and Geoffrey Hartmann. There are two theories, obvious mirror opposites, to describe the progress of poetry. There is the theory of the accumulated weight of the dead masters, who make it harder for the artist to achieve anything really new. In fact, this theory sees a steady deterioration in poetry with the passage of time. And there is the theory of the gradual enlightenment of the dark spirit of romance, in which the informed, critically aware artist rescues art from its dark, irrational origins. So, too, the critic is alternately the academic tapeworm or graverobber destroying even as he tries to *steal* from the artist, or he is one of a long succession of clerks, working towards the ultimate analysis, the final word, after which all such clerks can simply disappear.

But *Spring and All* suggests an alternative: that there is no real progress in art (and by extension, in criticism), but only, as Miller says, "an eternal re-enactment of the same dangerous encounter, since poetry must *always* return to its daemonic grounds" (emphasis added). Art becomes, then, "the perpetual replaying of the same drama in different forms." *Spring and All* is itself an interpretation of earlier texts (Rimbaud, the Surrealists), and even a self-conscious interpretation of itself. Williams rejects the concept of art as a mediating vision with its symbolic structures, correspondences, and assumptions of an extraterrestrial center, and undertakes instead the "deconstruction" of metaphysics, where the imagination is viewed as a force of nature and at one with it, but whose function it is to destroy and simultaneously recreate that nature. This is done by the imagination's power to name, which is not a copying but an imitation, that is, a repetition based on the recreation of physical objects (things) in the form of their names (also things). Ideas, then, literally become things by transforming or incarnating the syntactical energy of words into verbal substances (Miller's theological grounding surfaces here in his evocation of the idea of logical transubstantiation, pun begetting pun). What this suggests for criticism, Miller says, circling back to his beginning, is that meaning is not something there to be extracted from the text; it is, rather, the *product* of interpreting the text, which suggests that meanings alter with the nature of the specific encounter, that there is no Meaning, only meanings. With the inclusion of this essay, Miller offers us the most significant essay available on the nature of Williams's truly radical poetics. Attention to what he has written will undoubtedly clarify the poetic assumptions and strategies of epistemological confusion and revelation which make up a good part of *Paterson*.

In his "William Carlos Williams: Objectivist Mathematics" (1966), L. S. Dembo also asserts that dualism in Williams is reconciled. But that reconciliation, epistemological and moral in its nature, occurs in the formulations of a metalogic which Dembo calls an objectivist mathematics, where the phenomenological, the "mass of detail," is interrelated "on a new ground." For Williams, poetic language has the power to immediately reveal the poet's encounter with bare reality and bare beauty. The poet's language is honed to become in effect a "geometry of emotions" where objective description carries within itself a precise emotional weight. Williams's linguistic strategies do not "conquer" meaning; instead, they free beauty in the process of expressing its meaning. This epistemological process is in fact the significance of the "Beautiful thing" episode of *Paterson* III. For Dembo, all of the other ways to salvation which *Paterson* offers—such as literature, religion, and economics—prove not only inadequate; they are false. Pound's economics may be present, finally, only to underwrite their own insufficiency. What Paterson learns is modest enough: that the poet does not triumph. Instead he learns how, with imagination, to survive.

A. Kingsley Weatherhead's chapter on Williams in his 1967 study, *The Edge of the Image*, is almost exactly as long as Miller's chapter in *Poets of Reality*, but its yield is embarrassingly small by comparison. There is the sense in Weatherhead's encounter with Williams of someone desperately trying to hack his way through to some kind of illumination, sometimes knocking off flecks of light, but finally defeated before Williams's poetics. "If I had had the advantage of reading *Poets of Reality* before I wrote this essay," he humbly confesses at one particularly confusing juncture, "my task would have been easier and I would have written better." Few critics are willing to display *that* kind of courage. Essentially, Weatherhead makes a case that Williams is a poet of Coleridgean fancy, where Williams's wider meaning is achieved by a kind of violent juxtaposition, and where the object in all its singularity moves only partially towards the symbolic, without giving up its own hard identity. Weatherhead also has some intelligent things to say about Williams's employment of the variable foot and his conscious subordination of grammatical syntax in order to reinforce the centrality of the image. But it is not an essay remarkable for its paraphrasable content; its energy is local, fitful.

Joseph Riddel, reviewing Miller's *Twentieth Century Views* collection in *Modern Language Journal* (January 1968), focused on Miller's introductory essay which is, as he noted, "an abbreviated version of his provocative chapter in *Poets of Reality*" (both published in 1966). Miller's argument was so much in Williams's own terms, he underscored, "that it is disturbing no one has really explored its metaphysical assumptions before." All of the other essays in Miller viewed Williams as solidly within the Romantic world view, with its profound chasms between object and self. But Miller saw that Williams had early moved beyond this dualism to a self resigned to the flux of history and a poetics stemming from the rhythms of one's place. Given this unmediated view of language (a language which apprehends reality directly, without benefit of symbol), Williams's task was "to rediscover the primal oneness of word and thing . . . and thus restore the reality that language once had." Riddel also pointed out that, if one kind of dialectic was resolved, there was still in Williams the dialectic—a polemics, in fact—of getting a hearing for his view of poetry. What Riddel was stressing, even where he reserved the right to disagree with his friend, was that Miller was the first to elucidate Williams's radical difference from the romantic and modernist traditions, to really see the direction from which Williams was coming.

Only Richard A. Macksey's essay in Miller's entire collection comes close to Miller's viewpoint, and these two, colleagues while Miller was still at Johns Hopkins, were in close contact on the Williams question. In fact, there is one section in Macksey's essay, on Williams's rites of passage, which reads like a synoptic version of Miller, or vice versa. Macksey's thesis chartering the various descent-ascent curves throughout Williams's poetic career has also proven influential. He enumerates five such curves: (1) the initiation in *The Wanderer*; (2) the improvisations in *Kora in Hell* and *Spring and All*; (3) the descent through memory into the American ground in *In the American Grain*; (4) the ritual entry into *Paterson* by way of *The Wedge*; and (5) the resolution of annihilation by the acceptance of love in "Asphodel." Critics following Macksey have accepted the importance of these curves as integral to Williams, but have altered their precise numerology and configuration.

Working apart from Miller, and with an eye focused on Pound, Hugh Kenner has managed to throw off, almost as if with his left hand, some particularly illuminating pages on Williams's linguistic strategies—his "principle of syntactic leverage," as he calls it—in his superb study, *The Pound Era* (1971). In two short chapters on Williams, "Syntax in Rutherford" and "The Jersey Paideuma," Kenner shows, by his readings of "Poem" ("As the cat . . .") and "Young Sycamore," what Williams meant by his insistence that the poem is a machine made of words. "Poem" is "one sinuous suspended sentence, feeling its way and never fumbling. Its gestures raise anticipatory tensions, its economy dislodges nothing. The cat is as much an emblem of the sentence as the sentence is of the cat." Kenner's glance at *Paterson* in "The Jersey Paideuma"

is directed at the "intense but tacit" *paideuma* ("a people's whole
congeries of patterned energies," a living culture) which Williams
witnessed as small-town prophet to his townspeople, raising their
unarticulated cry into the occasion of *Paterson*. Still, there is a
sense in reading *The Pound Era* that Williams is at the periphery
of the literary movement which magnetized around Pound, tacitly arraigned there as an American cousin, a disciple rather than
an equal, the spokesman for a place which is only the shadow of
London, Paris, or even Rapallo.

In the hands of less skillful critics, however, there are attendant
dangers in the radical reevaluation of Williams which critics like
Miller and Kenner have accomplished. It has led other critics to
interpret Williams as if he were one of Charles Olson's sons rather
than one of his fathers. So we find for example, William Heyen
writing in an otherwise good review (*Sat R*, Nov. 14, 1970) that
we must "blow our minds clear of the chaff of conventional notions of unity" and "dismiss our traditional sense of logic, . . . our
ideas of truth and language and meaning in poetry." This is certainly true and, by now, even safe enough. But to write that
Williams was "a poet of the lower mind" who "wanted no directing consciousness to inform his work" and "no authorial intrusion
on raw material" is simply wrong-headed, at best misleading. Even
in his improvisations Williams was a highly conscious craftsman,
using a method of apparent randomness, but controlled by an
oblique pattern.

Recent Essays on Paterson

A majority of the essays written on Williams in the last decade
have focused on one or another of the poems, and *Paterson* continues to receive the lion's share. In that period, more than twenty
essays on *Paterson* have appeared, including sections of larger
studies, as well as three book-length commentaries. But it is also
true that only a few of these essays offer radically new interpretations or even treat the poem satisfactorily. So, while there are several interesting general overviews and comments on this image or
that line, it is not until 1970 that the most important new essays
begin to appear. Richard Gustafson's "William Carlos Williams'
Paterson: A Map and Opinion" (*CE*, April 1965) may be of help
to the high-school student. Roger Seamon's "The Bottle in the
Fire: Resistance as Creation in William Carlos Williams' *Paterson*"

(*TCL*, April 1965), reprinted in Engels, expounds upon the significance of the fired bottle in *Paterson* III, reading it as a symbol for poetry as act or process, as well as product, reconciling in itself the conflict between reality and the poetic process as it becomes a design "in immediate contact with the world." Such a poetics is an achievement not without its costs, Seamon cautions, since it means a loss of those ordered responses associated with the romantic artifact.

Sister Macaria Neussendorfer's long essay, "William Carlos Williams' Idea of a City," published in *Thought* in 1965 and reprinted in Engels, provides a good, generalist introduction to the poem. It is useful for its unweaving of some of the poem's many strands, but it seldom stays with an idea, and its section on *Paterson* V, which closes the essay, drags the whole discussion down with it. (There is also too much uncritical paraphrasing of Jarrell). But Sr. Neussendorfer's remarks on Williams's search for an adequate language, on the *experiencing* self as the center of the poem's attention, on the idea of the modern city as symbol (Paterson vs. London or Jerusalem or Cathay), on the shifting, surrealistic nature of many of the images (a view of the poem reinforced and clarified by Sr. Quinn in 1971), and on the poem as verb and as process are still viable entrances into *Paterson*.

David R. Weimer's chapter on Williams's urban imagery in his 1966 study, *The City as Metaphor*, focuses on Williams's ambivalent associations with New York City and Paterson. Williams saw New York as both a symbol—"meaningful *primarily* in its relationship to the artist," a relationship composed of "power, harassment, and disillusion"—and as a source of poetic (and erotic) energy. This was a reality which Williams was never able to manage in his poetry or his fiction. But Williams was able to handle his "other" city, Paterson, because he could internalize it, using it as both symbol and condition of the poet's, and society's, aggravated solipsism and divorce from the ground.

Donald Eulert's note, "Robert Lowell and W. C. Williams: Sterility in 'Central Park' " (*ELN*, Dec. 1967) outlines the kind of eminent domain (and homage) Lowell's "Central Park" (1965) pays to Williams. "Central Park" is a reenactment of Paterson's spring excursion up Garrett Mountain in Book II (1948), transferred now to New York's Central Park. One might also note Lowell's two poems in *Notebook* in praise of Williams, in one case for his abiding love of life and in the other for maintaining over an entire lifetime his intellectual honesty. Lowell's second point is sharpened by juxtaposing two related sonnets: "The New York Intellectual" (the title of an article written by Irving Howe in 1968), and "In the American Grain." Here Lowell takes Howe's liberal humanism, protected, isolated, and financially patented by Howe's "iron smile" and *New Yorker* rhetoric, a political stance safe from the mobs at that moment turning Columbia University into an armed camp, and measures it against Williams's radical honesty which cost him so dearly in terms of his literary reception and his income, but which kept his writing particularly free from taint.

Bernard Duffey's 1967 essay, "Williams' *Paterson* and the Measure of Art," reprinted in Engels, is concerned with that very duality between things and ideas which Miller was at pains to prove does not exist in Williams. In fact, Duffey sees Williams as concerned not so much with things as with ideas in *Paterson,* with finding some way in which what is outside himself can be incorporated into the self. He sees the first four books as sequential failures to redeem his world: the failure of history in Book I, of religion in II, of the library (humanistic knowledge) in III, and of science and economics (our modern projectors) in IV. However right he may be in this, he is certainly wrong in lumping the fire with the library as failures in Book III. Like Pearson before him, but with a differing emphasis, Duffey sees Williams as moving beyond the dualities of *Paterson* to a poetics which would "accept outright its own idealistic loyalties," as in "Choral: The Pink Church" (despite its 1946 date), and then moving to a poetics "sufficient to itself as it is sufficient to its creator and independent of 'things.'" What Duffey upholds (and Pearson questions) is Williams's late acceptance of the world of art, a self-contained world referring to nothing outside itself, self-sufficient as a mode of order, validated by reference to itself and to its own sense of the measure of things. Duffey, Miller, and Pearson split, then, on the nature and significance of Williams's last phase, Duffey and Miller reading it as a reconciliation of dualities in the imagination; Pearson reading it rather as a capitulation of those dualities before the all-devouring mind.

Thomas W. Ashton's (formerly Lombardi) "William Carlos Williams: The Leech-Gatherer of *Paterson* (*MQ,* July 1968) is a reading of the poem focusing on Williams's strategy of accretion, a piling up of the poem's images until they reveal their oblique pattern. Ashton's approach to the poem, his sensitivity to image clusters and juxtapositioning, is accurate and at moments brilliant. He sees in the poem's emphasis on the flux of things a similarity to Jackson Pollock's action paintings and, in its weaving of image strands, its likeness to the Unicorn Tapestries; it is, aptly, "an imagistic fugue." Ashton unravels something of the circular structure of the first four books, its dream sequentiality, with the poet-wanderer waking from the "dream of the whole poem" at the end of Book IV. In fact, Ashton demonstrates about the best that can be done with the (relatively) unassisted play of the mind over the surface of the text, and suggests, too, what the methods of formalist criticism can and cannot do with the poem.

Of the five essays of *Paterson* which appeared in 1970, only two are of real use. The others range from the puerile to the middling. Charles Doyle's "A Reading of 'Paterson III' " in *Modern Poetry Studies* is the weakest. Its summary conclusion that Dr. Paterson "arrives at no positive point in his search, but [that] he can see his own situation clearly" is not only not much of a conclusion, it is simply wrong. G. Morris Donaldson's reading of *Paterson* I and II (*WCR*) is not so much wrong as simply weak. Donaldson allegedly used the manuscripts at Yale "to open up as much as possible the poem's potential energy," but his reading has no substance, Williams's own words giving the essay whatever value it possesses. Thomas LeClair's "The Poet as Dog in *Paterson*" (*TCL*), traces another of the poem's image clusters. LeClair's essay occasionally yields up some significant commentary, as when he suggests that the man in tweeds combing the collie bitch in *Paterson* II is the university man influenced by the new traditionalism of Eliot, although he is probably a figure for Eliot himself. LeClair's thesis is a safe one: that "the dogs in *Paterson* have their prime importance as figurations of the poet." The various metamorphoses of the dog figure, however, have been left largely unattended to.

Powell Woods's "William Carlos Williams: The Poet as Engineer," reprinted in Mazzaro, employs a useful distinction borrowed from Claude Levi-Strauss between the poet as *bricoleur* and the poet as engineer. The bricoleur is the jack-of-all-trades, using tools and materials not designed for the job to be done, and making do with what is already available. Translated into the world of poetics, he is one who uses a language already plastered or smeared with connotation, with tradition. T. S. Eliot is Woods's primary example here. The artist as engineer, on the other hand, sees the word as "a potential 'tool,' as a structuring rather than a structural unit to be used in the *imitation* rather than the representation of nature." What this kind of poet is after is the dissolution of "complex residual or artificial structures" in order to "transcend the constraints imposed by a particular state of civilization," and Williams is his primary example of the "engineer poet." Woods is also one of those who has an argument with Miller: he does not see the destruction of the duality between the ego and the other, but rather an intensive interaction between the two, a movement in the late poems, and particularly *Paterson* V, towards a "self-transcending constructionism" on the level of form and vision, towards the open-ended structure, a dialectic of "becoming." There is, then, on the level of semantics, "a purgatorial reductionism," but on the level of epic structure, there is, in Levi-Strauss's terms, "the bridge, forever extended and improved."

Fifteen years after her pioneering essay on *Paterson*, Sr. Bernetta Quinn reappears on the Williams scene with two essays on aspects of landscape in *Paterson*. The first, "*Paterson:* Listening to Landscape," is included in Jerome Mazzaro's collection of critical essays, *Modern American Poetry*, and marks the fifth essay on *Paterson* published in 1970. The second, a cousin to the first, is called "*Paterson:* Landscape and Dream" and appeared in the Williams number of the *Journal of Modern Literature* in the following year. "Listening to Landscape" is a reading of *Paterson*'s symbolic geography as exterior and interior landscape, and it draws richly from Sr. Quinn's long steeping in Williams's geographic and literary sources, as well as his manuscripts, in a way that Zabriskie's 1953 essay on the geography of *Paterson* could not do. She knows Williams's library, his home, his manuscripts, as few other critics have been privileged to know, and she uses that material over the surface of the poem with sensitivity and intelligence. The essay is the best map we have of *Paterson*, more generically akin to tribute than to criticism.

Sr. Quinn's other essay, "Landscape and Dream," demonstrates the dream-like quality of *Paterson*, the entire epic seen as a dream more real than waking reality, where logical rigidities yield "like ice in March" and the mind flows with the river, its mirror-self, bearing witness to Paterson's citizens in the "plate-glass" of a corporate dream. In this world barriers are minimized, and self and other inter-penetrate. Paterson moves in a world not far removed from Alice's looking-glass world, revealing dreams within the dream, a world where poetry and dream lose their distinctions in the subconscious, the fertile ground of the imagination. Sr. Quinn sees *Paterson* V as Williams's mastery of the dream-technique, where as craftsman he finally learns how the imagination may dispense with the boundaries of space and time. What is interesting here is Sr. Quinn's view of the connection between Williams's middle and late periods as a mastery of dream technique. For her reading shifts the balance between self and other in favor of the self, thus implicitly reducing Miller's assertion at the end of his *Poets of Reality,* that time and space are truly annihilated in Williams's late poems, to something in the nature of a magician's disappearing act. When we look through Sr. Quinn's glasses, Miller's metaphysical resolution of the great romantic dilemma seems almost grounded in the kind of calculus which Lewis Carroll, in one of his quieter moments, would have applauded.

Besides Sr. Quinn's essay, there are three other *Paterson* essays in the May, 1971, *Journal of Modern Literature:* James C. Cowan's "The Image of Water in *Paterson*"; Louis L. Martz's "*Paterson:* A Plan for Action"; and Cary Nelson's "Suffused-Encircling Shapes of Mind: Inhabited Space in Williams." Cowan's essay is by far the slightest; it is largely a rehashing of what earlier critics have said, together with a few significant glosses. Louis Martz's essay suggests, in its quiet, yet persuasive way, that we ought to think of *Paterson* towards the end of Book III as reaching its "sense of full achievement" in the apprehension, realization, and creation of the beautiful thing *in the mind* itself. Martz sees Dr. Paterson as having learned to take up things lovingly within the mind and so transform them. In this light, Book IV becomes a new start using new forms and materials "foreign" to the earlier books. What such a reading does—and it is attractive—is to allow us to see *Paterson* V not merely as a coda, but to see Books IV, V, and the unfinished fragment of VI as new starts in what is generically a romantic epic which must flow on "as long as the author's consciousness exists."

Cary Nelson's essay is an important and fresh approach to the question of what happens when we read *Paterson*. It is a structuralist reading in three parts on the nature of the space or field inhabited by consciousness (Williams's as well as ours) when it approaches one of Williams's poems. Nelson understands correctly that flowers and flowering (object and process) are Williams's primary metaphors for what the mind itself does when it encounters Williams's poems which are either about flowers or which use the flower analogue. In Williams, consciousness inhabits the poem's space, becoming a dynamic vortex revolving about a central emptiness (as flowers bloom where there was—and

will be—nothing). Nelson is another of those in disagreement with
Miller's view of Williams, for he does not see external space as
finally annihilated, but as suffused and encircled by the activity
of the mind, in among the spaces of the page where the letters
exist, shaping, altering, activating them with consciousness, forc-
ing space itself into a verbal act. The symbol which most adequately registers what the mind does in encountering *Paterson* is
the falls themselves, where energy is localized, arrested in all of
its "hesitant, poised motion." There is perhaps too much in the
way of pyrotechnics in Nelson's reading of *Paterson;* one senses,
too, that Nelson's argument is struggling out from under him.
But the essay remains an important discussion of Williams's understanding of the dynamics of consciousness which anticipates our
own shock of confrontation and eventual recognition in reading
Paterson.

The Spring 1971 issue of the *Massachusetts Review* carried the
first half of Donald M. Kartiganer's impressive study of form in
modern literature, which contains a discussion of *Paterson* as the
purest example of process poetry. Called "Process and Product:
A Study of Modern Literary Form," Kartiganer's essay examines
the emergence in modern literature "of two distinct kinds of illusion possible in literary form": the sense of rigorous control
(product) and that of comparative looseness and fragmentation
(process). The process poem maintains a sense of continuous beginning; it is a highly self-conscious form which gives the impression of constantly recreating itself, of beginning again. *Paterson*
contains within itself a collection of disparate, jagged fragments
"which the poet can send flowing down the same broad channel."
The unifying *mythos* becomes here a "thing to be questioned
even as it is pursued," for Williams's ultimate commitment is to
the poem's own continuing movement, where the naked divinity
reveals itself fitfully, at moments, within the river of time.

Kartiganer, one of J. Hillis Miller's most attentive readers, sees
that Williams's profound philosophical resignation to existence
determines his strategy to "meet rather than to control objects,"
that, in order for the poet to meet the "Beautiful thing," he must
himself undergo transformation, destroying and simultaneously
recreating himself. What Kartiganer seems to be suggesting here
is that Dr. Paterson's marriage entails a transformation by acceptance of things as they are without destroying the radical integrity
of either Kora or himself. Interestingly, Kartiganer sees the an-
terior creation of Eliot's *Four Quartets* as a mode of the process

poem transforming itself into product. Here process "becomes a necessary step in the creation of product, of a context which delivers the poem, complete, from the very limitation of chaos out of which it is built." But in terms of radical modernism, Williams's poem has clearly taken the greater risk by moving again into the chaos of Book IV, maintaining its open-ended stance despite the lamentation of so many critics, their expectations frustrated, standing on the shores of the filthy Passaic. The best of these essays on *Paterson* show us that the poem's energy fields have hardly been tapped, that those falls still speak to us in ways for which we are only now finding an adequate critical language with which we can respond.

Charles Olson's prolific glossings and notations, scattered among a large number of published and unpublished sources, together constitute one of the most interesting and important commentaries on *Paterson* by a poet consciously working in a tradition aligned to Williams's own. Since Olson's death in 1970, critics have begun to sort out and evaluate his debt to Williams (and, by extension, Pound). Part of the story of Williams's influence on Olson, and of Olson's shifting senses of Williams's achievement, especially in *Paterson*, has been told from two widely divergent points of view by two capable critics. Marjorie Perloff's "Charles Olson and the 'Inferior Predecessors': 'Projective Verse' Revisited" in *English Literary History* (Summer 1973) charts the derivative element of Olson's famous 1950 "Projective Verse" essay, much of which Williams reprinted in his own *Autobiography* the following year. Using a synoptic plotting with Olson on one side and Pound and Williams facing him, Marjorie Perloff makes a strong case for Olson's wholesale conscription of ideas from the two men he later called his "inferior predecessors." Robert von Hallberg's essay, "Olson's Relation to Pound and Williams" (*Contemporary Literature*, Winter 1974), is far more pro-Olson, and, using the large collection of unpublished materials in the Charles Olson Archives at the University of Connecticut, among other collections, charts Olson's varying and ambiguous literary relationship to both Pound and Williams. Olson was vitally concerned with creating what he considered a more viable methodology for the modern long poem. While he admired the achievement of his predecessors in the *Cantos* and *Paterson*, he also scored them on several accounts, pointing to the myopic egocentricity of the *Cantos* and the failure of Williams to transcend historical time in *Paterson* by not going back far enough into history to find the mythological center of the polis which would have effectively erased or at least subsumed its industrial history. Olson also rejected, according to von Hallberg, Williams's pastoral conception of the American city. As Olson put it (*Selected Writings*, 84), "Bill, with all respect, don't know fr nothing abt what a city is," that is, his sense of Paterson as a city with a public life was, if not absent, certainly not developed in the poem. Both Perloff and von Hallberg show that Olson fluctuated in his sense of Williams's achievement, but von Hallberg notes that some of Olson's negative criticism of Williams was a defensive reaction against Williams's mixed reactions towards Olson's own work. If it is true, too, that Olson's understanding of Williams's poetics was far from complete, Olson's own poetry is clearly in the Pound-Williams line, itself the highest form of critical praise. Williams himself, after a decade of fluctuation, gave, in a 1961 interview with Walter Sutton, the laurels to Olson over Ginsberg. Olson's own shorter lines, closer in length to Williams's own, were for Williams more in touch with the central American idiom than Ginsberg's longer lines, which, Williams insisted, didn't "seem to fit in with the modern tendency at all." Ginsberg, Williams concluded, would have done better work if he'd listened "to what Olson was doing."

Other Essays, 1963-1973

If *Paterson* has understandably received most of the critics' attention, there have been attentive readings of Williams's other writings, particularly of some of the more neglected earlier works. Philip L. Gerber has given us an interesting and valuable study of Williams's critical reception up to 1920 in his "So Much Depends: The Williams Foreground," printed in Mazzaro's anthology. Gerber's essay places Williams in the flurry of literary experimentation in America in the years between the Armory Show of 1913 and 1920, when Williams finally "made" it in the big anthologies. Gerber is particularly good on showing the esthetic relationships between Williams and painters like Demuth, Steiglitz, Hartley, and Stuart Davis, as well as his connections with the little magazines, particularly *Others*, and the proliferating anthologies. But, strangely, he omits any discussion of either *Kora in Hell* or the "Prologue," which, although not published in book form until 1920, were written in 1917 and 1918. George Monteiro's "Dr. Williams' First Book" (*BB*, 1969) is by contrast simply a descriptive note on a copy of Williams's first, extremely rare volume, *Poems* (1909), inscribed to Charlotte Herman (Williams's early love and later his sister-in-law) at Brown University.

Neil Myers's "Sentimentalism in the Early Poetry of William Carlos Williams" (*AL*, Jan. 1966) dismisses the charges of sentimentalism brought against the poet by figures ranging from Stevens to Joseph Bennett. Examining the poetry collected in the early volumes up through *Spring and All*, Myers sees a struggle going on in Williams to handle sentiment firmly, to accept feeling while rejecting the stock response. If Williams often did slip into sentimentalism in the early poems, he also learned to control his feelings by formal means. Myers raises some interesting questions about the problem of tonal control in the early Williams, a problem which could profitably be examined over the entire range of his work.

Richard J. Calhoun's " 'No Ideas but in Things': William Carlos Williams in the Twenties" (1966), offers a brief discussion by a nonspecialist of some of Williams's themes and ideas in the poetry he wrote during the twenties. It discusses briefly Williams's diction as well as his ideas on the local, the American idiom, divorce, love, death, the role of the artist, and the act of perceiving. Calhoun asserts modestly that Williams was concerned with ideas, but ideas rising out of a close look at the things around him.

Three veteran critics have handled aspects of that difficult prose poem, *Kora in Hell*. Sherman Paul's "A Sketchbook of the Artist in His Thirty-Fourth Year" in *The Shaken Realist: Essays in Modern Literature in Honor of Frederick J. Hoffman* (1970) sets *Kora in Hell* in its own moment, focusing on the pressure of Kandinsky's *Über das Geistige in der Kunst*, 1912 (translated in 1914 as *The Art of Spiritual Harmony*) on Williams's early poetics. Paul argues, rightly, that Pound, and later Taupin, insisted too hard on the *Improvisations* as a derivative example of literary modernism (a little Rimbaud forty years late), and that Williams was right when he pointed instead to their "placement in a world of new values," which links them in spirit with his other experimental writings. Paul focuses on the *Improvisations* as "the pursuit of the imagination by the imagination"; it is a world where the self can freely dispose of and recreate the self.

Joseph Riddel's "The Wanderer and the Dance: William Carlos Williams' Early Poetics" (1970), back-to-back with Paul's essay, argues again for a basic acceptance of Miller's thesis that Williams rejected the dualist tradition of romanticism, and attacks Breslin's study for rejecting Miller's formulation. But Riddel also hesitates to follow Miller's thesis that Williams reconciled the mind/object duality; rather, he feels that Williams only resigned himself to "an affirmation of the finite" without achieving a new metaphysical synthesis. Williams's poetics insist upon the poem as process, with the poet constantly searching after a new measure of things in a world in constant flux (a view which comes close to Charles Olson's vitalist conception of energy). The concept of the whole poem, either as a complete formal unity, or as an object purified of its contingency is, for Williams, deathlike. *Kora in Hell* opts, then, for a continual search for a new and adequate language.

Joseph Evans Slate's "Kora in Opacity: Williams' *Improvisations*" (*JML*, May 1971) discusses the genesis and publishing history of *Kora in Hell*, first in the *Little Review* and later, in 1920, in book form. Slate makes especially clear the abiding presence of Pound in the *Improvisations*; it was his baiting of Williams, calling the improvisations which appeared in the *Little Review* "incoherent," which pushed Williams into adding his "explanatory" notes, at the same time that he defended this method by noting that Pietro Metastasio had used it long before in a book which Pound himself had once left at Williams's home. Slate also takes Pound, Taupin, and J. Hillis Miller to task for stressing too strongly the similarity of the *Improvisations* to Rimbaud's *Illuminations*, arguing that they lack the "high formality" of those French prose poems.

Besides J. Hillis Miller's essay, discussed earlier in this chapter, Neil Myers has also written an essay on *Spring and All* (*MLQ*, June 1965). Myers takes exception to Hoffman's misleading description of the poetry in *Spring and All* as examples of "still life." Rather, he insists, *Spring and All* "is also full of a powerful inward tension, of strongly contrasting elements put together in coherent, graceful patterns under great stress." Throughout his chapter, Myers struggles towards a satisfactory technical vocabulary which will explain *how* Williams's poems work.

Marta Sienicka's "Poetry in the Prose of '*In the American Grain*' by William Carlos Williams," which appeared in *Studia Anglica Posaniensia* in 1968, is of very limited value and adds nothing new to previous discussions of Williams's use of history. But Alan Holder's "*In the American Grain*: William Carlos Williams on the American Past" (*AQ*, Fall 1967) gives us an excellent

introduction and overview of the book's major themes, nicely sup-
plementing Breslin's and Whitaker's discussions. Holder sees the
"American failure story" as one of the book's major themes, and
points to the outright failure or incomplete successes of Eric The
Red, Columbus, Montezuma, Ponce de Leon, De Soto, Sir Walter
Raleigh, and Aaron Burr (he might have added Poe and even Lincoln). Holder sees that failure (descent) for Williams can breed
valuable characteristics, as Williams shows in his sympathetic treatment of the black. The fact that the two American successes—
Franklin and Washington—succeeded only at a terrible personal
cost should make us reconsider our assumptions about success and
failure in America. Holder also sees a group of New World heroes
—Perè Sebastian Rasles, Aaron Burr, Daniel Boone—pitted against
Williams's villains, the Puritans, who never came in close contact
with their new world, and who feared the place and the people
they found here. Holder's view that Williams saw the Indians as
noble savages is not really correct, although earlier critics also felt
the same way. He qualifies himself later in his essay when he explains Williams's insistence that we accept the beauty-violence
duality which is at the heart of Williams's vision of America.

Neil Myers offers us a formalist reading of Williams's *Two Pendants: for the Ears* (*JML*, May 1971). Myers sees the poem as
Williams's effort to release his will, to "force" the imagination to
remake his own dissolving self as he confronts the fact of his aged
mother's imminent death, a dying which occurs amidst the background of the riotous profusion of spring and the promise of
Easter. Myers's reading is superficial and in several biographical
points wrong, but he has still managed to throw some light on this
neglected poem's image structures.

Myers's earlier reading of *The Desert Music* (*Cr*, Winter 1970)
is comparatively stronger. Spinning off from Sherman Paul's book-
length study of the poem and grounded in Macksey's elucidation of
the descent-ascent theme, Myers sees the poem "clearly organized as
a 'descent,' moving toward a clearly defined moment of awak-
ening." Williams's images of the dancer and the egg reveal a
"stark, dynamic" poet-critic partaking of the same energy as the
nature around him and moved to create a poem "*beside, impelled
by*, and *counter* to flux."

Besides Mazzaro's essay collected in *William Carlos Williams:
The Later Poems* (1973), there are three other readings of Wil-
liams's "Of Asphodel, that Greeny Flower." In "The Old Poets"
(*JH*, 1968), Richard A. Macksey notes that both Williams and

Stevens wrote some of their finest poetry in their seventies. He reiterates several of the same points he made in his 1966 essay in
Miller's anthology, particularly about Williams's ritual entry into
a new world with *The Wedge* (1944). "Of Asphodel" is another such entry, but this one into the world of memory. Beginning as a "private and public confession," the poem transforms
itself into "a consolation at the close of a long career and an exultant epithalamion." Helge Normann Nilsen's "Notes on the
Theme of Love in the Later Poetry of William Carlos Williams"
(*ES*, June 1969) is stained by a viscous emotional style throughout; it reads almost like an address to the flower children. The
late poems, including "Asphodel," she says, concern themselves
with the restorative power of love and poetry.

My own "The Satyr's Defense: Williams' 'Asphodel'" (*CL*,
Winter 1973), is a reading of the poem's strategy of presentation
measured against the poet's biographical background, which sees
"Asphodel" as a complex, highly organized poem employing a
veritable calculus of persuasion. Williams pleads in the poem for a
new imaginative order—a celebration of the light—to supplant the
old classical synthesis of Homer. In place of eros and entropy
(Helen and murder), license and divorce, he calls instead for eros
and renewal (Kora and cyclical rejuvenation), license and acceptance through understanding. The steps in his wife's (and our)
understanding lead us to a recognition that our real father—that
dark underground figure—is, in fact, Pan. In the reaffirmation of
the myth of Persephone, of perpetual renewal, Williams is once
again renewed as artist. In identifying Persephone (Kora) with his
wife, and in winning her renewed acceptance, Williams is renewed as a man. The mask of sentimentality is at all points manipulated by a master strategist.

In his "William Carlos Williams: Traditional Rebel" (*MRR*,
Winter-Spring 1967), Peter Meinke has given us a close reading
of "Self-Portrait," one of the "portraits" in *Pictures from Brueghel*. Meinke's comments on the nervous rhythms and fluid syntax
are particularly helpful. Joel Conarroe's "The Measured Dance:
Williams' 'Pictures from Brueghel,'" (*JML*, May 1971), points
up the similarities in aesthetics and temperament between Brueghel and Williams. Conarroe's emphasis is on a reading of the
organic relationships between the sections and the poem as a
whole, which, he shows, yields an unresolved pattern of ascent
and descent. "Children's Games," which closes the sequence, acts

as a coda, recapitulating themes developed in the earlier sections as these are played out again by the children, seriously intent upon their games—*homo ludens* reenacted on a smaller scale.

Williams's short stories still continue to receive relatively little attention. In his 1965 essay, "The Short Stories of William Carlos Williams" (*Spectrum*), Benjamin Sankey could remark that, for "all his willingness to improvise and take chances, Williams can perhaps be described as a reactionary—convinced of the value of serious narrative, but not committed to the fairly specialized short story *genre*," writing as he did on "the old principle of alternating narrative and interpretive comment." But Joseph Slate, in his "William Carlos Williams and the Modern Short Story" (*So R*, Summer 1968), sees Williams rather as an "esthetic revolutionary," pointing out that most of the early critics and anthologizers of Williams's fiction simply missed what Williams was doing. Williams, Slate maintains, consciously shared the language and the limitations of the poor, maintaining a strategy of the isolated moment and the presentation of the apparent randomness of things. Williams's social function was to arrest the child-like emotions of self-destruction, violence, and irrational behavior and give them an objective value, to *imitate* the destruction of impersonal violence creatively in the imagination. He learned that it was in times of crisis, such as during the influenza epidemics of 1917–18 or the economic depression of the thirties, that the secret life of these people was revealed. So, in the violence of destroying the old forms, Williams sought to create forms nearer and nearer the truth about us. Williams's eschewal of the point of view was another strategy to bring us closer to the shape of the action as it had really occurred. So wary was Williams of generic distinctions that narrative elements appear in his essays, his autobiography, and his letters, and essay elements keep recurring in the fiction.

Williams's drama has likewise received almost no attention. In fact, only one essay has appeared in the last ten years, and Williams shares that essay with three other American poet-playwrights: Cummings, MacLeish, and Robert Lowell. Katherine J. Worth's commentary on Williams in "The Poets in the American Theatre," in *American Theatre* (London, 1967), is an introduction to Williams as a playwright which simply reiterates the same points made by earlier critics that Williams "integrated verse into a prose texture for special effects of contrast and illumination."

Williams's Measure

Williams's metrical theory and practice is still an important issue, both for scholars and, of course, for practicing poets. Harvey Gross's brief section on Williams in his 1964 study, *Sound and Form in Modern Poetry*, focuses its discussion not on Williams's characteristic measures—indeed it does not even touch on these—but on such uncharacteristic, "traditionally" oriented pieces as "The Dance," with its percussive anapests, and the approximate blank verse of "The Yachts." He treats an Objectivist poem like "Between Walls" as an example of "spatial heresy," where the poem necessarily undergoes a form of paralysis as the "words detach themselves from their meanings." Paul Ramsey's 1971 essay, "William Carlos Williams as Metrist: Theory and Practice" (*JML*), takes the same basic stance towards Williams's prosody that Gross does. Ramsey maintains, without a serious investigation of the theory, that Williams does not sufficiently describe his own practice. Ramsey uses an accentual-syllabic grid in order to show that Williams often employs quite traditional means to achieve his metrical effects. Certainly "The Yachts" approaches blank verse (as it also approaches or departs from a modified *terza rima*), and a poem like "Metric Figure" may make a fine example of "short-long free verse." But Ramsey, like Gross, avoids the significant departures from the norm, those poems where Williams was using a new basis of measurement. (Ramsey's sudden shifting from a discussion of the details of prosody to his wholesale ontological attack on *Paterson* is a most puzzling non sequitur.)

On the other side, in her *Testimony of the Invisible Man: William Carlos Williams, Francis Ponge, Rainer Maria Rilke, and Pablo Neruda* (1970), Nancy Willard insists that "there is no theoretical poetic form" in Williams, "no grammar of poetry. There is only poetry." And again, that if "you want to talk about form in Williams' poems, you will have to remember that they were written without rules and that the conventional tools of metrical analysis are inappropriate to him." But it does not take much critical acumen to see that the two halves of that sentence don't necessarily fit together. In his *American Free Verse: The Modern Revolution in Poetry* (*ND*, 1973), Walter Sutton devotes two chapters to Williams's metrical experiments and to a general discussion of some of Williams's subjects and themes. Sutton adds little that is new to our understanding of Williams, but he does place him in the free verse movement and offers as well a handy redaction of Williams's general development.

The real battle over Williams's new measures, however, is still a matter of sporadic skirmishing which continues intermittently in the reviews. Christopher Ricks reviews a new book of Creeley's for the *New York Times Book Review*, even though he admits he cannot adequately *hear* Creeley. Another British reviewer, recently discussing Tomlinson's "Written on Water," writes that the poet has still not been accepted by the English, "for somehow they get a wild smell of Williams off his work." Certain damaging assumptions, such as that Williams's staggered tercets are an idiosyncratic, indeed mystical, signature which will somehow "work" for Williams but for no one else, have been attacked forcefully by Robert Duncan. In "A Critical Difference of View" (*SB*, 1969), Duncan chides Hayden Carruth for his attack on Tomlinson for using staggered tercets in *A Peopled Landscape*. Duncan strongly insists that Williams "meant every development in his art and particularly the music of his later poetry to furnish the 'rite' or mode of a new poetics." What Williams discovered, in fact, was "the common law of our American speech that every utterance has at least one and only one major stress in relation to which subsidiary stresses are organized."

Williams and Olson continue to be linked together in discussions of "composition by field." Ted Whittaker's "Presumptions" in the *Open Letter* for April, 1966, is one such commentary, where Yvor Winters comes in for some heavy drubbing. Milne Holton's "To Hit Love Aslant: Poetry and William Carlos Williams" (1969) contains another brief discussion. More significantly, Mary Ellen Solt has continued to listen closely to Williams. In her introduction to *Concrete Poetry: A World View* (1968), she sees in Williams "a patterned use of the pause (space) in the late step-down line poems and semantic serial patterns running vertically through all the poems." In short, she sees a similarity between the late poems and the spatial forms of concrete poetry because Williams was able "to bring space (pause) into the structure as a formal element." Williams, she insists, "carried the stress line as far as it can go." The next logical step is concrete poetry, where "meter" becomes structurally accommodated to space itself. But whether Williams would have agreed to let himself be godfather to concrete poetry, or that measure could make this leap without destroying itself is doubtful. In this whole battle of the traditionalists and the experimenters, one thing remains certain. Until prosodists come around to *hearing* as Williams heard, and said he heard, they will be playing the game with a whole set of rules which simply do not apply.

Recent Studies in Influence

Still other critics have discussed influences on Williams, the most responsible being Mike Weaver's *William Carlos Williams: The American Background*. K. L. Goodwin's small section on Williams in his *The Influence of Ezra Pound* (1966) treats Williams's literary relationship with Pound only superficially. Not only does Goodwin lack a sufficient understanding of *Paterson's* density, but he has used neither the essays Williams wrote on Pound nor the other available manuscript sources which suggest just how deeply Pound did influence his friend. Goodwin touches on Pound's ideogrammic method and the usury motif, and is fairly full on the early Pound-Williams contacts (to 1914), but that still leaves another half century virtually unattended to.

Joseph Slate's "William Carlos Williams, Hart Crane, and 'The Virtue of History' " (*TSLL*, Winter 1965), is a more responsible study of influences. While Crane and Williams never met, they did have some "business" correspondence and they appeared in many of the same magazines and anthologies in the mid-twenties. Furthermore, contemporary critics like Waldo Frank, Allen Tate, and Yvor Winters tended to lump them together when discussing American experimenters. Slate is cautious in discussing influence, but (following Horace Gregory's lead) he is convincing in demonstrating Crane's aggrandizement of Williams's *In the American Grain,* and in showing how both were concerned with the American artist's fear of failure, a revitalized Whitman, a heroic Columbus, and the centrality of the Indian to the American consciousness. Slate is also correct in seeing Crane's presence as "old Tim Crane" in Book I and elsewhere in *Paterson*. Crane is there, however, not only as one who created an American epic, but probably also as a presence to be exorcised, a heavyweight to be beaten.

In his chapter on Williams, "In the American Grain," from his *American Poets from the Puritans to the Present* (1968), Hyatt Waggoner places Williams in the Emersonian tradition. But Waggoner's essay, despite some noteworthy commentary on Williams's

esthetic relationships with his mother, Pound, and Eliot, is dangerously uninformed—"dangerously" because the tone of Waggoner's
essay is so positive, giving the assumption of wide reading in
Williams where this is simply not the case. In 1968, Waggoner was
still accusing Williams of being "guilty of intellectual innocence
and confusion," and insisting that "we must *not* approach his
poetry by way of his work as a 'theoretician.' " Waggoner's contention that Williams had not read very much Whitman and had
digested less is untrue; and even if it were true that Williams did
not read Whitman deeply, that is no criterion for judging literary
influence, as both Hopkins and Hart Crane's reading of Whitman
attest. (On this point, Galway Kinnell's reading of Whitman's
influence on American poets in his 1972 essay, "Whitman's Indica-
tive Words," also misses the mark. Before there was Ginsberg's
Howl, there was "The Bridge" and *Paterson;* influence takes more
shapes than the lexical.)

Hans Galinsky's "An American Doctor-Poet's Image of Germany: An Approach to the Work of William Carlos Williams"
(*SG,* 1968), is a study of influences of another kind. Galinsky
traces some of Williams's images of Germany and of German-
Americans in his writing. There is a potentially good idea here,
but Galinsky's woefully incomplete tabulation and his superficial
treatment of the significance of his material seriously hobbles the
usefulness of his essay.

In "William Carlos Williams and the Past: Some Clarifications"
(*JML,* May 1971), James Guimond shows that Williams "was
willing to accept the past under certain conditions." If his own
primary allegiance was to the present, to immediate human concerns, to his own moment, still, he was attracted to those artists in
the past who had likewise celebrated their own place and time—
Homer, Chaucer, Villon, Whitman. Williams's discontent was
with the grand literary tradition, which grounds one's own voice
under with the insistent, weighty echoes of the dead.

The Longer Commentaries

Overviews and a Bibliography

The decade following Williams's death also saw a flurry of
book-length critical studies of the poet by American academics.
These studies arrived at first slowly, tentatively, and then with a

spiral of activity lasting from 1968 until late 1970. Most of these studies were either critical introductions to the poetry and prose or readings of one or the other of the long poems, including three full-length studies of *Paterson*. Linda Wagner's 160-page *The Poems of William Carlos Williams: A Critical Study* (1964) cracked the long freeze which had followed Vivienne Koch's 1950 new critical study. Wagner was followed in 1966 by Alan Ostrom's 170-page *The Poetic World of William Carlos Williams* and in 1967 by Walter Scott Peterson's *An Approach to Paterson*, part of the Yale College series of outstanding theses by Yale undergraduates. The year 1968 saw the publication of four books: Emily Mitchell Wallace's *A Bibliography of William Carlos Williams*, an exceptionally thorough tabulation of Williams's books and contributions to innumerable little magazines and journals, as well as his translations, broadsheets, leaflets, and recordings, all complete up through mid-1967; Thomas R. Whitaker's *William Carlos Williams* for the Twayne series; Sherman Paul's reading of *The Desert Music*, called *The Music of Survival: A Biography of a Poem by William Carlos Williams*; and James Guimond's *The Art of William Carlos Williams: A Discovery and Possession of America*.

In late 1969 Bram Dijkstra's *The Hieroglyphics of a New Speech: Cubism, Stieglitz, and the Early Poetry of William Carlos Williams* was published by Princeton. Then, in 1970, four more books on Williams: Linda Wagner's companion study to the poetry, *The Prose of William Carlos Williams*; Joel Conarroe's *William Carlos Williams' Paterson: Language and Landscape*; a strange agglomerate called *The Williams-Siegel Documentary*, edited by Martha Baird and Ellen Reiss; and James E. Breslin's *William Carlos Williams: An American Artist*. The third commentary on *Paterson*, *A Companion to William Carlos Williams' Paterson* by Benjamin Sankey, appeared in late 1971. In early 1973 Cornell published Jerome Mazzaro's *William Carlos Williams: The Later Poems*, concentrating on *Paterson* and after. Except for Emily Wallace's bibliography and Dijkstra's study of the influence of cubism and the American school of painting on Williams's early poetry, then, American scholar-critics have concentrated their energies on presenting readings of Williams's poetry (and prose) to an audience finally ready to listen to it.

Emily Wallace's *A Bibliography of William Carlos Williams* placed Williams scholarship on a new footing by showing Williams's remarkable productivity, much of it in the ephemeral,

hard-to-trace little magazines. This book has proven indispensable
to every scholar-critic writing on Williams since its publication
in 1968. Using Donald Gallup's bibliographies of Pound and Eliot
for its model, Wallace's own bibliography is virtually complete up
through 1967, cataloguing Williams's 50 books and pamphlets (including Rosenthal's *Reader*), the nearly 100 books for which he
wrote introductions or contributed something, some 635 articles
or contributions to periodicals since 1912, and an impressive array
of miscellany, including broadsheets, leaflets, greeting cards, off-
prints, musical settings, recordings, radio scripts and transcripts,
statements on dust jackets, and his single medical article, published
in *Archives of Pediatrics* in August, 1913. Wallace also provides
us with a necessarily incomplete checklist of translations of Williams into a polyglot assortment of languages: French, Spanish,
Portuguese, German, Italian, Arabic, Czechoslovakian, Greek,
Hungarian, Japanese, Norwegian, Polish, Russian, Bengali, perhaps even Vietnamese. She has also provided us with relevant quotations from Williams's own letters which treat, in large part, the
actual genesis of his books, and she also gives us extracts from
early or pertinent reviews. (Emily Wallace is now at work on
what will probably be a four-volume edition of Williams's letters
for New Directions, which will go a long way towards giving us
the man in all of his fascinating complexity, for Williams was a
voluminous writer and there are literally thousands of as yet unpublished letters written over sixty years.) What *all* of Williams's
work reveals—the letters, the essays, the unpublished material—is
what Wallace suggests in her considered introduction to her bibliography: that Williams's lifetime of writing all converges towards what he himself once called the "Complete Collected Exercises Toward a Possible Poem."

Linda Wagner's 1964 commentary on Williams's poetry has its
faults. Its style, particularly in its first parts, is often so general
and unrelieved that it is an effort to read it. It contains a conception of Williams's view of human nature which is embarrassingly
two-dimensional. And it insists on coining critical terms where the
older ones, or, better, Williams's own, will serve. While such
coinages as "symbolic" and "transitional metaphor" are not particularly helpful in describing Williams's practice, they do describe ways in which Williams's metaphors undergo metamorphosis, enlargement, proliferation.

But her study is generally reliable, informative, and organized
around a discussion, in successive chapters, of Williams's poetics,

his use of imagery, his colloquial style, his pervasive use of metaphor, and his variable measures. It is in *Paterson* and the late poems that Wagner sees Williams's fullest achievement. Wagner's discussions of Williams's metaphors for the modern mind in *Paterson*, for example, or her descriptions of Williams's late symphonic arrangements, such as "The Orchestra," are good, sharp, and to the point. So is her overall discussion of the changes Williams wrought in his search for measure, a search which went even beyond the triadic line to a short, tight stanza without punctuation in the poetry he wrote after 1958. *Paterson* is seen as a search in its very unfolding for a redeeming language, as a study of its various verse forms shows. But, finally, Wagner reads the poem as "a study of man's search for relationships with other people," for which language is the means. Her use of the manuscript collections at Yale and Buffalo helps to give her study a clarity and a density which several subsequent studies, using the same collections, manage to miss.

On the other hand, her companion study, *The Prose of William Carlos Williams*, published six years later, shows a greater unevenness, an intermixture of competent analysis with the worst kind of plot summary, as in her treatment of *A Voyage to Pagany*. Wagner's chapters on *Kora in Hell, Spring and All, The Great American Novel, In the American Grain*, the short fiction, the novels, the plays, *Yes, Mrs. Williams*, and the prose sections of *Paterson* in no way make up a definitive or even satisfying study of Williams's prose. Her strategy in this study was first to argue for the overall unity of the man's work, for "the interrelationships between his prose and his poetry," next, to survey the prose pieces generically and chronologically, and then to fold the prose back into a study of the late poems, where she saw the twin lines of poetry and prose converge once again. Why Professor Wagner strains so hard to give us plot redactions like, "There is a deep love . . . a love complicated by Evans' remaining a bachelor even though he is nearly forty," is puzzling, unless she believed her readers would not be able to get hold of copies of Williams's early books. The prose is flabby, redundant, wasteful, badly in need of a final, severe cutting. Relatively speaking, the best sections are, again, those that treat the late poems, such as the section first published in the *Kenyon Review* in 1967 as "A Bunch of Marigolds." (Of the earlier poems, such as *Spring and All*, Louis Martz, Neil Myers, J. Hillis Miller, and James Breslin have all given us superior readings.) What is a reader to make of Wagner's analysis of

"The Pot of Flowers": "Progressing as would the eye, Williams' poem moves, in meaningful rhythm, down the picture to the leaves of the plant and, finally (and perhaps not too poetically), to the pot." One can hear Williams groaning at that one. Still, one is thankful for Professor Wagner's stirring up of the river bottom of manuscript collections once again and for her bibliography.

Alan Ostrom's *The Poetic World of William Carlos Williams* (1966) is a mixed bag, though not quite the "hodgepodge" which Bernard Duffey called it in his review (*CL*, Summer 1968). The book's major weaknesses are an overly abstract initial chapter and the absence of strong transitions among the numerous discussions. One has no way of knowing what subject Ostrom will treat next, and the chapter headings, phrases taken from the beginning of *Paterson*—which Ostrom sees as Williams's summative work—are of little help. Ostrom is strongest on what he calls Williams's major period, from *Al Que Quiere!* through *Paterson* IV (1917–51). He dismisses the earlier poetry as apprentice work, and, less pardonably, sees the last four books marred by the use of symbols which are "arbitrary rather than organic parts of the wholes." He fails to even mention *In the American Grain*. Again, he has made not only a number of factual errors, such as that "Two Pendants: for the Ears" is addressed to Williams's ninety-year-old grandmother rather than to his dying one-hundred-year-old-plus mother, but he is also guilty of embarrassingly simplistic statements about subject/object dichotomies and the nature of romanticism in Williams.

However, there are whole slabs of Ostrom's study which are worth close attention. Among these are his discussions of the importance for Williams of the local, the marriage of reality and the imagination to create new orders, and the themes of divorce, unity, human sexuality, the natural versus social conventionality, city versus country. There are discussions, too, of Williams as a moral poet, of his mythopoeic method, and the underlying reasons for his accretive technique, his strategy of perception, his elliptical syntax, his melding of prose and poetry, his search for a new idiom (an ideal speech made from the defective language at hand), and the strategy of the submerged metaphor. He is particularly good in demonstrating *how* Williams's ideas are created in the process of generating the poem itself. There are a number of fine close readings of some of Williams's difficult lyrics, such as "The Ball," "The Motor-Barge," "Pot of Flowers," "Sparrows Among Dry Leaves," "Aigeltinger," even "The Red Wheelbarrow." It is,

then, in its parts rather than as thesis-statement that Ostrom's study
works. Williams's poetic world remains fragmented, intractable in
this critic's handling, pulled together only at the level of the most
traditional categories. There are moments when it seems as if Williams's complex but single world will be yanked into focus, as
when Ostrom speaks of Williams's strategy of accretive, juxtaposed images "built one upon another like the layers of a pearl
deposited . . . upon a center of irritation," thus "expressing a . . .
broken world, a world without logical connections, without *overt*
or *perceptible* connections of any sort" (emphasis added). But
Ostrom has left out too much, has focused on too narrow a range
of Williams's created world; he slides too easily into the flux of
his own style to have made anything like a definitive statement.

Thomas R. Whitaker's volume, *William Carlos Williams* (1968),
written for Twayne's United States Authors series, is a remarkably tight and illuminating study of Williams in 164 pages of
text. Its limitations are those of space; one senses that Whitaker
might easily have relaxed into a longer study without being prolix or wasteful. The book is the tip of the iceberg: clear, sharp,
pointed. Whitaker has the necessary critical vocabulary, the
sense of critical tact, the skill in uncovering amidst an uneven
plentitude of writing Williams's main lines of development. Opening with a precise and convincing chapter on "Attention," which
Whitaker presents as "a useful key to his writing," the book treats
the significant developments in Williams's poetry and prose chronologically. Chapter 2 focuses on the poetry from 1909–18, showing Williams's early ability to cope with traditional versification
and his conscious eschewal of that mode, the development of his
own idiom in *Al Que Quiere!*, and his descent into the chaos of
his own imagination in order to free it from restrictions and blockage. In chapter 3, Whitaker treats the poetry from 1918 to 1934:
The *"Transitional"* Poems (which are finally given their correct
place in Williams's chronology, written as most of them were
between 1918 and 1921), *Sour Grapes, Spring and All*, and the
Collected Poems 1921–1931, including *The Descent of Winter*.
For Whitaker, this was a period of "poetic descents, explorations,
and refinements," of "new Cubist constructions that enact the
swift transit of the attention or raise the disorder of the moment
to the plane of abstract design." Chapter 4 treats "the longer prose
fictions of the 1920s: *The Great American Novel* (1923), *In the
American Grain* (1925), *A Voyage to Pagany* (1928), and *January: A Novelette*, which Williams wrote in 1929 but which was

not published until 1932. Whitaker's treatment of the first two in particular is brilliant and his commentary on the dialogic strategy of *In the American Grain* reveals one of the reasons for that book's insistent relevancy to our own moment. Whitaker's fifth chapter deals with the most important examples of the later prose fictions and the plays: *The Knife of the Times* (1932), *Life Along the Passaic* (1938), *Make Light of It* (1950), the *White Mule* trilogy, the late short story, "The Farmers' Daughters" (1957), and the plays, particularly *The First President, Many Loves*, and *A Dream of Love*, the last of which Whitaker sees as Williams's best play, genuinely complex and enacting a poignant dialogue between Thurber and his wife, Myra.

Chapter 6, a short essay, deals briefly with the poems published between 1935 and 1950, "a time of poetic uncertainty and often of dearth" for Williams, a time when he was pushing towards "a new measure implicit in the spoken language, and a more sustained utterance." While Williams's output during these years was large—it included *An Early Martyr, Adam and Eve and the City, The Broken Span, The Wedge,* and the *Collected Later Poems*—there was, as Whitaker shows, a great deal "of imperfect and fragmentary experimental work, along with some very fine poems." Much of this period was, of course, taken up with the writing of *Paterson*, to which Whitaker devotes chapter 7. In twenty pages Whitaker manages to elucidate *Paterson*'s central concerns and its mode, where "risk and value inhere in the attempt to render the living movement of the imagination that questions and transforms all our conventions." There is an uncanny precision in the way Whitaker can go to the core of this poem. "Perhaps *Paterson* may be most usefully described as a listening, and a speaking," he notes. It is "a *way* of language—both a process and a path," seeking "all along its way, amid its own recognized evasions and failures . . . a more authentic saying of what it is to exist in a present world." Whitaker probes the poem's protean, metamorphic quality with admirable concision. Critics of *Paterson* would do well to observe the encompassing trajectory of a comment like this: "Wonders sardonically merge—the Great Falls, a hydrocephalic dwarf, the shrewd and secretive brain of Hamilton (who thought to make Paterson a monopolistic industrial center), the heterogeneous population drawn to the city by the mills—all within the analogously river-filled mind of the speaker himself." That sentence reveals something of Williams's strategy of "by multiplication a reduction to one." Chapter 8, dealing with the late poems, however, shows an unfortunate falling off from the earlier chapters. Whitaker's explanation of the variable foot as being not a culmination but, rather, another interim measure, is correct, and his discussion of the vulnerable persona in these late poems helpful. But he does not apparently see that Williams's digressions, as in "Asphodel," are themselves part of Williams's strategy of revelation. In all, however, Whitaker has managed to sift and order Williams's ambitious opus into a volume which is a marvel of economy, order, and grace.

James Guimond's *The Art of William Carlos Williams: A Discovery and Possession of America*, for all its unevennesses, its more than occasional flirting with the banal commonplace, stands as a solid, competently researched and written commentary on Williams's entire corpus. It is a book which is in need of a final thinning, a more economical use of sources, but it handles, often with critical sensitivity, the major lines of Williams's development and his themes. Daniel Hoffman called these themes, in his review of Guimond's study (*Times*, Apr. 6, 1969), "certain unexamined *idées fixes*." There is an untidy sprawl in the way Guimond moves about, especially in the early chapters of his study, which is not helped by calling his chapters one, two, three, and so forth. But his chapter breaks are essentially chronological, like Wagner's and Whitaker's. Chapter 1 deals with the early poetry, particularly with a reading of *The Wanderer* as a seminal study of Williams's developing themes, and especially the Kora myth. Guimond's strategy is to cull from whatever sources he can to elucidate the subject under discussion. His search for sources seems to have been fairly thorough and his use of these sources to connect and explain the sometimes hopelessly disparate comments Williams made is at times strained, but more often helpful. Chapter 2 treats Williams's development from about 1916 to about 1928 when he was, as Guimond sees it, "influenced by two major concerns": the artist's contact with his own locality, and his imaginative possession of that place. There is a good discussion of Williams's similarities to the American painters, Charles Sheeler and Charles Demuth, which also delineates precisely the stylistic and temperamental differences between the two painters. But one keeps stumbling up against such embarrassments as this: "[Williams] became convinced at that time [1930] that poetry should be serious and difficult rather than entertaining. He also became a staunch advocate of an 'antipoetic' theory of beauty whose chief tenet was that beauty and ugliness were parts of a single whole." The first statement is simply astounding; the second is more troublesome and would take too many qualifiers to allow assent.

Chapter 3 contains an excellent discussion of the call, especially by New York intellectuals (as well as by D. H. Lawrence), in the late teens and early twenties, for a new look at America, even as expatriates were sailing to Paris. Guimond establishes the long-range influence of figures like Van Wyck Brooks, Randolph Bourne, and Waldo Frank on Williams's *The Great American Novel, In the American Grain,* and even *Paterson.* Chapter 4 is a study of Williams's Objectivist phase, which Guimond sees as including not only the poetry but the fiction of the thirties, including *White Mule* (1937) and *In the Money* (1940).

Chapter 5 is a discussion of Williams's "anti-poetic" poetry in the late thirties. Guimond, aware of Williams's distaste for the term, nevertheless insists on perpetuating it as "a valid generalization." The antipoetic, as he sees it, included for Williams not only those subjects traditionally "unfit" for poetry, but, interestingly, the poor, the cast-offs of society, which Williams treated so sensitively in his short fiction of the thirties, in such pieces as "Jean Beicke," "Pink and Blue," and "Old Doc Rivers." Guimond calls the latter "Williams' most comprehensive and sensitive diagnosis of the poverty of his environment and the flawed perfections which were endemic to it."

Chapter 6 treats the background of *Paterson,* Williams's articulation of "his entire environment," and some of the major themes of the poem: Paterson, the man/city; the passive, fecundating female-nature principle; the divorce between the two created by the man/city's misuse of power; the failure of communication. Where chapter 6 gives us the coordinates of *Paterson,* chapter 7 focuses on the interrelatedness of the proliferating details. For in *Paterson,* Guimond argues, "Williams attempted to increase his readers' vision of their localities by presenting the local details of his environment in a deliberately fragmentary manner." This chapter is a reading of the river-like development of the original four books, and particularly of the metamorphosis of Dr. Paterson from the cold, scientific observer of his place to the more vulnerable lover who undergoes the necessary descent in order to find the beautiful thing in his place. Guimond also points to some of the ways in which *Paterson* developed out of the short stories and the early poems. In the early poems, Williams shows an "extraordinary clarity of vision achieved by the exclusion of all inessentials." But the short stories and *Paterson* both "begin with only an apprehension of value, a sense that something within the subject is essential." There is a good deal of truth in this, but it does not go very far in explaining such elliptical lyrics as the "rapid transit" poems of *Spring and All.*

The final chapter and conclusion treat several of Williams's chief concerns in the late poems (after 1951). There is an especially good discussion of the essential, almost mythic, differences between men and women in Williams's poetry, of the dilemma Williams saw between the man who seeks after many flowers and the woman who needs constancy in order that the single cell may expand and encompass its world, a tension which leads to divorce or infidelity unless the man's imagination constantly renews the woman, creating an identity between the virgin and the whore. There is also a good discussion of the artist's relationship to the radically "unpoetic," to deformity, pain, and disease, which art can make bearable. There is also a useful discussion of Williams's new measure.

In his "Conclusion," Guimond, followed Macksey, suggests that Williams's career was a series of peaks, followed by descents which led to depths of chaos and to consequent renewal. There were four peaks: 1914–16, culminating in *The Wanderer;* the mid-twenties, culminating in *In the American Grain;* 1938 to 1947, when Williams moved towards and into *Paterson;* and 1951 to 1955, which included "The Desert Music" and "Asphodel." Williams's depths were reached about 1923 (in *Spring and All*); in the early '30s; and again in the late '40s, which Guimond says accounts for the concomitant falling off in the poetry of Books III and IV of *Paterson.* Finally, Guimond makes it clear that to think of Williams as a primitive is a mistake. Rather, he was a great experimenter, a competent but not a finished critic, always willing to sacrific theory "so that he could discover anew the 'rare element' of life which he loved so faithfully." On balance, Guimond's treatment of Williams, for all its flaws of prolixity and occasionally puzzling misinterpretation, reveals a critical sensitivity which has meditated long and hard on a vast welter of published and unpublished material, shaping much of it into a sense of what Williams's critical intelligence and fertile experimentation achieved.

James Breslin's *William Carlos Williams: An American Artist* (1970) is very likely the best overview of Williams we have, although Whitaker's earlier study comes close. There is a range of intelligence, literary background, and critical acumen that places this 230-page study above most of the other critics. Breslin's approach is measured and balanced, his enthusiasm omnipresent but restrained, his style readable and lucid. What Breslin does is pretty much what Whitaker did in his study: first fix Williams's early development, next, place Williams in his literary and cultural milieu, and then focus on the major texts while providing incisive comments on the rest. As major, Breslin chooses *Spring and All, In the American Grain,* the fiction (with special attention to the two collections of short stories, *The Knife of the Times* and *Life along the Passaic*), *Paterson,* and "Asphodel." Breslin's method or organization is, as he himself tells us, "developmental as well as generic: Williams seems to have proceeded almost systematically from one literary form to the next as his career advanced."

Breslin has made errors, as in his identification of the unicorn in *Paterson* V with "that beauty Paterson had found in the girl in the basement in Book III." (Actually, the unicorn is the type of the imagination, the one-horned, satyr-like beast in his recurrent search for the Virgin, the feminine principle, the language, whom he will marry and thus whore.) There is bound to be a renewed critical hassle over Breslin's judgment that the early *Spring and All* is probably "superior to the works of the middle fifties" because the late poems often "sink into [a] sort of soggy, uplifting didacticism." Still, Breslin's emphasis on the early poetry is, at this juncture, a correct one, as is his statement that "*Spring and All,* for its startling originality and tensed force, must be ranked as one of the major documents of modern literature." As difficult and undigestive as some of Williams's statements on radical poetics in the twenties were, they remain, as Hugh Kenner noted nearly twenty years ago, one of the most important nuclei of modernist esthetic thought we have, and still one of the most neglected. Wallace Stevens knew what he was talking about when he called Williams "a prodigious theorist" in 1934.

In his chapter on *Paterson,* Breslin is careful to suggest the tentativeness of his own reading. If he insists perhaps too hard on the poem's "primitive and experimental" nature, taking Williams's own defensive contention (paraphrased by Breslin) that *Paterson* was "a rough and profuse start from which some later summative genius may extract and polish," still he gives us a sharp sense of the poem's texture, its "multi-dimensional quality," its "buried system of recurrences." But even more, he shows us that he has an ear, that he can attend closely to the various voices in the poem, including its comic element, something almost *no* critic has treated.

In summing up *Paterson*, which he calls a "pre-epic," Breslin sees
that its structure imitates "the process of disintegration [which]
releases forces that can build a new world. It confronts, again and
again, the savagery of contemporary society, but still affirms a
creative seed." Breslin's study has its shortcomings, which the
Williams specialist could point to and argue over. But for a satisfying introduction into the world of Williams, Breslin's is the
book: readable, tight, and intelligent.

Three on Paterson

Walter Scott Peterson's *An Approach to Paterson* is the first
full-length study of Williams's cubist epic. Published in 1967 in
the *Yale College Series* of outstanding undergraduate writing, the
study grew out of a seminar in modern poetry conducted by Yale
professors Louis Martz and Harold Bloom. *An Approach to Paterson* is, essentially, an *explication de texte* of *Paterson* I-IV, with
emphasis on Books II and III, and with *Paterson* V viewed as
a coda already attended to by Peterson's mentor, Martz, in his
1960 "The Unicorn in Paterson." Peterson's is a book which undergraduates have found helpful in threading their difficult way
through *Paterson*'s maze, and Peterson shows that he can handle
the poem's lexis with sensitivity and imagination. But he does not
seem to have heard its kinds of music, and he hardly touches on
Williams's constant experimentation with the line, which is, in fact,
a central preoccupation of the poem. Nor did Peterson make much
use of the large collection of Williams manuscripts available in the
Yale collection of American literature.

There is an enunciation of the poem's major themes, but these
are treated in an overly simplified, two-dimensional fashion. The
poem's central argument, as Peterson sees it, is "that man's loving
and imaginative 'marriage' to the particulars of his local world can
ultimately save him from the death-in-life of 'Puritan divorce.' "
Paterson becomes for Peterson a kind of rewriting of *In the
American Grain*. And his own study was undertaken because
none of the existing criticism on *Paterson* set out to investigate,
systematically and at length, just "how" the details of the poem
"work." The study has the markings of much serious undergraduate writing: the effusive complimenting of the rabbi by the
ephebe; the first nervous locking of horns with the older critics
(or those who have already found their way into print); the early

enthusiasms (as here, Peterson's initial contact with Blake—via
Bloom—who is lugged in from time to time and made to add his
difficult luminosity to the landscape of *Paterson*); the eschewal of
most of the earlier criticism and a concomitant braving of the text
alone, with the young critic in the guise of an Odysseus-*manqué;*
the solemnity of the proceedings; the sense of the grim rightness
in one's own discoveries. But for all this, the study is a brave undertaking and, until an indisputably first-rate book-length study of
the poem is given us, students will be grateful for this pioneer
vademecum.

   Paterson: a poem so alinear and so fragmentary it is no wonder
that even ten years after Williams's death its grand design should
have been only imperfectly and even now only partially explained
by the critics. What are we to do with the most radically experimental and successful long poem written in our time, a poem
which has gathered to its magnetically energized fields such random effluvia as: letters from the distraught Marcia Nardi; the
urbane Edward Dahlberg; Ezra Pound at St. Liz's; a semiliterate
black woman; old, relatively unknown or forgotten writers like
Alva Turner and Fred Miller; and young ones like Gilbert Sorrentino and Allen Ginsberg; excerpts from medical journals, old newspapers, old history texts, texts on primitive societies; Mezz Mezz-
row's *Really the Blues; National Geographic;* Symonds on Greek
prosody; an old artesian well chart; a serio-comic flyer advocating
Social Credit; excerpts from a television interview with Mike Wallace? The central question which *Paterson's* critics have had to
face is the question of critical strategy (and critical tact), of how
best to approach *Paterson* in order to demonstrate, to manifest, its
underlying unity within a mass of such strange plenitude.

   In his *William Carlos Williams' Paterson: Language and Landscape* (1970), Joel Conarroe has attempted to come at the poem by
unweaving, or combing out—as Williams/Paterson himself tries to
do with the language—what he sees to be some of the central strands
or themes of the poem. For Conarroe, as for many of the earlier
critics and reviewers, these are: the man-city (Paterson as central
consciousness and Paterson as city-object); the river; the mountain
(the female counterpart, the source of the man-city's energy);
economics (usury, cancer, the blight); and the search for a redeeming language. But the essays, if very good in parts and in their
details, remain holistically insufficient and, finally, insensitive to the
poem's linguistic density, larger design, and symphonic elements.
The quality of Conarroe's analysis makes Williams's theses two-

dimensional and reductionary, collapsing *Paterson* into a parody of itself not much removed from the arguments for Social Credit in the flyer which Williams, with delicate irony and compassion, pasted to his poem.

For one of Williams's major strategies is to seem to lead the reader towards a standard critical response even while he is working the greater design which will alter our given response, until we realize with something of a jolt that we are in the mesh of a design which was there all the while, but which we saw only fitfully. This is so because the poem is constructed as a *process* of unfolding, of discovery, with Paterson-Williams as our Virgil taking us through this modern industrial hell in search of the beautiful thing, the radiant gist, Kore, by metamorphic turns the living *core*, the *cure* for our modern cancer, Kore the Virgin and Madame *Curie*, impregnated in the deepest sense by Mendelyeef's discoveries and finding the radiant gist, her mirror-self. *Paterson* is itself a brilliant analog for Williams's own search for the meaning of his place. For Williams's artistic strategy is to take anything and shape it into the poem, the imagination energizing the discrete particles into a pattern, a force shaping the material without altering the hard particularity of things.

Book V offers a good place from which to take an example, because the design is more readily apparent here. We get a view here of *Paterson* "from the air," an overview, in which we see the poem as map, as Mendelyeefian chart, as tapestry, rather than, as in the mode of the *Cantos* or the earlier books of *Paterson*, a discovery by seaboard, with its more tentative journey. Book V yields up more readily the design governing the whole. The final section of the last book opens with a poetic translation of Pieter Brueghel's sixteenth-century painting, *The Adoration of the Magi*. Williams salutes here another artist who "painted/what he saw—many times no doubt/among his own kids but not of course/in this setting." What Williams celebrated in the great Dutch artist is not only the ostensible subject, the archetypal pattern of maid and child, but the way in which Brueghel caught the particular reality of his own place: the "armed men" with "features like the more stupid/German soldiers of the late/war" who keep looking askance at poor Joseph, "the potbellied greybeard," whispering their own explanations about the father of the baby; the three Magi "come, obviously from afar/(highwaymen?)" with gifts picked up or, "more properly," stolen. In the midst of all this human bustling is the beautiful thing, the maiden (Kore) and child, archetypes of the imagination, existing on another plane, "as from an/illustrated catalogue/in colors," like one of Juan Gris's early collages, which Williams so much admired. So Brueghel, like the fifteenth-century artisans of the Unicorn tapestries, has captured the archetype alive and well in the rough-edged world of discrete particulars, the flux energized by the presence of a radiant core, and all set dancing together in a new order.

A few pages later Williams gives us a long excerpt of a letter from Edward Dahlberg, describing the plight of "a highly intelligent author," a woman who had come to America and there had a child by a "wretched scribbler." Poor and forsaken, she had returned to Copenhagen with her "wonderful boy," where she tried to eke out an existence, all the while badgered by "the socialist police" for nonpayment of taxes. Conarroe's strategy in his gloss is to catch as many of the interweaving threads as he can, and so the primary homologous design of *Paterson* never comes into focus. Dahlberg's letter, he says,

concerns a woman author who lives in Copenhagen with an illegitimate son, and who, when questioned by the police about a bottle of wine she bought (she had not paid her taxes), answers, 'I am so poor, and so driven to despair by it that I had to have a bottle of wine to relieve me of my melancholia' (267). This unrelieved despair, coupled with illegitimacy, inevitably suggests Miss Cress, and in the poetry that follows Paterson speaks of the dog of his thoughts as having shrunk to " 'a passionate letter'/to a woman, a woman he had neglected/to put to bed in the past" (268). This allusion is very possibly to his old correspondent [Cress].

All of this is no doubt true, and Conarroe also stresses the theme of illegitimacy and the identity of whore with virgin. The logic of Conarroe's method is to recall as many verbal echoes as one is able: Dürer's *Melancholy*, other "beautiful things" broken by a vicious economic system, the pathetic release by wine of the old Italian woman, Mary, dancing alone on Garrett Mountain, and the bottle ravaged and transformed in the fire (of the imagination). But Conarroe's strategic metaphor is the strand rather than the core, and the result is that the major unifying design is left insufficiently attended to.

Benjamin Sankey's strategy in his *A Companion to William Carlos Williams' Paterson* (1971) is, in actual practice, less useful than Conarroe's, given the fragmentation of *Paterson*'s surface into hundreds of planes and dozens of styles. For Sankey attempts a running commentary, relying rather heavily on the manuscripts at

Yale and Buffalo, the raw working notes *coming over* into, not a "finished" poem, but another level of process. A running commentary on a poem which deliberately undercuts logical sequence for simultaneity is unworkable, becomes in fact a backwater, static and murky. And nowhere does the commentary fail more massively than in the short redaction, "A Note on Book Five," where Williams's design is given but a passing nod. Brueghel's painting is included, Sankey writes, because it is an example of the religious motif treated realistically. And the "concern with economics is carried along in a letter Williams prints from a friend describing conditions in some of the countries of post-war Europe."

But what Williams has given us in the juxtaposition of Brueghel with Dahlberg is no less than this: the eternal pattern of maiden and child, the Danish woman as modern counterpart of the sixteenth-century Virgin, the Danish police replacing the Flemish soldiers, Dahlberg playing a surrogate poor Joseph. Dahlberg's letter, pasted into Williams's epic collage, keeps its own design and purpose, its own hard-edged singularity as artifact, but resonates with a new significance beyond its original one as it is caught up in the larger archetypal pattern.

Sankey's commentary is described on the dust jacket as "the first book-length study of *Paterson* which uses manuscript material to help elucidate the poem." It is certainly the first to rely on this material so extensively, but it does very little elucidating. Conarroe's study, which also used the manuscripts, preceded Sankey's by nearly a year. Furthermore, Sr. Quinn as early as 1955 had used the materials at the Lockwood Memorial Library, and Linda Wagner had used both collections for her 1964 study. There is also the sense in Sankey's study that the author became increasingly disenchanted with *Paterson* as he worked out the commentary. Sankey faults Williams's tone as being often shrill and desperate, and he sees the argument of *Paterson* as both obsessive and self-conscious: "the poem threatens at times to become a discourse on poetry, or on the psychology of the writer. Even the 'things' appearing in the poem, particulars and objects described sharply and persuasively, are sometimes infected by the poet's self-concern. Williams may have meant *Paterson* to compete in its way with the work of Homer and Villon, but he is too obsessed with his own role to approach his subject matter as naively or as confidently as those poets had done."

It is difficult to believe that such a statement could be made seriously at any time since the appearance of Wordsworth's *The*

Prelude, and especially in a post-modernist age. There is no city, no polis, apart from the mind perceiving its reality; the subject is *Paterson* and not Paterson. Or, as Williams put it in "Young Love" (1923): "Clean is he alone/after whom stream/the broken pieces of the city—/flying apart at his approaches."

Williams himself begins *Paterson* by telling us that "the beginning is assuredly/the end—since we know nothing, pure/and simple, beyond/our own complexities," and ends Book V by returning to a statement of the limitations of consciousness, for "to measure is all we know,/a choice among the measures." The modern sensibility as refracted in the modern poem knows only its own designs, a "chess game/massively, 'materially' compounded," and the interplay of the parts as they "dance to a measure." We cannot finally know Paterson any more than we can know Stevens's New Haven or Fellini's Roma. Our knowledge of place remains imperfect, and only what is measured by the imagination finally counts. For, as James Breslin says in his chapter on *Paterson*, all serious long poems since the early nineteenth century tend "to be more concerned with 'the growth of the poet's mind,' and to view this growth as a series of discrete moments (or episodes) rather than as a narrative action." We may view all three studies of *Paterson*, then, as prolegomena, approaches, to the poem, but one comes away with the sense of looking at driftwood spars, the flotsam and jetsam of three brave pilot ships which came through those falls badly battered.

Specialized Topics and Special Pleading

Sherman Paul, Guimond's dissertation advisor, with a number of good book-length studies of American figures like Thoreau and Randolph Bourne already to his credit, has given us a fine essay on Williams's *The Desert Music. The Music of Survival: A Biography of a Poem by William Carlos Williams* (1968) is a one-hundred-page genetic study of that late poem which illuminates much of the interior landscape of Williams's poetic world. Paul is an intelligent and seasoned close reader; he approaches the poem by showing us some of the pressures which converged in March, 1951: Williams's near-fatal apopletic stroke; his sense of achievement, with its concomitant premonitions of closure, of death; the presence of Eliot, of the ghosts of the avant-garde of the twenties; the fall of his friend Bob McAlmon; the ambivalence of the desert, the night, chaos, as

both "the supplying female" and the alien other. His discussions of
the dance of the imagination and of Williams's sense of culture as
opposed to what Eliot in particular was propounding in the forties
is remarkably lucid and "right." His reading of the *Autobiography*
as a fiction of the vindicated American who stayed at home and
made contact with his place, and again as the older artist passing
on the new, viable texts to a younger generation (Charles Olson's
projective verse, the grandfather showing the grandson the Falls)
helps to demonstrate the *Autobiography's* sense of calculation in
which a rambling and naive "honesty" are in fact strategies in
creating that image of himself which Williams felt he needed. In
his presentation of the relationship between Williams and Mc-
Almon, however, Paul might have stressed the other, mercurial side
of Williams, who could also forget or dismiss at times his old friend,
an aging tubercular alcoholic living with his brothers and selling
trusses for a living (as Edward Dahlberg evokes him sensitively in
Alms for Oblivion as well as in his correspondence).

Bram Dijkstra's *The Hieroglyphics of a New Speech: Cubism,
Stieglitz, and the Early Poetry of William Carlos Williams*, pub-
lished by Princeton in late 1969, is a serious investigation into the
influence of cubism and the American "school" of Alfred Stieglitz
on the poetry and poetics of William Carlos Williams in the 1910s.
Dijkstra describes carefully the intellectual ferment among the
New York-based artists who clustered about Stieglitz's "291
Gallery." He demonstrates the range and importance of such
avant-garde magazines as Stieglitz's *Camera Work*, deZaya's *291*,
Rosenfeld's *Manuscripts*, Picabia's *391*, and Duchamp's *The Blind
Man, Rongwrong,* and *New York Dada*, magazines which helped
create a new visual imagination. He shows in particular how Williams's poems from about 1915 through the twenties approximate
cubist designs. Dijkstra is good, too, in showing how Paul Rosenfeld's essays on American painting in the *Dial* and in *Vanity Fair*
in 1921 and 1922, as well as Marsden Hartley's *Adventures in the
Arts*, directly influenced Williams's concern with the American
and with the local.

Unfortunately, Dijkstra also allows his thesis to run away from
him. His insistence that the roles of Pound, Whitman, and Stein
"must be considered secondary to the role played by painting in
general, and figures such as Alfred Stieglitz in particular," over-
states the case and tends to undermine much that he has carefully
established in the muzzy area of influence. Nowhere, for example,
does he evaluate Pound's emphasis (after Gautier) on line and

sculpture. Nor does he ever mention John Dewey's insistence on the importance of the local, even though Williams himself stressed this connection. Another shortcoming of Dijkstra's study—and a more serious one—is his assumption that Williams attempted to do with words exactly what the European post-impressionists and the American painters had done with paint. Williams did sometimes paint a verbal still life so that the poem can be checked against an "original": a photograph by Stieglitz, a painting by Juan Gris, Charles Sheeler, or Charles Demuth. But on the larger question of design, on the use of a poetic form similar in intention to the painters, it is here that Dijkstra falters. For direct copying, as Williams knew, leads to stasis, and led to the dead end of objectivism for him in the late thirties. It is the understanding of increasingly complex forms in artists like Cézanne and Tchelitchew, Lautrec and Brueghel, which led from the early still lifes like "Between Walls" and "On Gay Wallpaper" to the larger canvas of *Paterson*. Williams simply cannot be explained in terms of Stieglitz any more than Keats can be understood in terms of Leigh Hunt. Still, for all these caveats, Dijkstra's is an informative, worthwhile study. But his 1971 essay, "Wallace Stevens and William Carlos Williams: Poetry, Painting and the Function of Reality," a kind of groping towards a sociology of literary forms, reviews briefly and in a surprisingly superficial manner the role of painting in the development of the poetics of Stevens and Williams. Dijkstra's thesis is this: that Stevens tried to use paintings, usually of still lifes, as mediators between vulgar reality and his rage for order. The result was that he effectively cut himself off from living contact with the world around him, surrounding himself instead with second-rate European painters and cheap colored photo-postcard reproductions of paintings. In marked contrast was Williams, who employed the *theories* of American experimental artists like Demuth, Hartley, Dove, and Sheeler in order to *see* reality fresh and from a new perspective. But Dijkstra's theory "explains" neither Stevens's nor Williams's practice.

The Williams-Siegel Documentary (1970) is surely one of the strangest, most irritating, comic, and pathetic books Williams ever attracted. Only one other piece is more excessive: the baroness's two-part dadaist critique of *Kora in Hell* back in 1921. The "documentary" is clearly an embarrassment—an irritable embarrassment for Williams and his literary estate, a weary embarrassment for the critic, a comic embarrassment for the reader. Hugh Kenner seems to have found the exact tone for dealing with the thing in his review of the book (*NR*, Dec. 12, 1970). Admitting that Siegel had given us three of the most attentive pages a critic has written (referring to Siegel's commentary on "The Red Wheelbarrow" in his 1952 talk on Williams), Kenner also lamented the fact that three-quarters of the book dealt with "an apparently obsessive grievance." The book reads like a comedy of errors, with Martha Baird and Ellen Reiss editing the abortive epithalamion between Williams and Siegel. Briefly, Martha Baird sent Williams copies of Eli Siegel's poetry in October, 1951, and Williams sent back an enthusiastic reply. Williams was frequently generous to a fault, but this time he was trapped into extending himself more than he had expected, first into hearing Siegel lecture on Williams's poetry (Williams was pleased), and then into reciprocating by arranging for Siegel to participate in a poetry reading. But as Williams moved on to other things, the Siegels and then the members of the Society for Aesthetic Realism, sensing a waning of devotions, huddled around their stricken leader, with various members turning to whoever might be listening to keen that, yes sir, Siegel is "so humble and so great," "the greatest critic there ever has been." Williams was numbed into silence by the whole affair, and told to be more careful about whom he chose to compliment.

Jerome Mazzaro's *William Carlos Williams: The Later Poems*, published in the spring of 1973, closes off the first decade of criticism and scholarship since Williams's death. As its title suggests, Mazzaro's study concerns itself primarily with the poetics of Williams's last phase, and particularly with "Of Asphodel, that Greeny Flower" and the "Pictures from Breughel" sequence. But there is also a chapter on the analytical cubist strategy of *Paterson* and another chapter on the pervasive erotic pressure of the Williams lyric. Mazzaro himself sees his study as "a work of exegesis, in at least two traditional senses": exegesis both as a correlating of Williams's texts in order to map the development and metamorphosis of some of Williams's major poetic ideas, and as an interpretation, a glossing, of those texts. Of the five chapters which comprise Mazzaro's study, versions of four appeared in 1970: two (chapters 1 and 3) in the pamphlet series, *Intrepid* (Buffalo), under the title, *Of Love, Abiding Love*, and two (chapters 2 and 5) in *Modern Poetry Studies*.

Mazzaro's study has flashes of brilliance, but it is, overall, a disappointing book. Stylistically, it is prolix, composed of syntactic structures more concerned with the figure they make as they arc through space than with conveying information or elucidation. Mazzaro has the questionable habit of lugging in systems and information, particularly from his Renaissance training, which usually obfuscate rather than clarify Williams's texts. He seems to have little use for transitions. And he is unnecessarily tentative about a problem in poetics where further study of the critics who came before him, or even of Williams's own papers, would have clarified what he refers to as the "mystery." The yield is surprisingly light for surviving the book's lexical density; its direction is circuitous and cubistic, and one is puzzled by the failure of idea to grow naturally out of idea. The text needs a more severe pruning than it has received.

Mazzaro's major "finding" is that the poetry of Williams's late phase, which includes *Paterson* III and IV as well, is seriously flawed by Williams's own poetics. For Mazzaro sees in these poems an "ideological snarl in a poetic canon whose dialectic is already characterized by contradiction, vacillation, and reversal." But Mazzaro reaches this conclusion by assertion rather than by proof, largely because his own understanding of Williams's ongoing theoretical dialectic, his expectations for the poetry, is imperfect. This was, incidentally, the major fault of much of the early criticism directed towards Williams. The critic came to the poetry with a previously established set of criteria, and found those criteria frustrated when measured against a poetry which accordingly did not "function" or yield itself up. The solution was simple. The critic had to learn to rethink his categories and let himself approach the new, a thing which, admittedly, is never easy. For the earlier critics who did not have access to Williams's own theoretical writings which had appeared in almost impossible-to-attain books or in obscure little magazines, and who thus had no way of telling where to find the considered essay as opposed to the piece thrown off to meet an encroaching deadline, there is ample excuse for often making egregious blunders of judgment, particularly since a favorable critical climate for Williams just did not exist.

But this is not the case with Mazzaro, who has simply not listened long enough to Williams and particularly not to his many notes toward a radical poetics. As oblique as Williams is, there is often a clarity and precision about his statements, even amidst his polemics, which Mazzaro's baroque syntax seldom attains. Take an example. Mazzaro misunderstands the "cubist" nature of *Paterson*, insisting that the analytical cubist poem should be able to introduce "life" language into "literary" language so that art and nature seem to intermingle. But to articulate the dimensionality of *Paterson* in this way is to misunderstand Williams's own intentions for his prose borrowings from newspapers, journals, letters, pamphlets, charts, flyers, and even broadcasts. Once these are handled by the artist they become part of his material, informed now by a controlling, selecting intelligence. Henceforth, they can give only the *appearance* of being accidental. Whatever Williams meant the poem to do, he knew too well that, just as "foreign" materials magnetized to a cubist painting became part of that painting, so too words were, finally, only words, other objects. And yet Mazzaro gauges the relative failure of *Paterson* on his conception that Williams intended to bring over into words the exact equivalent of analytical cubism. Here J. Hillis Miller's reading of Williams's unitive epistemology, where word and thing each possess a reality which they share in common, is more helpful than Mazzaro.

But Mazzaro's study can be both illuminating and interesting, particularly in its development of two major themes in Williams's poetry: the Kora/Demeter myth as a symbol of the artist's descent in imagination into chaos and his ascent into form; and, as a corollary to this myth, the androgynetic basis of Williams's art, the artist as a composite of the male and female. This idea is an old one, with antecedents going back at least as far as Aristophanes's myth of the radical dispersal and return to complements in Plato's *Symposium*. Closer to our own time, it has been developed by, among others, Coleridge, Joyce, and Virginia Woolf. And, as documented direct influences on Williams, there is Otto Weininger's *Sex and Character* (1906), Dora Marsden, and, probably by way of Ezra Pound's translation, Remy de Gourmont's *Physique de l'amour* (1903). Mazzaro's reading of Jung to clarify Williams's notion of the woman is also generally helpful. Also useful is his discussion of the relationship between painting and literature, showing in particular Williams's proximity to movements like simultaneism and to painters like Stuart Davis. But it is also true that he rarely complements or extends the groundwork of critics like Dijkstra on Williams's relationship to figures like Sheeler, Demuth, Gris, and Stieglitz, or of Weaver on Williams's use of these figures as well as of Tchelitchew and Emanuel Romano. One senses in Mazzaro, rather, a parasitic relationship to these and other critics, using their findings to initiate and sustain his own discussion. What often happens, as a result, is that we find ourselves at a second remove from Williams, caught up in a mesh which exists not to clarify but to exhibit its own pyrotechnics. Perhaps the most disturbing thing about this study is that the reader may come away from it not only unconvinced and unrefreshed, but wondering whether he ought in fact to take the whole thing seriously. Mazzaro, nevertheless, is potentially a good critic, one to listen to in spite of the failures which his study of Williams contains. It is a question of focus, of moving too easily to the right or to the left with learned allusions or quotations which distract rather than enlighten. It is a question, too, of writing clearly, directly, and with constant attention on the artist himself, giving him the benefit of the doubt rather than attempting to display a critical one-upmanship which, rather than instructing the neophyte, only burdens him.

Conclusion .

This chapter, then, is a mapping of the critical strategies and the scholarly findings in the field of Williams in the decade since his death. We now possess several competent overviews and introductions; *Paterson* continues to be explored; and several critics have demonstrated the usefulness and importance of those early experiments in radical poetics: *Kora in Hell* and particularly *Spring and All*. The late poems continue to influence younger writers. Several of Williams's most important texts have been made available, although many still remain unpublished or are out-of-print. We need a much expanded letters and a new, enlarged collection of Williams's essays which will include the many introductions to books and the uncollected pieces in little magazines. We sorely need a biography of the man and a book on the Williams-Pound literary relationship which would incorporate some of the voluminous correspondence between the two men written over sixty years. We still need a study of Williams's sense of American history, which would cover not only *In the American Grain* but also the other prose and the poetry, including *Paterson*. We need another study of Williams and the painters. We have no full-length study of Williams as a theoretician and radical experimenter to dispell the myth of the anti-intellectual doctor jotting down poems between house calls.* There is also room for a book on Williams and his contemporaries, and another on Williams and the sons (and daughters) of Williams.

*Joseph N. Riddel's *The Inverted Bell: Modernism and the Counterpoetics of William Carlos Williams* (Baton Rouge: Louisiana State Univ. Pr.), which appeared too late for coverage here, addresses itself to this very question. Applying a structuralist grid derived from Heidegger and Derrida, Riddel gives us a brilliant but vastly uneven reading of Williams's post-modernist poetics.

The drama and the fiction have been calling for some time for serious attention. And there is still *Paterson* waiting for its summative critic. These are only some of the more obvious directions for Williams scholarship in the coming years. When we review the flurry of critical and scholarly activity which Williams has attracted in the past decade, it is clear that Williams has finally arrived, especially among the young. Youth has the republican advantage over the settled hierarchies of the past of being able to reduce the old statues to rubble and of recreating from the fragments a new household of acceptable presences.

References

Abbe, George
   1965. *You and Contemporary Poetry: An Aid to Appreciation.* Peterborough, N.H.: Richard R. Smith, pp. 48–53.
Alexander, Michael
   1966. "William Carlos Williams and Robert Creeley," *Agenda.* Summer, pp. 56–67.
Angoff, Charles
   1964. "A Williams Memoir," *Prairie Schooner.* Winter, pp. 299–305; reprinted in *Profile of William Carlos Williams,* ed. Jerome Mazzaro, pp. 33–38. Columbus, Ohio: Charles E. Merrill, 1971.
Anonymous
   1964a. "No Ideas but in Things," *Times Literary Supplement.* May 7, p. 396; reprinted in *T.L.S.: Essays and Reviews from the Times Literary Supplement* 1964, pp. 136–38. London: Oxford Univ. Pr., 1965.
   1964b. Response to Tomlinson, *Times Literary Supplement.* May 28, p. 455.
   1967a. "The Williams Grain," *Times Literary Supplement.* Apr. 13, p. 305.
   1967b. "Old New World," *Times Literary Supplement.* June 22, p. 556.
Baird, Martha
   1970. (and Ellen Reiss, editors) *The Williams-Siegel Documentary.* New York: Definition Pr.
Blackmur, R. P.
   1960 . "Introduction" to *American Short Novels.* New York: Crowell, pp. 13–15.
Bradley, Sculley
   1967. (and Richmond C. Beatty and E. Hudson Long) *The American Tradition in Literature.* 3rd ed., 2: 1540–56. New York: Norton.

Breslin, James E.

1967a. "William Carlos Williams and the Whitman Tradition," in *Literary Criticism and Historical Understanding: Selected Papers* of the English Institute, ed. Phillip Damon, pp. 151–79. New York: Columbia Univ. Pr. Revised and reprinted in *William Carlos Williams: An American Artist*. New York: Oxford Univ. Pr., 1970.

1967b. "Whitman and the Early Development of William Carlos Williams," *Publications of the Modern Language Association*, Dec., pp. 613–21; revised and reprinted in *William Carlos Williams: An American Artist*. New York: Oxford Univ. Pr., 1970.

1970. *William Carlos Williams: An American Artist*. New York: Oxford Univ. Pr.

Brooks, Cleanth

1960. (and Robert Penn Warren) *Understanding Poetry*. New York: Holt, pp. 172–75.

1965. "A Retrospective Introduction," in *Modern Poetry and the Tradition*, pp. vii–xxvii. Rev. ed. Chapel Hill: Univ. of North Carolina Pr.

Bruce-Wilson, Richard

1966. "The New American Decadence," *Delta*. Spring, pp. 22–28.

Butler, Gerald

1964. "The Measure of American," *Things (Hanging Loose)*. Fall, pp. 38–46.

Calhoun, Richard

1966. " 'No Ideas but in Things': William Carlos Williams in the Twenties," in *The Twenties, Poetry and Prose: 20 Critical Essays*, eds. Richard E. Langford and William E. Taylor, pp. 28–35. Deland, Fla.: Everett-Edwards.

Carruth, Hayden

1970. (editor) *The Voice That Is Great Within Us: American Poetry of the Twentieth Century*. New York: Bantam, pp. 49–50.

Clark, Thomas

1965. "Moving Images," *New Statesman*. July 23, p. 126.

Coblentz, Stanton

1967. *The Poetry Circus*. New York: Hawthorn.

Conarroe, Joel

1970. *William Carlos Williams' Paterson: Language and Landscape*. Philadelphia: Univ. of Pennsylvania Pr.

1971. "The Measured Dance: Williams' 'Pictures from Brueghel,' " *Journal of Modern Literature*. May, pp. 565–77.

Corman, Cid

1962. "*The Farmers' Daughters:* A True Story about People," *Massachusetts Review*. Winter, pp. 164–70.

Cowan, James C.

1971. "The Image of Water in *Paterson*," *Journal of Modern Literature*. May, pp. 503–11.

Cox, C. B.
1967. "Williams and Pound," *Spectator*. Apr. 14, p. 425.

Dahlberg, Edward
1964. *Alms for Oblivion*. Minneapolis: Univ. of Minnesota Pr., pp. 7–8, 20–27.

1967. *Epitaphs of Our Times: The Letters of Edward Dahlberg*. New York: Braziller, pp. 177–206.

1971. *The Confessions of Edward Dahlberg*. New York: Grosset, pp. 201–2, passim.

Davie, Donald
1964a. *Ezra Pound: Poet as Sculptor*. New York: Oxford Univ. Pr., pp. 120–25, passim.

1964b. "Two Ways Out of Whitman," *Review*. Dec., pp. 14–19.

Dembo, L. S.
1966. "William Carlos Williams: Objectivist Mathematics" in *Conceptions of Reality in Modern Poetry*, pp. 48–80. Berkeley: Univ. of California Pr.

Dickey, James
1964. "First and Last Things," *Poetry*. Feb., pp. 321–22; reprinted in *Babel to Byzantium*. New York: Grosset, 1968.

1966. "William Carlos Williams: The Yachts," in *Master Poems of the English Language*, ed. Oscar Williams, pp. 901–2. New York: Trident. Reprinted in *Babel to Byzantium*. New York: Grosset, 1968.

Dijkstra, Bram
1969. *The Hieroglyphics of a New Speech: Cubism, Stieglitz, and the Early Poetry of William Carlos Williams*. Princeton, N.J.: Princeton Univ. Pr.

1971. "Wallace Stevens and William Carlos Williams: Poetry, Painting and the Function of Reality," in *Encounters: Essays on Literature and the Visual Arts*, ed. John Dixon Hunt, pp. 156–72. London: Studio Vista.

Donaldson, G. Morris
1970. "William Carlos Williams: *Paterson* Books I and II," *West Court Review*. June, pp. 3–10.

Donoghue, Denis
1965a. *Connoisseurs of Chaos*. New York: Macmillan, pp. 16–17, 199–200, passim.

1965b. "Dark Angels," *Manchester Guardian Weekly*. July 29, p. 11.

1966. "The Long Poem," *New York Review of Books*. Apr. 14, pp. 18–20.

Doyle, Charles
1970. "A Reading of 'Paterson III,' " *Modern Poetry Studies*. No. 3, pp. 140–53.

Duffey, Bernard
1967. "Williams' *Paterson* and the Measure of Art," in *Essays on American Literature in Honor of Jay B. Hubbell,* ed. Clarence Gohdes, pp. 282–94. Durham, N.C.: Duke Univ. Pr. Reprinted in *Studies in Paterson,* ed. John Engels, pp. 61–73. Columbus, Ohio: Charles E. Merrill, 1971.
1968. "Stevens and Williams," *Contemporary Literature.* Summer, pp. 431–36.
Duncan, Robert
1969. "A Critical Difference of View," *Stony Brook.* Nos. 3/4, pp. 360–63.
Ehrenpreis, Irvin
1965. (editor) *American Poetry.* Stratford-upon-Avon Studies 7. London: E. Arnold.
Ellmann, Richard.
1973. (and Robert O'Clair) *The Norton Anthology of Modern Poetry.* New York: Norton, pp. 284–87.
Engel, Bernard
1966. "A Democratic Vista of Religion," *Georgia Review.* Spring, pp. 84–89.
Engel, John
1971. (editor) *Studies in Paterson.* Columbus, Ohio: Charles E. Merrill.
Eulert, Donald
1967. "Robert Lowell and W. C. Williams: Sterility in 'Central Park,'" *English Language Notes.* Dec., pp. 129–35.
Ferry, David
1965. "The Diction of American Poetry," in *American Poetry,* ed. Irvin Ehrenpreis. London: E. Arnold.
Fields, Kenneth
1967. "The Free Verse of Yvor Winters and William Carlos Williams," *Southern Review.* Summer, pp. 764–75.
Finkel, Donald
1964. "An Old Review," *Prairie Schooner.* Winter, pp. 367–72.
Furbank, P. N.
1964. "New Poetry," *Listener.* Apr. 16, p. 645.
Galinsky, Hans
1968. "An American Doctor-Poet's Image of Germany: An Approach to the Work of William Carlos Williams," *Studium Generale.* pp. 74–93.
Garvin, Harry
1961. "William Carlos Williams' Journey to Marriage," *Annali Instituto Universitario Orientale.* pp. 203–14.
Gerber, Philip L.
1971. "So Much Depends: The Williams Foreground," in *Profile of*

William Carlos Williams, ed. Jerome Mazzaro, pp. 5–24. Columbus, Ohio: Charles E. Merrill, 1971.

Goodwin, K. L.

1966. *The Influence of Ezra Pound*. London: Oxford Univ. Pr., pp. 1–3, 143–57, 219.

Grigson, Geoffrey

1964. "That Greeny Flower," *New Statesman*. May 1, p. 691.

Gross, Harvey

1964. *Sound and Form in Modern Poetry: A Study of Prosody from Thomas Hardy to Robert Lowell*. Ann Arbor: Univ. of Michigan Pr., pp. 117–22.

Guimond, James

1968. *The Art of William Carlos Williams: A Discovery and Possession of America*. Urbana: Univ. of Illinois Pr.

1971. "William Carlos Williams and the Past: Some Clarifications," *Journal of Modern Literature*. May, pp. 493–502.

Gunn, Thom

1962. "New Books in Review: Things, Voices, Minds," *Yale Review*. Autumn, pp. 129–38.

1965. "William Carlos Williams," *Encounter*. July, pp. 67–74; reprinted in part in *William Carlos Williams: A Collection of Critical Essays*, ed. J. Hillis Miller, pp. 171–73. Englewood Cliffs, N.J.: Prentice-Hall, 1966.

Gustafson, Richard

1965. "William Carlos Williams' Paterson: A Map and Opinion," *College English*. Apr., pp. 532–34, 539.

Halpert, Stephen

1969. (and Richard Johns) *A Return to Pagany: The History, Correspondence, and Selections from a Little Magazine 1929–1932*. Boston: Beacon Pr., pp. 9–12, 124–28, passim.

Hamburger, Michael

1970. *The Truth of Poetry*. New York: Harcourt, pp. 31–35, 252–54.

Hamilton, Ian

1964. "Poetry," *London Magazine*. July, pp. 65–69.

Hardie, Jack

1971. " 'A Celebration of the Light': Selected Checklist of Writings about William Carlos Williams," *Journal of Modern Literature*. May, pp. 593–642.

Harrison, Keith

1964. "Places and People," *Spectator*. May 29, p. 731.

1967. "No Things but in Ideas: Doctor Williams and Mr. Pound," *Dalhousie Review*. Winter, pp. 577–80.

Hays, H. R.

1969. "An American Voice: The Continuing Presence of William Carlos Williams," *Voyages*. Spring, pp. 34–39.

Heal, Edith
1965. "A Poet's Integrity," *Little Review*. Autumn, pp. 115–19.
Heyen, William
1970a. "The Poet's Leap into Reality," *Saturday Review of Literature*. Aug. 1, pp. 21–24.
1970b. Review, *Saturday Review of Literature*. Nov. 14, pp. 31, 39–40, 45.
Hoffman, Daniel
1969. "A Poet of the Quotidian, Dedicated to the Imaginative Possession of Experience," *New York Times Book Review*. Apr. 6, pp. 5, 30.
Holder, Alan
1967. "In the American Grain: William Carlos Williams on the American Past," *American Quarterly*. Fall, pp. 499–515.
Holton, Milne
1969. "To Hit Love Aslant: Poetry and William Carlos Williams," in *Private Dealings: Eight Modern American Writers*, ed. David J. Burrows, pp. 50–69. Stockholm: Almquist and Wiksell.
Ignatow, David
1964. "Williams' Influence: Some Social Aspects," *Chelsea*. Jan., pp. 154–61.
Josephson, Matthew
1962. *Life among the Surrealists*. New York: Holt, pp. 72–77, 253–54, passim.
Kartiganer, Donald M.
1971. "Process and Product: A Study of Modern Literary Form," *Massachusetts Review*. Spring, pp. 297–328.
Kenner, Hugh
1962. "The Drama of Utterance," *Massachusetts Review*. Winter, pp. 328–30.
1963. "William Carlos Williams: In Memoriam," *National Review*. Apr., p. 237.
1965. *Studies in Change: A Book of the Short Story*. Englewood Cliffs, N.J.: Prentice-Hall, pp. xi, 100, 166.
1968. "Syntax in Rutherford," *Poetry*. Nov., pp. 119–25; reprinted in his *The Pound Era*, pp. 397–406. Berkeley: Univ. of California Pr., 1971.
1970. "Red Wheelbarrow Revisited," *New Republic*. Dec. 12, pp. 22–24.
1971. *The Pound Era*. Berkeley: Univ. of California Pr., pp. 397–406, 506–17, 541–44.
LeClair, Thomas
1970. "The Poet as Dog in *Paterson*," *Twentieth Century Literature*. Apr., pp. 97–108.
Levin, Harry
1970. "William Carlos Williams and the Old World," *Yale Review*.

June, pp. 520–31; reprinted as "Introduction" to *A Voyage to Pagany*, pp. ix–xx. New York: New Directions, 1970.

Lewis, R. W. B.

1973. (and Cleanth Brooks and Robert Penn Warren) *American Literature: The Makers and the Making*, 2: 2142–53. New York: St. Martin's.

Litz, A. Walton

1964. "William Carlos Williams," in Lawrence B. Holland, Nathaniel Burt, and A. Walton Litz, *The Literary Heritage of New Jersey*. New Brunswick, N.J.: Rutgers Univ. Pr., pp. 83–130.

Lombardi, Thomas (Ashton)

1968. "William Carlos Williams: The Leech-Gatherer of *Paterson*," *Midwest Quarterly*. July, pp. 333–49.

Macksey, Richard A.

1966. " 'A Certainty of Music': Williams' Changes" in *William Carlos Williams: A Collection of Critical Essays*, ed. J. Hillis Miller, pp. 132–47. Englewood Cliffs, N.J.: Prentice-Hall, 1966.

1968. "The Old Poets," *Johns Hopkins Magazine*. No. 1, pp. 42–48.

Mariani, Paul

1972. "Towards the Canonization of William Carlos Williams," *Massachusetts Review*. Autumn, pp. 661–75.

1973a. "The Satyr's Defense: Williams' 'Asphodel,' " *Contemporary Literature*. Winter, pp. 1–18.

1973b. "A Williams Garland: Petals from the Falls, 1945–1950," *Massachusetts Review*. Winter, pp. 65–148.

Marshall, Tom

1970. *The Psychic Mariner: A Reading of the Poems of D. H. Lawrence*. New York: Viking, pp. 239–41.

Martz, Louis L.

1971. "*Paterson*: A Plan for Action," *Journal of Modern Literature*. May, pp. 513–22.

Mazzaro, Jerome

1970a. "Dimensionality in Dr. Williams' 'Paterson,' " *Modern Poetry Studies*. No. 3, pp. 98–117; revised and reprinted in *William Carlos Williams: The Later Poems*. Ithaca: Cornell Univ. Pr.

1970b. "Williams, Kora, That Greeny Flower," in *Of Love, Abiding Love, Intrepid* 17, Buffalo, pp. 5–29; revised and reprinted in *William Carlos Williams: The Later Poems*. Ithaca: Cornell Univ. Pr.

1970c. "Asphodel, Williams, the Tragic Foot," in *Of Love, Abiding Love, Intrepid* 17, Buffalo, pp. 30–54; revised and reprinted in *William Carlos Williams: The Later Poems*. Ithaca: Cornell Univ. Pr.

1970d. "The Descent Once More: 'Paterson V' and 'Pictures from Brueghel,' " *Modern Poetry Studies*. No. 6, pp. 278–300; revised and reprinted in *William Carlos Williams: The Later Poems*. Ithaca: Cornell Univ. Pr.

1971. (editor) *Profile of William Carlos Williams*. Columbus, Ohio: Charles E. Merrill.

1973. *William Carlos Williams: The Later Poems*. Ithaca: Cornell Univ. Pr.

Meinke, Peter

1967. "William Carlos Williams: Traditional Rebel," *Mad River Review*. Winter-Spring, pp. 57–64; reprinted in *Profile of William Carlos Williams*, ed. Jerome Mazzaro, pp. 107–14. Columbus, Ohio: Charles E. Merrill, 1971.

Meserole, Harrison

1969. (and Walter Sutton and Brom Weber) *American Literature: Tradition and Innovation*. Lexington, Mass.: Heath, pp. 3365–67.

Miller, J. Hillis

1966a. "William Carlos Williams" in *Poets of Reality: Six Twentieth-Century Writers*, ed. J. H. Miller, pp. 285–359. Rev. ed. New York: Atheneum.

1966b. (editor) *William Carlos Williams: A Collection of Critical Essays*. Englewood Cliffs, N.J.: Prentice-Hall.

1967. Review, *American Literature*. May, pp. 237–39.

1970. "Williams' *Spring and All* and the Progress of Poetry," *Daedelus*. Spring, pp. 405–34.

Monteiro, George

1969. "Dr. Williams' First Book," *Books at Brown*. 23: 85–88.

Mottram, Eric

1964. "American Poetry in the Thirties: Some Revisions and Bearings," *Review*. Nos. 11–12, pp. 25–41.

1965. "The Making of Paterson," *Stand*. 7, no. 3: 17–34.

Myers, Neil

1965. "William Carlos Williams' *Spring and All*," *Modern Language Quarterly*. June, pp. 285–301.

1966. "Sentimentalism in the Early Poetry of William Carlos Williams," *American Literature*. Jan., pp. 458–70.

1970. "Williams' Imitation of Nature in 'The Desert Music,' " *Criticism*. Winter, pp. 38–50.

1971. "Williams' 'Two Pendants: for the Ears,' " *Journal of Modern Literature*. May, pp. 477–92.

Nelson, Cary

1971. "Suffused-Encircling Shapes of Mind: Inhabited Space in Williams," *Journal of Modern Literature*. May, pp. 549–64.

Nilsen, Helge Normann

1969. "Notes on the Theme of Love in the Later Poetry of William Carlos Williams," *English Studies*. June, pp. 273–83.

Noland, Richard
  1964. "A Failure of Contact: William Carlos Williams on America," *Emory University Quarterly*. Winter, pp. 248–60.
Neussendorfer, Sr. Marcaria
  1965. "William Carlos Williams' Idea of a City," *Thought*. Summer,
  pp. 242–72; reprinted in *Studies in Paterson*, ed. John Engels, pp.
  89–122. Columbus, Ohio: Charles E. Merrill, 1971.
Norman, Charles
  1960. *Ezra Pound*. New York: Funk and Wagnalls, pp. 1–7, 23–25,
  225–28, 265–69, 317–19, passim.
Olson, Charles
  1968. *Mayan Letters*. Ed. and with preface by Robert Creeley, New
  York: Grossman, passim.
Ostrom, Alan
  1966. *The Poetic World of William Carlos Williams*. Carbondale:
  Southern Illinois Univ. Pr.
Parsons, Ann
  1970. "The Art of Process," *Nation*. Nov. 23, pp. 534–36.
Paul, Sherman
  1966. "Seeing Williams with Fresh Eyes," *Nation*. Oct. 10, pp.
  356–57.
  1968. *The Music of Survival: A Biography of a Poem by William
  Carlos Williams*. Urbana: Univ. of Illinois Pr.
Peterson, Walter Scott
  1967. *An Approach to Paterson*. New Haven, Conn.: Yale Univ.
  Pr.
Press, John
  1965. "Recent Poems," *Punch*. July 7, p. 29.
Quinn, Sr. Bernetta
  1970. "*Paterson: Listening to Landscape*," in *Modern American
  Poetry: Essays in Criticism*, ed. Jerome Mazzaro, pp. 116–54. New
  York: McKay.
  1971. "*Paterson:* Landscape and Dream," *Journal of Modern Litera-
  ture*. May, pp. 523–48.
Ramsey, Paul
  1971. "William Carlos Williams as Metrist: Theory and Practice,"
  Journal of Modern Literature. May, pp. 578–92.
Riddel, Joseph E.
  1968a. Review, *Modern Language Journal*. Jan., pp. 44–46.
  1968b. Review, *Criticism*. Fall, pp. 358–62.
  1970. "The Wanderer and the Dance: William Carlos Williams'
  Early Poetics," in *The Shaken Realist*, eds. Melvin J. Friedman and
  John B. Vickery, pp. 45–71. Baton Rouge: Univ. of Louisiana Pr.
Rosenthal, M. L.
  1965a. "William Carlos Williams," *Spectator*. June 25, pp. 822–23.

1965b. "Gurlie, Joe, and Spider," *Spectator*. Aug. 20, pp. 241–42.

1966. "William Carlos Williams: More than Meets the Eye," Introduction to *The William Carlos Williams Reader*. New York: New Directions.

Rosenthal, Raymond

1967. "The Way the Land Lies," *New Leader*. Jan. 30, pp. 23–24.

Sankey, Benjamin

1965. "The Short Stories of William Carlos Williams." *Spectrum*. Spring, pp. 19–27.

1971. *A Companion to William Carlos Williams's Paterson*. Berkeley: Univ. of California Pr.

Schott, Webster

1966. "A Gigantic Poet Who Wrote American," *Life*. Nov. 18, pp. 8, 16.

1970a. "Doctor Williams: Beautiful Blood, Beautiful Brain," *American Scholar*. Spring, pp. 305–9; reprinted as Introduction to *William Carlos Williams: Imaginations*, pp. ix–xviii. New York: New Directions.

1970b. (editor) *William Carlos Williams: Imaginations*. New York: New Directions.

Seamon, Roger

1965. "The Bottle in the Fire: Resistance as Creation in William Carlos Williams' *Paterson*," *Twentieth Century Literature*. Apr., pp. 16–24; reprinted in *Studies in Paterson*, ed. John Engels. Columbus, Ohio: Charles E. Merrill, 1971.

Sereni, Vittorio

1964. "W.C.W.· An Italian View," *Prairie Schooner*. Winter, pp. 307–16.

Shapiro, Karl

1964. "Is Poetry an American Art?" *College English*. Mar., pp. 395–405; revised and reprinted in *To Abolish Children and Other Essays*, pp. 45–62. Chicago: Quadrangle, 1968.

1967. "Our Heroes Off Their Horses," *Washington Post Book Week*. Feb. 26, pp. 17–18.

Sienicka, Marta

1968. "Poetry in the Prose of 'In the American Grain,' by William Carlos Williams," *Studia Anglica Posnaniensia*. No. 1, pp. 109–16.

Slate, Joseph Evans

1965. "William Carlos Williams, Hart Crane, and 'The Virtue of History,'" *Texas Studies in Literature and Language*. Winter, pp. 486–511.

1968. "William Carlos Williams and the Modern Short Story," *Southern Review*. Summer, pp. 647–64.

1971. "Kora in Opacity: Williams' Improvisations," *Journal of Modern Literature*. May, pp. 463–76.

Smith, Barbara H.
1968. *Poetic Closure: A Study of How Poems End*. Chicago: Univ. of Chicago Pr., pp. 257–60.
Solt, Mary Ellen
1968. "A World Look at Concrete Poetry," Introduction to *Concrete Poetry: A World View*. Bloomington: Indiana Univ. Pr., pp. 47–54, 58–59.
Sorrentino, Gilbert
1970. " 'Art is a Country by Itself,' " *Nation*. Dec. 14, pp. 635–36.
Sutton, Walter
1965a. "Criticism and Poetry," in *American Poetry*, ed. Irvin Ehrenpreis, pp. 175–95. Stratford-upon-Avon Studies 7. London: E. Arnold.
1965b. "A Conversation with Denise Levertov," *Minnesota Review*. Oct.–Dec., pp. 322–38.
1973. *American Free Verse: The Modern Revolution in Poetry*. New York: New Directions, pp. 118–51, passim.
Symonds, Julian
1967a. "New Poetry," *New Statesman*. May 12, p. 658.
1967b. "Moveable Feet," *New Statesman*. June 16, p. 849.
Talbot, Norman
1965. "The Poetry of William Carlos Williams, 1883–1963," *Poetry Australia*. Dec., pp. 31–38.
Tanner, Tony
1967. "Transcendentalism and Imagism" in *The Reign of Wonder: Naivety and Reality in American Literature*, pp. 87–93. New York: Cambridge Univ. Pr.
Taubman, Robert
1965. "Portrait of a Baby," *New Statesman*. July 23, pp. 126–27.
Tomlinson, Charles
1964a. "Black Mountain as Focus," *Review*. Jan., pp. 4–5.
1964b. "Robert Creeley in Conversation with Charles Tomlinson," *Review*. Jan., pp. 24–35.
1964c. "Pictures from Brueghel," *Times Literary Supplement*. May 21, p. 435.
1967. "Dr. Williams' Practice," *Encounter*. Nov., pp. 66–70.
1972. *Penguin Critical Anthologies: William Carlos Williams*. Baltimore: Penguin.
Toynbee, Philip
1967. "Semantic Frontiersman," *Observer* (London). Dec. 17, p. 21.
Waggoner, Hyatt
1968. "In the American Grain," in *American Poets from the Puritans to the Present*, pp. 369–86, 615–17. New York: Dell.
Wagner, Linda
1963. "*Pictures from Brueghel* and William Carlos Williams," *American Weave*. Winter, pp. 37–39.

1964a. "William Carlos Williams: Giant," *College English*. Mar., pp. 425–300.

1964b. "William Carlos Williams: Classic American Poet," *Renascence*. Spring, pp. 115–25; revised and reprinted in *Poems of William Carlos Williams*. Middleton: Wesleyan Univ. Pr., 1964.

1964c. "Metaphor and William Carlos Williams," *University Review*. Autumn, pp. 43–49; revised and reprinted in *Poems of William Carlos Williams*. Middleton: Wesleyan Univ. Pr., 1964.

1964d. "The Last Poems of William Carlos Williams," *Criticism*. Fall, pp. 361–78; revised and reprinted in *Poems of William Carlos Williams*. Middleton: Wesleyan Univ. Pr., 1964.

1964e. *The Poems of William Carlos Williams: A Critical Study*. Middleton: Wesleyan Univ. Pr.

1965. "A Decade of Discovery, 1953–1963: Checklist of Criticism, William Carlos Williams' Poetry," *Twentieth Century Literature*. Jan., pp. 166–69.

1967a. "A Bunch of Marigolds," *Kenyon Review*. Jan. pp. 86–102; revised and reprinted in *Prose of William Carlos Williams*.

1967b. "Dr. Williams' Prescription," *Laurel Review*. No. 2, pp. 23–28.

1969. "William Carlos Williams: The Unity of His Art," in *Poetic Theory/Poetic Practice*, ed. Robert Scholes, pp. 136–144. New York: Modern Language Assn. Revised and reprinted in *Prose of William Carlos Williams*. Middleton: Wesleyan Univ. Pr., 1970.

1970a. "Spring and All: The Unity of Design," *Tennessee Studies in Literature*. 15: 61–73; revised and reprinted in *Prose of William Carlos Williams*. Middleton: Wesleyan Univ. Pr., 1970.

1970b. *The Prose of William Carlos Williams*. Middleton: Wesleyan Univ. Pr.

1973. "William Carlos Williams" in *Sixteen Modern American Authors*, ed. Jackson R. Bryer, pp. 573–85. Durham, N.C.: Duke Univ. Pr.

Wallace, Emily Mitchell

1966. "William Carlos Williams Bibliography," *Literary Review*. Summer, pp. 501–12; revised and reprinted in "Introductory Note" to *Bibliography of William Carlos Williams*, pp. ix–xx. Middleton: Wesleyan Univ. Pr., 1968.

1967."Pound and Williams at the University of Pennsylvania: 'Men of No Name and with a Fortune to Come'," *Pennsylvania Review*. Spring, pp. 41–53.

1968. *A Bibliography of William Carlos Williams*. Middleton: Wesleyan Univ. Pr.

1973. (editor) "Interview with Williams in 1950," *Massachusetts Review*. Winter, pp. 130–48.

Weatherhead, A. Kingsley

1965. "William Carlos Williams: Poetic Invention and the World

Beyond," *English Literary History*. Mar., pp. 126–38; revised and reprinted in *The Edge of the Image*. Seattle: Univ. of Washington Pr., 1967.

1966. "William Carlos Williams: Prose, Form, and Measure," *English Literary History*. Mar., pp. 118–31; revised and reprinted in *The Edge of the Image*. Seattle: Univ. of Washington Pr., 1967.

1967. *The Edge of the Image: Marianne Moore, William Carlos Williams, and Some Other Poets*. Seattle: Univ. of Washington Pr., pp. 3–57, 96–169.

Weaver, Mike

1966. "Introduction to a Modern Portrait," *Form*. Sept. 1, pp. 20–21.

1971. *William Carlos Williams: The American Background*. New York: Cambridge Univ. Pr.

Weimer, David R.

1966. *The City as Metaphor*. New York: Peter Smith, pp. 104–22.

Welland, Dennis

1965. "The Dark Voice of the Sea: A Theme in Modern American Poetry," in *American Poetry*, ed. Irvin Ehrenpreis, pp. 197–219. London: E. Arnold.

Whigham, Peter

1963. "William Carlos Williams," *Agenda*. Oct.-Nov., pp. 25–32.

1966. "Acknowledgments" to *The Poems of Catullus*. Baltimore: Penguin, pp. 9–10.

Whittaker, Ted

1966. "Presumptions," *Open Letter*. Apr., pp. 18–24.

Whitaker, Thomas R.

1968. *William Carlos Williams*. New York: Twayne.

Willard, Nancy

1965. "A Poetry of Things: Williams, Rilke, Ponge," *Contemporary Literature*. Fall, pp. 311–24; revised and reprinted in *Testimony of the Invisible Man*, pp. 1–15. Columbia: Univ. of Missouri Pr., 1970.

1967. "Testimony of the Invisible Man," *Shenandoah*. Autumn, pp. 42–49; revised and reprinted in *Testimony of the Invisible Man*, pp. 110–15. Columbia: Univ. of Missouri Pr., 1970.

1970. "A Local Habitation: William Carlos Williams," in *Testimony of the Invisible Man*, pp. 16–42. Columbia: Univ. of Missouri Pr.

Woods, Powell

1970. "William Carlos Williams: The Poet as Engineer," *Modern Poetry Studies*, No. 3, pp. 127–40.

Worth, Katherine J.

1967. "The Poets in the American Theatre," in *American Theatre*, pp. 86–107. London: St. Martin's.

Youdelman, Jeffrey
1969. "Pictures for a Sunday Afternoon: The Camera Eye in *Paterson*," *Concerning Poetry*. Fall, pp. 37–42.
Zitner, S. P.
1967. "Art as Redemption," *Poetry*. Oct., pp. 41–42.

Abbreviations

ELN	*English Language Notes*
ER	*Evergreen Review*
ES	*English Studies*
EUQ	*Emory University Quarterly*
Ex	*Explicator*
GG	*Golden Goose*
GR	*Georgia Review*
H	*Harper's*
HH	*Hound and Horn*
Hop R	*Hopkins Review*
HR	*Hudson Review*
JH	*Johns Hopkins Magazine*
JML	*Journal of Modern Literature*
KR	*Kenyon Review*
L	*Listener*
Lau R	*Laurel Review*
LM	*London Magazine*
Lit R	*Literary Review*
LR	*Little Review*
MASAL	*Papers of the Michigan Academy of Science, Arts and Letters*
MD	*Modern Drama*
MGW	*Manchester Guardian Weekly*
Minn R	*Minnesota Review*
MLJ	*Modern Language Journal*
Mod R	*Modern Review*
MPS	*Modern Poetry Studies*
MQ	*Midwest Quarterly*
MR	*Massachusetts Review*
MRR	*Mad River Review*
N	*Nation*
Nat R	*National Review*
ND	*New Directions*
NEW	*New English Weekly*
New M	*New Masses*
New Review	*New Review: An International Notebook for the Arts Published from Paris*
NL	*New Leader*
NMQ	*New Mexico Quarterly*
NQ	*Notes and Queries*
NR	*New Republic*
NS	*New Statesman*
NV	*New Verse*
NY	*New Yorker*
NYRB	*New York Review of Books*
Ob	*Observer* (London)

OL	Open Letter
O/W	Orient/West
PA	Poetry Australia
Penn R	Pennsylvania Review
Per	Perspective
PMLA	Publications of the Modern Language Association
Post	Washington Post Book Week
PR	Partisan Review
PS	Prairie Schooner
QQ	Queen's Quarterly
R	Review
S	Shenandoah
SA	Studi Americani
SAP	Studia Anglica Posnaniensia
Sat R	Saturday Review of Literature
SB	Stony Brook
SG	Studium Generale
So R	Southern Review
Sp	Spectrum
SR	Sewanee Review
Sym	Symposium
TCL	Twentieth Century Literature
TCV	Twentieth Century Verse
Things	Things (Hanging Loose)
Times	New York Times Book Review
TLS	Times Literary Supplement
trans	transition
TSL	Tennessee Studies in Literature
TSLL	Texas Studies in Literature and Language
UKCR	University of Kansas City Review
UR	University Review
V	Voyages
VQR	Virginia Quarterly Review
WCR	West Coast Review
WR	Western Review
YR	Yale Review
YULG	Yale University Library Gazette

Index

Names, books, and essays listed only in the References at the conclusion of each chapter are not included in the Index.